Second Star to the Right

Second Star to the Right

PETER PAN IN THE POPULAR IMAGINATION

Edited by
ALLISON B. KAVEY
LESTER D. FRIEDMAN

RUTGERS UNIVERSITY PRESS
New Brunswick, New Jersey, and London

Library of Congress Cataloging-in-Publication Data

Second star to the right : Peter Pan in the popular imagination / edited by Allison B.
Kavey and Lester D. Friedman.
    p. cm.
  Includes bibliographical references and index.
  ISBN 978-0-8135-4436-6 (alk. paper) — ISBN 978-0-8135-4437-3 (pbk. : alk. paper)
  1. Barrie, J. M. (James Matthew), 1860–1937. Peter Pan.   2. Barrie, J. M. (James
Matthew), 1860–1937—Adaptations.   3. Children's stories, English—History and
criticism.   4. Peter Pan (Fictitious character)   5. Barrie, J.M. (James Matthew),
1860–1937—Characters.   I. Kavey, Allison, 1977–   II. Friedman, Lester D.
  PR4074.P33S43 2009
  822'.912—dc22   2008011254

A British Cataloging-in-Publication record for this book is available from the British Library.

Visit our Web site: http://rutgerspress.rutgers.edu

Manufactured in the United States of America

*For Rae-Ellen Kavey, who always leaves the light on
and the window open*

Contents

ACKNOWLEDGMENTS

ANY ANTHOLOGY REPRESENTS the combined efforts of both its editors and its contributors; the wheel cannot turn properly without all of its spokes. We were fortunate to have a group of diverse writers who were not only enthusiastic and diligent, but who were often playful as well. Many had a personal connection with the Pan narrative at some point in their histories, a few as participants in productions during their younger days. The resulting interdisciplinary volume, from our earliest discussions of it, to holding the finished product in our hands, was an enjoyable enterprise. We hope that these essays shed some light on one of the most popular and enduring children's narrative ever conceived. We would like to express our appreciation to the staff at Rutgers University Press, who make the sometimes rocky process of publishing as easy as possible. In particular, we wish to thank Leslie Mitchner, who green-lighted and guided the book, Rachel Friedman who never left the red telephone, Rick Delaney, who edited it with such sharp eyes, Marilyn Campbell and Anne Hegeman who saw it through production, and Nancy Wolff who provided the index.

ABK ACKNOWLEDGMENTS

I was warned by my colleagues, with varying degrees of cynicism and sarcasm, that editing a book—much less an interdisciplinary collection of essays—was enough to make anyone crazy. Apparently I lucked out, because this was almost as fun as a weekend in Neverland. I would like to thank Les Friedman for his kindness, patience, and sense of humor as we navigated the lagoon of coediting. I must thank the students in my Research Methods class from the spring of 2007 who got over their horror at being forced to do serious work on a children's book and produced smart and interesting responses to *Peter Pan*. My colleagues in History, Justice Studies, and Gender Studies at CUNY John Jay College have also been exceptional sounding boards and very supportive of this interdisciplinary adventure. My mother, Rae-Ellen Kavey, deserves all credit for reading me *Peter Pan* when I was tiny and for kindly listening to her bizarre academic child. Finally, I would like to thank Andrea Woodner, who has prompted me to think better and more clearly about Peter Pan, epistemology, and the ties between memory and belief. "I do believe in fairies."

LDF ACKNOWLEDGMENTS

In the interest of full disclosure, I must admit that this anthology was not my idea; the impetus for the volume came from Allison, and I owe her a debt of gratitude for the fairy dust that sparked such an exhilarating project. My thanks to her for gently but persistently prodding me out of my comfort zone and into Neverland. At Hobart and William Smith Colleges, I am fortunate to have a supportive group of colleagues and administrators. Specifically, I am indebted to Teresa Amott, Provost, for supporting my work both financially and intellectually. As always during this process, I had the encouragement and patience of family and friends, including my parents, Eugene and Eva Friedman, and my children, Rachel and Marc Friedman. I owe a special, and continued debt to my friend, Delia Temes, and my wife, Rae-Ellen Kavey, both of whom offered valuable suggestions and insights as the anthology took shape.

Peter Pan Chronology

May 9, 1860 James M. Barrie is born in Kirriemuir, Scotland.

1902 J. M. Barrie publishes his first Peter Pan story, "The Little White Bird, or Adventures in Kensington Gardens."

1904 *Peter Pan* premieres at the Duke of York Theatre in London, with Nina Boucicault as Peter Pan.

1905 *Peter Pan* opens in New York City, with Maude Adams in the lead role.

1906 J. M. Barrie publishes *Peter Pan in Kensington Gardens*, which tells the story of Peter's escape from the nursery and his adventures among the birds and fairies.

1911 J. M. Barrie publishes *Peter and Wendy*, which develops the story of the Darling children and their adventures with Peter Pan in Neverland.

1912 Sir George Frampton's statue of Peter Pan erected in Kensington Gardens.

1915 The sinking of the *Lusitania*, on which Peter Pan producer Charles Frohman drowned after paraphrasing the line, "To die will be an awfully big adventure."

1929 J. M. Barrie gives the copyright for *Peter Pan* to Great Ormond Street Children's Hospital.

June 3, 1937 J. M. Barrie dies; the bequest of the *Peter Pan* copyright is reaffirmed.

1953 Disney's animated version of *Peter Pan* hits American silver screens.

1954 Staging of Broadway musical of *Peter Pan* premieres with Mary Martin in the starring role. NBC airs the first televised *Peter Pan* based on the Martin performance. It was shown three more times on television before 1960, when it was color videotaped and shown in 1963, 1966, and 1973.

1974   Cathy Rigby assumes the role of Peter Pan on stage and on television.

1979   Sandy Duncan takes the role of Peter Pan in the Broadway revival.

1991   Steven Spielberg releases the film *Hook*.

2000   Diarmuid Bryan O'Connor's new statue of Peter Pan is unveiled outside Great Ormond Street Children's Hospital.

2001   Director P. J. Hogan releases *Peter Pan*.

2002   Walt Disney Studios releases its animated sequel, *Return to Neverland*.

2004   Director Marc Forster releases the film *Finding Neverland*.

2006   Geraldine McCaughrean publishes an authorized sequel, *Peter Pan in Scarlet*.

Second Star to the Right

A friend characterized it as a "Peter Pan view," and now I can't see it any other way. I lie awake thinking of someone with a hook for a hand, and then, inevitably, of youth, and whether I have wasted it.

—David Sedaris, *When You Are Engulfed in Flames*, 2008

Introduction

FROM PEANUT BUTTER JARS
TO THE SILVER SCREEN

Allison B. Kavey

"It's only a play, mother, it doesn't matter."
—Peter Llewelyn Davies, *Finding Neverland*
(dir. Marc Forster, 2005)

"Never Neverlands beneath our skin"
—Lindsay Mac, "Small Revolutions"

WHEN I WAS SEVEN YEARS OLD, my figure skating club chose to stage *Peter Pan* on ice for its annual show. Because I was by far the smallest girl who could do a camel spin, I was chosen to skate the part of Tinker Bell. My mother spent three weeks of all-nighters sewing my fairy costume, a tiny green dress with a satin petal skirt. In it, on the day of the show, I felt downright puckish—mischievous, small, pretty, and awfully proud to be skating with stars like Kitty and Peter Carruthers whom I had only seen on TV. Better than all of that, though, was the ultimate reward for playing Tinker Bell: I didn't just get to skate, I got to *fly*. Slightly more than two decades later and a foot and a half taller, I'm still in thrall to the story of the boy who wouldn't grow up and his flitting fairy friend. But I know now that, like the adult Wendy, I've committed the ultimate sin and grown too big and too old to fly. This book attempts to regain the buoyant and compelling sense of excitement that was so easy to have when I was seven and the obvious thing to do was to fly across the ice next to my Peter, retrieve the shadow that he had so carelessly left behind when he was flirting with that wretched little girl, and leave for Neverland.

Because this is a collection of essays, not a monograph, its very existence confirms that I am not the only academic living in Peter's shadow. Les and I were astonished when, after batting around the idea for a Peter Pan book for years, we finally agreed to do it and started searching for contributors. Much to our surprise, fellow academics greeted us not with traditional mutterings and polite refusals such as, "Oh, I'd love to but I'm already committed to five other projects," but nearly all responded with genuine enthusiasm and personal stories about their own connections with the narrative. In fact, many of our friends and colleagues revealed that they too had been thinking about Neverland and leaped at the chance to write about it.

What is it about Peter Pan that has allowed him to permeate Western popular culture and become an enduring icon? There are some easy answers, of course. For an ever increasing number of men and women in the early twenty-first century, the worship of youth and beauty demands painful and extensive plastic surgery, resulting in more face-lifts and tummy tucks as the wrinkles and pounds accumulate at an alarming rate over time. In an age of schedules and responsibilities that start increasingly earlier and earlier in childhood, the desire to withdraw into a place entirely of your invention, one that responds to your every daydream and nightmare, is incredibly seductive. The importance of family, a virtue hammered home by the Darling children's return to the nursery, is easy to appreciate, especially when families live farther apart and spend less time together than ever. So you begin to understand the branding of a bus line that promises a quick and affordable escape on America's highways, and the peanut butter that smacks of wholesome lunches served by a loving parent to a smiling tot, and the hundreds of Halloween costumes donned by small children in the quest to become Lost Boys, Lost Girls, Tinker Bell, and Peter Pan. They all partake in the liberating fantasy of flight, the aching desire to remain youthful, and the reckless longing to return to Neverland.

But like the salmonella that contaminated ConAgra's Peter Pan peanut butter in February of 2007, our cultural infatuation with the eternal boy has a poisonous side. Pop psychologist Dan Kiley's "Peter Pan Syndrome" indicts men who are egotistical and manipulative, who refuse to assume adult roles and responsibilities, and who fly from emotional relationships. Pixie and angel dust have become synonyms for an entirely different kind of flight than Barrie intended. Attacks regularly leveled at men who play with gender and/or sexuality include the word "fairy" as the most pleasant term amid a litany of curses. Multiple references to Peter Pan abound in popular media representations of children gone wild. Take, for example, the television series *Angel* (1999–2004). The reappearance of Angel's (David Boreanaz) son Connor (Vincent Kartheiser), kidnapped as an infant and transported to a Hell dimension, dressed in animal skins and kicking some serious ass (primarily his father's), prompts colleague Charles Gunn (J. August Richards) to say, "Angel, Peter Pan here doesn't stop."[1] What becomes apparent from reading the chapters in this book is that we don't just love Disney's sweetly confident Peter Pan, though Susan Ohmer describes why that film still holds such a significant place in the American psyche, but also Brian's cocky bastard Peter imitations in *Queer as Folk*. We admire Peter's flexibility, which has allowed him to dominate stage, page, screen, and merchandising for one hundred years, and has permitted his story and the characters with whom he plays to be appropriated by a multitude of identity groups. But this is an intellectual answer to what I believe is an inherently emotional response to Peter Pan.

The remarkable thing about this book, this boy, and any of the movie versions is that nearly every woman I know has her own story to tell about seeing Peter Pan. They're not stories about textual analysis or close readings of screen images. Instead they relate tales of watching Mary Martin dressed as Peter and hearing her say, "Never gonna be a man, catch me if you can," and knowing that there might be other girls who would rather dress as boys than marry and raise children, or deciding, in the third year of medical school during a pediatric rotation, that the Lost Boys were not lost, but in fact dead children. I know of no other story, neither Tolkien's Ring trilogy nor even the Harry Potter series, that consistently inspires such personal and intense reactions in adults. But wasn't this supposed to be a children's story? As Martha Stoddard Holmes demonstrates in her essay, *Peter Pan* occupies a select literary niche—stories originally written for children, but now primarily read by adults and absorbed by children through other media, such as films. Like the best children's stories, it reveals the nastiest aspects of childhood, rather than simply genuflecting at the altars of innocence and youth. Unlike others, though, the Pan narrative reflects adult reactions to children's selfishness, as, at the behest of the narrator, readers are asked to reconsider mothers, "those toads." Like its curious namesake, this story is really liminal, straddling age groups and meaning different things to all of us at different moments in our lives.

Although the stories have very little in common beyond superficial elements, the most consistent literary comparison to *Peter Pan* is Lewis Carroll's *Alice in Wonderland*. Both deal with English children of comparable ages who escape the real world for a parallel reality inhabited by weird and wonderful beings. But the similarities end there. Alice wants desperately to find her way back to England, while Peter chooses to spend eternity inside his personal landscape. Alice's adventures are remarkably physical and often center around her own body, which allows for an easy comparison with the growing emotional and physical pains of adolescence. Peter and his friends, on the other hand, clearly interact with others, though not always nicely. Finally, Alice gets lost inside an exotic landscape that comes complete with a beguiling menagerie of droll, outlandish, and seemingly mad characters, while Peter, the Darlings, and the Lost Boys exist in both the corporeal world of London and the fantasy realm of Neverland. The frequent pairing of the two books often reflects modern assumptions about Carroll's and Barrie's sexuality, rather than a close reading of the actual stories, and reveals more about the predilections of psychoanalytical critics and biographers than about the texts—or their authors.

Jacqueline Rose's *The Case of Peter Pan* (1984) is both the most frequently cited scholarly work on the narrative and the most egregious example of the argument that Barrie's desire—for children, to be a child—permeates the text and inevitably confounds its title character. She first published the study during a time when critics routinely overlaid fiction with a dizzying array of psychoanalytic categorizations, plunking authors (even long-dead ones) on the couch and publicly dissecting their psyches. Such explorations often focused on salacious revelations of an author's previously unrevealed depravities, charges impossible either to prove definitively or to retort posthumously. Rose's new introductory essay to a 1993 reissue of the book shows the assumptions that shaped her original argument and telegraphs its promulgation of late-twentieth-century paranoia:

> If there is widespread sexual abuse of children, then it is not so much the innocence of childhood as the boundary between adult and child, their status as stable and knowable entities, that starts to shake. Child abuse confronts us with the violence of limits flouted and transgressed. Bodies open where they should remain closed, and a defining space is invaded— the space which conceptually as well as physically is meant to keep children and adults apart.[2]

Throughout her analysis, Rose consistently conflates the sexual abuse of children with the literary text of *Peter Pan*. Did I miss a crucial scene in Barrie's story? If this line of reasoning is correct, then Beatrix Potter should be posthumously hanged by animal welfare groups for the ideas in *Peter Cottontail*—and I do not want to think about what could happen to poor William Shakespeare for *As You Like It*.

I remember well the days of open bodies and endless discussions of desire, but I support two corrections that have changed the direction of literary scholarship since the early 1990s. The first argues that what people write cannot be taken as a direct reflection of their hidden desires. The tale is not the author and the author is not the tale. Anyone who can disentangle

Barrie's secret desires and hidden addictions from the language he employs to relate the events in *Peter Pan* is more psychic than psychoanalyst. In this often opaque text, desire is everywhere, nowhere, nebulous, defined, pervasive, and absent. It is, like Peter, a cipher, and far too carefully constructed to be the reflection of a single man's sexuality. The second correction comes from historians whose influence on literary scholarship remains inconsistent but contains an important message: don't make unfounded biographical assertions based on fictional evidence. Since the Llewelyn Davies boys have consistently assured Barrie biographers that they remained unmolested, the least we can do is believe them. They are, after all, the victims whose voices many scholars claim they want to recover. I wish those writing about *Peter Pan* would listen to what they actually say about "Uncle Jim" and his many kindnesses to them.

The 2006 collection of essays edited by Donna White and C. Anita Tarr obeys these correctives, and it admirably avoids the trap of equating Barrie with the narrator in *Peter Pan* or of considering the text to be an extension of its author's desire.[3] Its goal is similar to ours: to understand what shaped the narrative and how it influences today's culture. The collection's many arguments can be narrowed to three themes: Peter Pan is liminal, which made him both appealing and problematic for Edwardian culture and has kept him fresh in ensuing decades; the book is a product of its time, as a reaction to girls' culture, or a part of the fin de siècle equation of life as art, or in the genre of late-nineteenth-century children's literature (fairy, pirate, or otherwise); and the text exemplifies the problems of race, class, and gender. The anthology's weaknesses, however, are located in the theoretical apparatuses employed to deconstruct—or torture—this narrative. From Jacques Lacan to Judith Butler, from center-periphery theory to the white man's burden, *Peter Pan* is made to serve many masters, not all of them particularly kind. We have taken a different approach, which privileges the production of *Peter Pan* in its various iterations across mediums and takes seriously the problem of audience and reception.

Given these previous discussions, director Marc Forster's *Finding Neverland* (2004) clearly walks the very lines so successfully navigated by the author and his story. In what initially appears to be a sloppy and often syrupy conflation of biography and fictional narrative, Forster offers a rigorous and disciplined separation of the author and the character, insisting on the radical distinction between the two. A single scene directly addresses the question of Barrie's sexuality and desire. It takes place on the sidelines of a cricket match when a team member traps Barrie (Johnny Depp) into responding about the time he spends with Sylvia Llewelyn Davies (Kate Winslet) and her sons. Notably, both parties are considered potential objects of his desire in this instance, while only the growing attachment between Sylvia Llewellyn Davies and Barrie raises the ire of Mrs. Du Maurier (Julie Christie) and Mrs. Barrie (Radha Mitchell). Barrie responds with bewildered shock to his friend's pronouncement that "There have also been questions about how you spend your time with those boys and why." In a low voice defined by a combination of horror and shock, Barrie answers, "That's outrageous. How could someone think something so evil? They're children, innocent children. I don't think people will give credence to such nonsense."[4] But academics have given "such nonsense" credence for several decades, relentlessly filling an evidence vacuum with innuendos, snide assumptions, and psychoanalytical theories. The question is clearly not whether Barrie desired Peter Llewelyn Davies and his brothers, but how and why Peter Pan has become such an entrenched part of modern culture.

It isn't only through books that Peter has entered children's imaginations. In Britain during the early twentieth century, upper- and middle-class parents frequently took their small children to the theater. Often, they saw pantomimes or children's ballets, but sometimes they saw plays especially written to entice and enchant youngsters. *Peter Pan* was such a play, and it was seen by thousands of children throughout Britain after its debut in 1904. The production was so tremendously popular that it jumped the Atlantic and appeared in New York in the 1920s, then toured the country, remaining a favorite through many changes of company and venue. As Patrick Tuite's chapter reflects, the play was fundamental to the careers of several significant twentieth-century actresses because it offered them unique opportunities to experiment with gender and stagecraft. Many lesser-known thespians have also taken to the boards dressed as Peter, the Lost Boys, Captain Hook, the Darlings, and even Nana. *Peter Pan* remains a consistent favorite for school plays because of its large cast and broad appeal. In fact, the first hit from a Google search for the keywords "Peter Pan play" takes you to Childrenstheatreplays.com, a website specializing in theatrical adaptations of favorite stories for schools and children's theatrical companies.[5] But not every child has the good fortune to act in, or even see *Peter Pan* on stage. In 2007, electronic visual media are the most popular venues, and the appeal of *Peter Pan* is most commonly measured in Nielsen ratings and at the box office.

Disney can take a great deal of the credit here, both for introducing new viewers to the *Peter Pan* story and for making it sufficiently saccharine and moderately sexualized to keep young Americans happily watching. As Murray Pomerance shows in his essay, the Disney studios entirely revised Tinker Bell, taking her from a flashing light to a fleshy blond bombshell, known more for her cleavage and her impishness than for fairy incorporeality. But

Disney had no easy time with *Peter Pan*; Susan Ohmer's chapter demonstrates that the images that millions of children have consumed since the movie's debut in 1953 took nearly two decades to create and reflect the changing nature of the Disney studios more than that of the original play or book. Disney did maintain a few aspects of the original stage productions, including having the same actor, Hans Conried, voice Mr. Darling and Captain Hook, and clothing Peter Pan entirely in green—much as Barrie described him: "clad in skeleton leaves and the juices that ooze out of trees."[6] It also did what only a multimillion-dollar megacorporation can: it commodified Peter and his friends into an endlessly flowing stream of merchandise. Now, at the Disney website, you can purchase a Peter Pan costume *and* a popup tent; Tinker Bell mugs; *and* messenger bags—and a Tinker Bell costume . . . for your pet. (Someone e-mail Paris Hilton immediately![7]) For any child who manages to escape kindergarten without having been stuffed into a costume, thrust onto stage, or trotted out the door to beg for candy, an unremitting series of Peter Pan–laden moments await at almost every stage of childhood and early adolescence.

The televised movie *Peter Pan*, especially the version with Mary Martin, is frequently compared with *The Wizard of Oz* (1939) as an iconic childhood viewing experience. As Teresa Jones argues, however, *Peter Pan* has a lot more to offer than the eventual return to gingham, pigtails, and sepia-and-white shots of Depression-era Kansas. Peter, at least, gets to stay in Neverland with his best friend and fairy, while the Darlings and the Lost Boys live out their choice to return to the nursery and grow up. Peter gets to keep coming back to the window and steal away generations of Darling women, leaving Wendy for Jane and Jane for Moira, and on into infinity. The fates of girls in both these movies are remarkably similar—go home. Whether that's back to the nursery or somewhere on the original side of the rainbow, they must grow up, which means getting married, having children, and growing old. Poor Dorothy, poor Wendy: no wonder we envy Peter Pan and make him the subject of our fantasies; he gets to move between Neverland and the nursery, forever navigating the space between the window and the second star to the right with reckless grace. Michael Maguire made an art of personifying Elphaba, the Wicked Witch of the West, in *Wicked* (1996), which has been a smash hit on Broadway as well as a *New York Times* bestseller. But even after all of his efforts, the witch remains a creature of Oz, just as Dorothy is inherently a Kansan. Peter, the Lost Boys, and even the more vehemently human Darling children can move between their cozy beds and Neverland, which makes it more possible for us to move with them, leaving our nightlights behind for the eerie twilight of London and Technicolor dawn of Neverland.

Neverland and Oz are also inherently different. L. Frank Baum created a place with a clear geography, climate, and political system that existed before Dorothy showed up and will continue after she leaves, with only a few lives— most notably the witches'—being utterly changed. Oz does not need Dorothy, and Dorothy certainly, as she makes clear when she leaves, does not need Oz. But as I argue in my essay, Neverland needs Peter—it slumbers, freezes, hibernates while he is away; it mourns when he does; it triumphs when he does. Its inhabitants slow down their usual routines in his absence, following each other in a repetitive circle of Redskins, Lost Boys, pirates, and animals that is broken only when Peter shows up and initiates the next adventure. The landscape also responds to Peter's needs, seeming to anticipate things that will come in handy for him and maintaining them until he wants them, at which point it gives them up without a backward glance. The best example of this is the Neverbird, who gives Peter her nest so that he can escape drowning on Marooners' Rock in the lagoon. At that moment, John's top hat conveniently appears, Peter loads the bird's eggs into it, and then steps into the nest. (You might ask why he didn't just get into the top hat, since he obviously could have fit, but that suggests a significant lack of appreciation for the story and too much appreciation of logic, which has only a small foothold in Peter's world, for he is, in fact, a child.) I want a landscape that does this for me!

But, as any Peter aficionado would tell you, I can't have one, because I'm a girl. I think it is sad that so many lesbians see a place for themselves in a play where a woman played the part of an eternal boy, while all of the literal female characters dreamed only of marriage and childrearing. I entirely agree that gender bending is good fun for all, but the possibilities for women qua women in the story are stifling. Wendy always made me faintly ill with her prim manners and fondness for darning socks. I like the modern Wendy portrayed by P. J. Hogan in *Peter Pan* (2001) only slightly better, since she exchanges her profound power as the teller of stories to deliver the fated kiss that saves Peter but dooms her to a life of heteronormative servitude in full Edwardian style. Despite the fact that she is the only genuinely nice character in the entire story, I can say nothing but nasty things about Wendy. She tries not to be selfish, she takes care of other people, she has emotional range. But she trades so much for so little, and that ultimately makes me both sad and angry.

It is Mrs. Darling who gives hope to all female readers and viewers of *Peter Pan*; even in the face of a silly husband and three demanding children, she manages to keep the deepest secret of the innermost box of her Chinese-box personality, and a single kiss, for herself. I've always liked her for that, even before university when I decided that she was obviously hiding in this sham marriage until the preposterous Mr. Darling died so that she could go live by herself. In her flat, she would think and eat cookies all afternoon, and occasionally have great sex with Virginia Woolf. Even though one of these people was fictional and the other was real, I did not care. They would easily sort out this small detail, as they would determine who would get the chocolate biscuits. What I like about Mrs. Darling is the same thing that I like about Peter. They both depend upon other people's need of them to exist, and yet they maintain identities independent of the people who need them. Peter is eternally a child and no longer of this world, so he lives through the fantasies of children who need him—and Neverland. He does not think of himself in terms of those children, however, but instead believes that he is no "ordinary boy," but a "wonderful boy" (Barrie, 148).

Mrs. Darling, a master of performing domestic femininity, remains an excellent wife for Mr. Darling and an attentive mother to her three children. And yet she still keeps a part of herself separate from those who need her. Both she and Peter are pros at navigating between worlds without losing their sense of who they are or where they were going in the first place. Peter has Neverland, while Mrs. Darling has the nursery, which responds to her mood, her desires, and her perambulations by accommodating her, until the sprite shows up and hijacks it for his own purposes. As Murray Pomerance shows, the domestic space and soft light of the nursery are always in sharp opposition to the bright and dashing light that accompanies Peter, though both kinds of electricity were associated with femininity in early-twentieth-century publicity. That light is, of course, Tinker Bell, the faithful fairy who started out as a flashing light and wound up Julia Roberts. Of all the women who love Peter, Tinker Bell is the simplest and the most tragic, if only because she is so small that she can only hold one emotion at a time (Barrie, 111). Like Mrs. Darling, Tinker Bell is limited in one way that Peter is not—she is, like the other female characters, stubbornly categorized as human or fairy, while Peter Pan is flexibly preternatural, moving from boy to bird to fairy and back. This final comparison makes it clear that being a woman in Barrie's world is inherently frustrating, and being human—growing up, growing old, dying—is fundamentally limited.

Just ask Captain Hook. It's fine for me to think that Neverland's responsiveness to Peter's every wish is charming and seductive, but imagine endlessly waiting for your foe to return from hearing bedtime stories so that you can resume your life of piracy and plans for revenge. Imagine literally being named, in some ways invented, by the wretched cocky brat who sliced off your hand. Combine that with a near obsession with good form crafted in the dark halls and bright playing fields of Eton College, and you have James

Hook: a tormented man haunted by the desire to behave well even while he guts his lackeys and stalks a little boy who simply refuses to die. Is this any life for a man? Surely not, and so it is always with gratitude that I watch Hook fall to his death, though I worry that he will eventually emerge from the crocodile and perpetually (re)perform the whole battle to the death just because Peter wishes his nemesis back to duel—over and over again. Masculinity in *Peter Pan* is, to say the least, complicated. As Lester Friedman explores in his essay, James Hook is a collage of English masculinities that compete with each other to determine how he behaves and whether he is right to do so, a continuous conversation that would make anyone crazy, and which probably drives Hook into the drink at the end.

Combine all of these frustrated expectations with the fact that Captain Hook is Mr. Darling, and you might well consider clawing your way out of this plot. To say that James Barrie acutely depicted the suffocating, limited opportunities for expression available to bourgeois men of his period is like saying that Peter Pan can fly. Mr. Darling demonstrates the multitude of ways in which sending men to offices where they judge their success through the respect and fear they engender in underlings and are rewarded for speaking languages that their wives and children cannot understand is a remarkably bad idea. Is it any surprise that this man who cannot fix his tie and tricks his younger son into taking medicine winds up living in a doghouse? Absolutely not. But how different is Mr. Darling from Hook? Both men steal for a living, one through the august institution of a bank and the other more honestly as a pirate. Both men are disturbed by the wanton lighthearted disregard that children show for their accomplishments. Both men are terrified by what other people think of them and change their behavior accordingly. Both men want children to love them. Both men are locked in a struggle to the death with time and responsibility. Suddenly, the banker and the pirate, though clad very differently, seem to have a lot in common, and those similarities serve as a commentary on the stringent boundaries placed on men by the cultural expectations of the early twentieth century.

And what of Peter? Always a boy, always attractive, always desired, always living in a self-reflective, constructed reality, he replicates the most appealing aspects of childhood. Even as I sit here at my computer working on a gorgeous July day in the Hudson Valley, I remember the long, wonderful summer afternoons of my childhood. Then, I lounged under a tree with my book and imagined a new world in which I could demonstrate the incredible skills that would make everyone want to admire the cleverness of me. Mostly, though, I envy Peter's lack of memory: imagine the freedom of never knowing the disappointment that you have caused, the tears you have prompted, the anger you have engendered. Imagine every "I love you" having the intensity of that first, daring expression. Of course, bigger problems come with a missing memory than simply being unable to come up with my students' names. There are some memories I would hate to lose, and certainly moments I would loathe to relive. But I am jealous of the freedom—from age, from fear, from want—that has made Peter Pan the envy of the gay male world. As Davis Munns illustrates in his essay, gay men have exceptionally good reasons to want to be Peter Pan, since they also occupy two worlds with competing sets of expectations and regularly show allegiance to one over the other. In the real world, cocky bastards are rejected for failing to display good form at work, on the playing field, at home, while in the twilight world of gay clubs, beautiful men with perfect confidence become the focus of everyone's desire. These men are Hook by day, fighting fat and age with iron at the gym, but they all want to be Peter (or at least with him) at night in the dance clubs. It is no surprise that the anthem of *Queer as Folk* is a remix of the old Dylan song "(I Want to Be) Forever Young."

But the death drive is never far from Peter Pan. The boy who would not grow up sometimes wants to die, simply because it would be a new experience. In the moment on the rock in the lagoon where Peter watches the waters rise over his body, knowing that he will drown, we are terrified for him. Unlike his readers and viewers, though, he moves past the fear to remark, "To die will be an awfully great adventure" (Barrie, 152). As Linda Robertson explains in her chapter, the man who brought Peter Pan to America would paraphrase this remark on the deck of the sinking *Lusitania* after handing away his life vest, and it would be broadcast as a remarkable display of bravery and fortitude in the face of certain death. The British war machine would then adopt the line as a means of recruiting young men to the fields of Flanders, where they would experience terror, rats, exhaustion, and pain—with death as their only escape. George Llewelyn Davies, the eldest of Barrie's adopted sons, was lost in that war, as were 8,538,315 other soldiers from both sides.[8] The fact that Peter Pan to some extent helped lead these young men into the killing fields of World War I literally boggles the mind, at least until you notice that the U.S. Army now advertises for recruits with a video game.

From pop culture to gay culture to the military machine, the *Peter Pan* narrative has been indelibly stamped upon significant aspects of twentieth-century Western culture. Peter is alternately a charming figure of fun, an enchanting image of everlasting youth, a runaway, an irresponsible adolescent, a lost child, a sexual object, and an action hero. His green tights have graced the legs of some of the most attractive and talented actresses of the twentieth century, and his character has pushed public gender-bending past the boundaries charted by Shakespeare's Rosalind in *As You Like It* (1599) and Middleton and Dekker's Moll in *The Roaring Girl* (1611). And if you gave me the chance to go back to that moment when I was flying, tiny and light and fast, next to Peter, I'd walk away from this computer, tie on my skates, and never look back.

NOTES

1. *Angel*, created by Joss Whedon and David Greenwalt (WB network, 1999–2004), season 4, episode 20.
2. Jacqueline Rose, *The Case of Peter Pan or the Impossibility of Children's Literature* (New York: Routledge, 1993), xi.
3. Donna White and C. Anita Tarr, *J. M. Barrie's Peter Pan In and Out of Time: A Children's Classic at 100* (Lanham, MD: Scarecrow Press, 2006).
4. *Finding Neverland*, directed by Marc Forster, Miramax, 2004.
5. The Children's Theatre Project. www.childrenstheatreproject.com, accessed July 20, 2007.
6. J. M. Barrie, *Peter and Wendy* (New York: Oxford University Press, 1991), 77. Subsequent citations appear parenthetically in the text.
7. Disney Store. http://disney-store.shopping.co.uk , accessed July 20, 2007.
8. Spartacus Educational. http://www.spartacus.schoolnet.co.uk/FWWdeaths.htm, accessed July 20, 2007.

CHAPTER 1

Tinker Bell, the Fairy of Electricity

Murray Pomerance

FOR MORE THAN a hundred years now, onstage and onscreen, we have gazed wonderingly at, and often through our credulous applause revivified, Tinker Bell, sometimes embodied by nothing more than a well-choreographed flicker and sometimes made manifest through the performance of a human actor. She was once to be called something else. Andrew Birkin unearths notes of J. M. Barrie's from October 14, 1903, under the rubric "Fairy," mentioning "Fairy Tippytoe—3 inches high."[1] If Tinker Bell, as she came to be called, was not the first fairy to be invoked on the London stage, she was in many ways the brightest, and surely original in her jealous and possessive attitude toward a male, even if that male was played—originally and then in a long and stable tradition, owing to the difficulties of stage-managing "his" flying—by a girl.

Tinker Bell has appeared (she has been the pretext for an appearance) in a long chain of stage presentations, in numerous motion pictures, as a variety of mass-marketed toys and associated ephemera, on animated television shows—including, of course, her iconic presence on *The Wonderful World of Disney*—and, perhaps most significant to contemporary addicts of popular culture, she is Paris Hilton's well-manicured Chihuahua. Always, however, Tinker Bell has been a presence that fascinates audiences less, I think, because of what she does or fails to do in Barrie's delightful tale than because she brings together three charming characteristics—magic, femininity, and electricity—in a single personification that is unmistakable, dramatic, and somehow deeply true, a personification that has now become something of a myth.

TINK LIVE AND ILLUMINATED

Barrie's Tink originally appeared to the British public as a boldly visible phenomenon, and was presented as such, "live" on the London stage, during a period of remarkable theatrical spectacularization. Wolfgang Schivelbusch reminds us that the theater had "the greatest appetite for light in the nineteenth century";[2] indeed, in the earliest theatrical staging that employed electrical light, Gilbert and Sullivan's *Iolanthe* (November 25, 1882), fairies were produced precisely through such illumination.[3] *Theatre* described "self-lighting fairies with electricity stored somewhere about the smalls of their backs," and raved that "the effect of this brilliant spark of electricity is wonderful."[4] *Peter Pan* was produced (with many of its settings, including that of the nursery, by Sir Edwin Lutyens) in an era when the stage often reflected wild inventiveness, such as could be enjoyed in the concoctions of Dion Boucicault, who directed the first production of *Peter Pan* with his daughter Nina as the first Peter and Jane Wren doing the musical bits as Tinker Bell. The fact that the play was a stage spectacular, therefore, or that Tinker Bell was a considerable spectacle inside it, did not suffice to make *Peter Pan* noteworthy at the time, though the *Times* called opening night a "pure delight."[5] At the turn of the twentieth century, actor managers such as Boucicault were constantly mounting lavish and elaborate productions, such as Herbert Beerbohm Tree's *The Tempest* (October 1904) at His Majesty's Theatre or W. S. Gilbert's *Harlequin and the Fairy's Dilemma* (soon renamed *The Fairy's Dilemma*) at the Garrick.

The spectacularizing of the British stage and significantly the creation of Tinker Bell were occurring at the same time as, and partly in response to, three broader cultural phenomena of the late nineteenth century that had overwhelmed the thinking of a considerable part of the audience, namely, theosophy, spiritualism, and Galvinism. The theosophists, who had organized themselves formally under Helena Petrovna Blavatsky as of 1875, followed Hamlet's lead in putting forward the thesis that there was more to heaven and earth than was dreamt of in our philosophies. They posited a world of harmonies and vibrations, of unseen forces, unifying the visible and the invisible specters, the living and the dead: in theosophy, fairies existed. Spiritualists claimed to manifest the world of ghosts by transcending the curtain between life and death, producing in séances and often in photographs tangible images of the departed, who were shown to inhabit the world of the living:[6] in spiritualism, fairy power could be made manifest. The noted American spiritualist Andrew Jackson Davis practiced "magnetic healing" in the mid-1840s. Influenced by the work of Franz Mesmer, spiritualists induced trances as a way of opening a pathway out of the mundane world.

In the Galvinism of the late nineteenth century lay Luigi Galvani's idea—in resonance with the thought of Nollet, Franklin, Volta, Cavendish, and numerous others[7]—of an electric body, a body that was itself a fount of electricity and that could be healed by electric charges when it was disabled: for Galvinists, the fairy could be electricity itself. "Things that flow (water, crowds of people, etc.)," Christoph Asendorf observes, "seem to move autonomously, to be without beginning and end."[8] Both fairies and electricity seemed to be such things.

Galvinism was the subject of a series of lectures presented from 1843 onward by William Sturgeon, and focused on animal and voltaic electricity:

> Galvanism, as represented by Sturgeon at least, was intimately linked to the processes of life. It arose directly, if serendipitously, from Galvani's interest in the relationship between muscular action and electrical agency.... [Galvani] came to regard "the whole animal frame as a natural electrical machine, in a continual state of excitement; and which, like the rubber and glass parts of the ordinary electric machine, has its muscular and nervous systems in different electrical conditions.[9]

According to Sturgeon, in Galvani's theory "the muscles and the nerves were the source of electric action."[10] The link between Galvani's theory, explored experimentally by his nephew Giovanni Aldini, who electrically stimulated the recently deceased body of an executed criminal to produce facial twitches, and Tinker Bell, is direct: Barrie's fairy is conceived through the narrative as a physical form resembling a tiny human body, and she exudes light. The progression in Tinker Bell's formation from 1904 through what we can see onscreen a hundred years later shows a notably increasing, even voluptuous, embodiment. In the 1904 production, Tink is a winking light that moves about the stage, but a light that is intended to be understood as emanating from a tiny fairy figure, one might say a tiny, barely visible Galvanic source shaped like a woman.

A foundation for the ability of an electrical conductor, such as Tinker Bell, to move around in a space while still maintaining its luminosity without a visible source of conduction had been laid by the Serbo-Croatian American physicist and inventor Nikola Tesla, with his work in Colorado Springs in 1899 and 1900. In carrying out high-voltage, high-frequency experiments he was able, some claim, to prove the conductive properties of the Earth itself, to manufacture artificial lightning, and to provide for electrical conductivity through the air. Much of this work is represented with a certain otherworldly aura in Christopher Nolan's film *The Prestige* (2006). Tesla and his principles of wireless conductivity were known worldwide when Barrie was conceiving Tinker Bell, and could surely have inspired the idea of an incandescent glowing, sparkling fairy type who could maintain brilliance while she teleported herself through space in a flash.

It was not until 1917 that actual physical images of fairies were circulated at all in the United Kingdom. Sir Arthur Conan Doyle, whose reputation would certainly have been significant to James M. Barrie, reports in lengthy detail in his book *The Coming of the Fairies* (1922) a case of two girls who saw, repeatedly played with, and then on two occasions ultimately photographed fairy spirits in a small glade behind their home in Yorkshire. This case excited much theosophical speculation at the time, especially since the images were repeatedly submitted to photographic experts who pronounced them genuine in all respects. (These events are replicated in two late–twentieth-century films, *Photographing Fairies* and *Fairy Tale: A True Story* [both 1997], and the capacity of the young girl to envision the fairy is a central aspect of the film *El Laberinto del Fauno* [2006].) Doyle himself rhapsodized:

> I must confess that after months of thought I am unable to get the true bearings of this event. One or two consequences are obvious. The experiences of children will be taken more seriously. Cameras will be forthcoming. Other well-authenticated cases will come along. These little folk who appear to be our neighbours, with only some small difference of vibration to separate us, will become familiar. The thought of them, even when unseen, will add a charm to every brook and valley and give romantic interest to every country walk. The recognition of their existence will jolt the material twentieth-century mind out of its heavy ruts in the mud, and will make it admit that there is a glamour and a mystery to life.[11]

Something of a susceptibility to fairy thought may have run in the Doyle family: his grandfather Charles had sketched fairies while incarcerated in the Montrose Royal Lunatic Asylum around 1889, and his uncle Richard made drawings for at least two books about fairies published in the middle and late nineteenth century.[12] Conan Doyle's fairies are described as virtually transparent, with wings of mauve, pink, or green, and with idiosyncratic bodies, and are clearly shown as lithe and beautiful young women hovering in the air in resplendent nudity. This, then, was at the very least one image of what the public could be expected to believe a fairy looked like, one reflection of what public thought at the time conceived in imaginative response to the suggestion of the presence of a "fairy," and one common reference among English readers for how fairies looked and behaved. Whether, in short, one believed or did not believe in the existence of these creatures in the world, this is how the creatures one did or did not believe in looked like. To match this reigning conception, and working in the wake of both theosophical and Galvanic thought, Barrie invented a fairy girl who was a moving light—whose capacity to illuminate could dim and die, if we did not express conviction in her—and whose attachment to her ageless companion was quite as aggressively feminine as that of the women in Barrie's audience to the husbands who were (at this time) the centers of their social world. She was a "Fairy of Electricity."

The fairy of electricity, painted by Raoul Dufy in the late 1930s (and now filling a room three stories high at Paris's Museum of Modern Art), had already been flashing alluringly at the Chicago Columbian Exposition of 1893 and was a central subject of fascination in the Paris Exposition Universelle of 1900, with the palais de l'électricité shining like a gargantuan jewel below the newly electrified Eiffel Tower (tallest structure on earth) and a sculpture of her capping its entryway. The fairy of electricity—and Tinker Bell, too—was a working sprite. Alexandre Fernandez writes of how in the late nineteenth century, electricity had been seen as a "fairy" form because of its association with luxury, play, and fun; and that it became, after its use as a utility, a servant.[13] But there is reason to wonder not only how unique and different the spheres of entertainment and labor are, or have ever been, but also how far either stood, at the turn of the twentieth century, from the development of electricity. "Increase of light and increase of labour," writes Winfried Sebald, "have always gone hand in hand."[14] Certainly what Barrie produces in Tinker Bell is a diligent worker and helper who is distinctly still a fairy, thus suggesting that the concept of the fairy does not belong to the trivial but is part instead of the fundamental world of work and pleasure together. In Tinker Bell, Barrie was embodying the idea and myth of "la fée électricité," an enchanter but also a servant.

The three aspects of Tinker Bell that typify her character and her presence in contemporary culture—her charged being, and thus her capacity to illuminate; her femininity, and thus her jealous love of Peter; and her identity as a fairy, and thus her dependence upon an audience's belief—all collapse into a single electric unity, since electricity at the turn of the twentieth century had been domesticated and thus brought into the domain of what was felt to be feminine control, and since for most of its users electricity daunted comprehension and worked as an unseen, magical force. When we watch Tinker Bell on the stage or on the screen, then, it is domestic femininity and otherworldly presence, linked as the fairy slave, that we see twinkling before us.

The development of electric light was hardly an overnight affair. Around 1882, the vacuum glass light bulb containing a carbon (carbonized bamboo) filament had been developed. But, because the burning carbon tended to vaporize, it produced only moderately bright light. By the early twentieth century, entrepreneurs such as the Germans Hugo Hirtz and Gustav Byng (founders of General Electric) and C. J. Robertson were experimenting with metallic filaments, using first platinum and then vanadium, niobium, osmium, and a mixture of osmium and tungsten called "osram." But of all metals, it was tungsten that could burn the hottest, to a temperature as high as just over 3,400 degrees Centigrade (6,170° F).[15] As Wolfgang Schivelbusch writes, "Just before the First World War, the tungsten filament was developed. This perfected incandescent lighting, which finally realized its full range, from a weak reddish glow right through to the blinding white light of a modern 300-watt light bulb."[16]

As a means of lighting, electricity improved upon its predecessor, gas, with cleanliness, silence, instantaneity of availability, and brilliance, not to mention its comparative ease and safety of production. David Nye describes the domestic advantage of the new electric light:

> One contemporary noted that with electric lamps, "In the billiard room the table is brilliantly lit, without danger of soil or soot marring the baize." Gas fixtures had to be washed of black soot almost daily, and they soiled wallpaper or fabrics. Molly Harrison found, "It was because of the collection of soot from gas and oil lamps that the Victorian housewife embarked upon the elaborate ritual of spring-cleaning. We hear nothing of it in earlier centuries. At the end of the winter they took down the heavy winter curtains, shook them outside. . . . Draperies, carpets, and upholstery had to have the loose soot beaten out of them, ceilings were washed and re-whitened, and the white summer curtains and the light chair-covers were put on."[17]

One should not interpret Nye as celebrating the liberation of the housewife, however, even though this soot-based version of spring cleaning faded as one of her rituals. As the human servants in the middle-class household came to be replaced by electrically powered devices, increasingly higher standards of housekeeping led to new standards of cleanliness; and women, who had been managing people, now had to make machines produce a world that could bespeak their proper feminine devotion and thoroughness.[18]

Mrs. Darling's performance of femininity and motherhood is shaped by the expectations for women of her generation and her class. While she would be expected to direct spring cleaning, she would not necessarily participate in it—she would have staff to do that for her (in the way that Peter had Tinker Bell, who as an electric force was also modern). Given that as a "tinker," this creature was originally a mender of fairy pots and kettles, and that in British society of the time such workers were typically Gypsies, the characterization, as Tracy Davis notes, was likely a reflection of the presence of Gypsies on the outer margins of Barrie's world—polite English society in the early twentieth century:

Tinker Bell's trade—like other gypsy service trades such as chair-bottoming and caning, umbrella repair, knife-sharpening, rat-catching, and agricultural implement repair—succumbed to industrial capitalism in cities and was waning even in the remote countryside of Edwardian Britain. As a gypsy-fairy, therefore, Tinker Bell was doubly threatened: her tinker livelihood was almost obsolete and her fairy habitat was fast disappearing except in the remotest parts of the countryside, both increasingly on the fraying edges of lived memory for those in the mainstream. . . . The will to believe in—and to understand—fairies and their kin was, by the turn of the century, in tension with the forces of industrialization, urbanization, imperialism, and nationalism. In 1801, 66% of the population of England and Wales were rural; by 1901, 79% were urban.[19]

Electrical illumination in the home was mother's fairy slave, after all, liberating her womanhood even as it simultaneously caught the eye of men and challenged the beliefs of everyone. To "believe in" Tink was to commit oneself to a preindustrialized spirituality and an outré social presence at the same time as to accept and marvel in the electrical possibilities of the future: it was to orient and disorient oneself simultaneously, to move in contradictory directions with the same impetus, to be both antimodernist and modernist in a single breath, and therefore to have an ecstatic experience.

Vigilant Light

Light—electric, gas, or candle-powered—might seem to have its own consciousness, even its own life. And light is, above all things, vigilant. Not long after our introduction to Mrs. Darling in *Peter Pan*, her hand is set to the problem of illumination. She is in the nursery with her fussy husband, preparing to go out for an evening by tucking her three children, Wendy, Michael, and John, into bed. "There are three beds," read the stage directions, ". . . Over each bed is a china house, the size of a linnet's nest, containing a night-light";[20] and now Michael is wondering whether he and his siblings will be safe for the night:

MICHAEL: Can anything harm us, mother, after the night-lights are lit?
MRS. DARLING: Nothing, precious. They are the eyes a mother leaves behind her to guard her children.

As eyes, the lights are presumably alert, aware, and cognitive, not to say loyal and diligent. They can be invoked, much as in *The Tempest* Prospero called up his spirit Ariel:

MRS. DARLING (with a last look round, her hand on the [nursery light] switch):
Dear night-lights that protect my sleeping babies, burn clear and steadfast
to-night.[21]

That Mrs. Darling feels she must implore the lights to "burn steadfast" does
not mean to guarantee that these night-lights are operated electrically, even
though by the early years of the twentieth century electricity was routinely
supplied to middle-class havens in Bloomsbury such as the Darlings' "corner
house" looking out "upon a leafy square."[22] The fragility of their illumination suggests instead that the night-lights are likely to have been either
porcelain lithophanes powered by candles (and decorated with little houses)
or else simple candles burning inside porcelain sculptures. The lithophane
was a plate or shade of porcelain, opaque and applied in layers so that the
densest layers transmitted the least light and a certain softened chiaroscuro
effect could be obtained in the bucolic or urban scene etched on the surface.
Whether or not they are lithophanes, the night-lights in the Darling nursery
are surely quaint little evocations of some nostalgic scene, suggesting comfort, the ease that comes with class dominance, and the romance that follows
from occupying a pleasing view. The night-lights are surely tiny representations of the electric light that by this time would have been flowing through
such a house under this woman's command, but, more crucially, they exemplify a pre-electric style of illumination, as we shall shortly see.

Mrs. Darling invokes a celebrated little prayer, or charm, to summon
the power of these little lights, which is nothing other than the protective
and maternal power of illumination. But as soon as she has left, a certain
spirit steals into the nursery, one described in the stage direction this way:
"Something uncanny is going to happen, we expect, for a quiver has passed
through the room, just sufficient to touch the night-lights. They blink three
times one after the other and go out."[23] In the novel form of the story (first
published in 1911 as *Peter and Wendy*), we find an account considerably less
stageable yet more animated, indeed utterly anthropomorphized:

> For a moment after Mr. and Mrs. Darling left the house the night-lights
> by the beds of the three children continued to burn clearly.
>   They were awfully nice little night-lights, and one cannot help wishing
> that they could have kept awake to see Peter; but Wendy's light blinked
> and gave such a yawn that the other two yawned also, and before they
> could close their mouths all the three went out.[24]

Here, mother's luminous nursery maids are delicate, genteel, and a little
self-absorbed, moved to yawn at a moment when diligence is called for, like
exhausted servants happy to be free of the mistress's observing eye.

The night-light as a bedside fixture was intended, of course, to assist reading in the dark, and in an early 1920s rhapsody about this practice, H. M. Tomlinson touts the power of the candle above all other possibilities, invoking, as he does, the very power of literary text to act as a light source itself:

> As the bed-book itself should be a sort of night-light, to assist its illumination, coarse lamps are useless. They would douse the book. The light for such a book must accord with it. It must be, like the book, a limited, personal, mellow, and companionable glow; the solitary taper beside the only worshiper in a sanctuary. That is why nothing can compare with the intimacy of candle-light for a bed-book. It is a living heart, bright and warm in central night, burning for us alone, holding the gaunt and towering shadows at bay. There the monstrous specters stand in our midnight room, the advance guard of the darkness of the world, held off by our valiant little glim, but ready to flood instantly and founder us in original gloom.[25]

This was a sensibility that could not have been foreign to Barrie as he composed his nursery scene, nor was it accidental that he considered the intimate embrace of literature in conceiving the Darlings and their abode. The house in which these night-lights burned so tentatively was "at the top of a rather depressed street in Bloomsbury. We have a right to place it where we will, and the reason Bloomsbury is chosen is that Mr. Roget once lived there. So did we in days when his *Thesaurus* was our only companion in London; and we whom he has helped to wend our way through life have always wanted to pay him a little compliment. The Darlings therefore lived in Bloomsbury."[26]

Just as through the night-light texts become available to the human spirit, through illumination in general the world becomes an accessible text. To understand is to see the light. To become aware is to have the light turned on. And if illumination is given over to the care of the Mrs. Darlings of the world, so, then, are knowledge, inquiry, exploration, and understanding products of a general kind of domestication and illumination that work inseparably together.

Mrs. Darling's darling lights, however, are about to be vanquished, not by darkness, for which we must wait to arrive at Neverland, but by an even greater light. For it is as a source of light supremely beyond these frail night-lights, a light that overshadows candle flame precisely as does the electric lamp, that Tinker Bell is first introduced. Cast as a fairy, she is, indeed, an embodiment of electric illumination as magical power. In the stage play this power is manifested principally through Tinker Bell's capacity for seemingly frictionless motion: "There is another light in the room now, no larger than Mrs. Darling's fist, and in the time we have taken to say this it has been into the drawers and wardrobe and searched pockets, as it darts about looking for a certain shadow." In the novel version, the power is that of incandescent intensity: "There was another light in the room now, a thousand times brighter than the night-lights."[27] The novel's text is careful to elucidate the true nature of Tink, lest a reader imagining this scene might chance to think Peter Pan really did travel around accompanied by a kind of tiny lamp: "It was not really a light; it made this light by flashing about so quickly." Tinker Bell is a source of illumination, a traveling power to illuminate, something like cinema. And in characterizing this brilliant, moving, cinematic light as fairy light, Barrie reflects upon the link between brilliant illumination, exciting movement, the optical spectacle—all as evident in cinema—and earlier optical phenomena that excited the eye through movement and intense illumination: the phantasmagoria, for example.[28]

An encyclopedia version of the tale, written early in the twentieth century and published in the 1920s, set out "The Story of Peter Pan" for young readers who might not have seen the play or read Barrie's novel. Here, too, Tinker Bell has a power that recalls the projects of both Wagner and Skriabin to meld color, illumination, drama, and musical sound: "Instantly a spot of light flicked into the room, and sprang round the walls, and over the ceiling, and down the beds, and across the carpet, making a tinkling sound wherever it flitted and whenever it settled for a moment."[29] This synesthetic mixture of illumination and musical sound further personifies the fairy by giving her a "voice" at the same time as it enchants the technological feature of the moving light, bringing it outside the confines of science and into the domain of art. Whereas the children's encyclopedia reconstructs Tinker Bell as a form that sings as it moves, as a product of its movement, the Barrie novel explicitly identifies Tink's music, "the loveliest tinkle as of golden bells," as "the fairy language," and associates it uniformly with the little creature's attempts to express herself.[30] In the play this language had been identified more tentatively, through a simile: "The answer comes as of a tinkle of bells."[31] Through Tinker Bell, then, light in its very brilliance— especially electric light—had personality, currency, linguistic fluency, and magical potency. As a creature to be seen, one whose fullness was realized as a specular quality, Tink brilliantly suggested the fixing of light upon film. In the late nineteenth and early twentieth centuries, photography was linked by many to spiritualism, to the desire to see beyond the empirical world, to the search for fairies, to the avant-garde presentation of a spectacle that transcended realism, to the trick of vision. So that the flitting, brilliant Tinker Bell of the 1904 stage play later became the tinkling fairy of the prewar novel suggests not only the principles of femininity and continual motion but also the synesthesia of harmonized art, the invocation of the photographic image, and the technological marvel of electricity.

Indeed, Tinker Bell is a missing link between electricity and the world of the supernatural, since this paragon of luminosity, this ungrounded, continually moving incandescence, is, as Peter explicitly informs Wendy in the play, also one of those fairy creatures who "are nearly all dead now . . . there ought to be one fairy for every boy or girl." But "children know such a lot now. Soon they don't believe in fairies, and every time a child says 'I don't believe in fairies' there is a fairy somewhere that falls down dead."[32] Tinker Bell's capacity to illuminate thus depends upon our (outmoded) conviction in her transubstantiality. In much the same way, the avidity of the general population for electric light in the early twentieth century flowed not from an understanding of the principles of incandescence and electrical resistance but from a belief in the magical power of technology, a belief that by throwing a switch one could have moonshine. (In a news account from 1950, in Devonshire, a school teacher picked up tiny Jimmy Baldson, so that he might flick the switch, high on the wall, that would bring electric light to their community. "A little nervously he pressed the switch down. Then, for the first time in his life, he saw electric light. He looked *down at me*, his face shining with delight: 'Tez like moonshine, Miss!'"[33]) Technology was itself a fairy.

Tinker Bell's Historical Moment

That "Tinker Bell" appears in the dramatis personae of *Peter Pan; or, The Boy Who Would Not Grow Up* does not mean the character had to be played by an actor. In the 1904 performance and in many subsequent stagings of the play, the bright light "no larger than Mrs. Darling's fist,"[34] produced by a stagehand holding a mirror, was associated with an offstage musician playing tiny bells. That she is a fairy was, for this performance, an ideological construct invoked as Peter tells Wendy, "I ran away to Kensington Gardens and lived a long time among the fairies."[35] That tinkling of bells, that "fairy language,"[36] Barrie insists producers reading his script should "hear" and digest, since he writes in a stage direction, as the spirit is freed from a chest of drawers, "Tink . . . darts about in a fury using language it is perhaps as well we don't understand."[37] From the beginning Tinker Bell was "not very polite":

PETER: She says you are a great ugly girl, that she is my fairy. You know, Tink, you can't be my fairy because I am a gentleman and you are a lady. (Tink replies)

WENDY: What did she say?

PETER: She said "You silly ass." She is quite a common girl, you know. She is called Tinker Bell because she mends the fairy pots and kettles.[38]

Barrie's dramaturgical technique here is a modification of Erving Goffman's "saying-for," a procedure in which a competent speaker articulates for an incompetent one (often a young child).[39] While saying-for can be used as a way of bringing prelinguistic children and pet animals into speaking society, it can also function, as it does here, to make manifest part of a discourse that is, for one dramatic reason or another, inaccessible to an audience's ears. (For a tour de force elaboration on saying-for, see Ch. LIX of *The Count of Monte Cristo*.) In this case, the audience is Wendy, and theatergoers watching the play identify with her in requiring Peter's translations as Tinker Bell "talks."

Tinker Bell was born at a particular historical moment, which is to say, there is a certain cultural, scientific, and artistic necessity that undergirds her curious domestic, fantastic, electrical nature. Toward the end of the nineteenth century gas lighting gradually gave way to electrical light, and European civilization (and the particular neo-European civilization that was America) changed forever. With electric light the day was lengthened,[40] work was expanded and more closely monitored, and, now that the world was more visible in its finest points and movements, time seemed to slow and even to stop (as present experience, situated in an eminently visible locale, seemed to expand outward into what had earlier been an area of shadow). From the early 1880s onward, even more can be said about electricity and culture. As Schivelbusch declares, "Electricity was believed to be, and was used as, a means of restoring exhausted energies."[41] It was at once a program, a revivification, a stimulant. It corseted the body and cured it of fatigue; it stimulated the growth of vegetables; the electric bath allowed one to be cleansed in health, and as though by magic; and by the early years of the twentieth century electro-shock techniques took form as a plan for therapeutically "exposing the body to electricity."[42] To be sure, since the Romans had cured headaches by touching patients with electrically charged sea creatures, electric shock was not novel in medical treatment; what was new was its diffusion and its commercially exploited scientific rationale. Very like a mother, electricity protected us, nursed us, shaped us, and guided us.

Tinker Bell would participate in this exciting development characterologically, because among other things she was a light source (casting, on her own, no shadow).[43] In that it came very early to be applied to both the body and the soil, that is, to matters of health or therapy and matters of fecundity, the spirit of electricity seemed from the beginning a female one, rather as Tinker Bell embodies it. For seventy-five years the principal application of electric power was toward the amelioration and redomestication of the home—"Starting just before 1900," Nye observes, "it became an integral part of both progressive and feminist housing designs,"[44] beginning with a newly clarified illumination that, thanks to the replacement of the revolving switch by the spring action quick-break switch, could be turned on and off at a wink, and culminating in the 1950s with the diffusion of radios and televisions and manifold household appliances designed for the "perfect home-maker." Karal Ann Marling lists some of the goodies that could typically be found in 1950s American homes:

> A hi-fi, a TV, and a nifty little transistor radio. Power tools. But most of all electrical appliances: a giant refrigerator-freezer, a washer-dryer combination, a toaster, a Hoover Constellation vacuum cleaner (in the shape of a space satellite), a portable mixer, a steam iron, a percolator, an immersible fry-pan, and a rotisserie with a see-through window. If the whirring, purring appurtenances of the suburban good life were driving women mad, they were nonetheless central to the definition of an *American* way of life.[45]

And once these possessions had come into one's world, status maintenance depended upon their visibility. Nye comments, "From the start, home electrification was not merely utilitarian. The novelty of the new force encouraged experimentation, and people took pleasure in festooning their homes and gardens with light, not in order to see better, but to see their possessions anew."[46] He gives an illustration, in fact, of a gentleman wearing an electric-light tie pin. Although electric light was relatively expensive, consumers like Cornelius Vanderbilt and J. P. Morgan could have generators built into their homes and put lights everywhere, outside and in, if only to show that they had the wherewithal to do so: "during the first quarter century only the wealthy had electricity in their homes, where it was primarily a form of conspicuous display," writes Nye.[47] And Schivelbusch prints an 1881 gravure by Poyet in which a ballerina dances with electric jewels affixed to her bosom and tiara.

The maternity that was at the center of the electric universe appeared either as Mother personified or as some embodiment of the maternal instinct—exactly the instinct Tinker Bell employs when, at the climax of *Peter Pan*, she twinkles into Peter's lair to drink the poisoned medicine the villainous Captain Hook has left for him. If the fairy light was not Mother herself, it was her device, her talisman. A 1936 advertisement for Siemens lamps, tagged "Used for lighting Big Ben and just as Reliable," showed a mother with two happy children at a drawing room window through which could be seen the specter of Big Ben, lit up at night. By her arm gesture of demonstration, the maternal figure is identifying herself with the light, owning it, making it hers to demonstrate, and also becoming a kind of standing beacon inside the home, an electric monument if not a monument to electricity. "Mother," quotes Brian Bowers from a Croydon diary, "could see the benefit of electricity in other places and consequently lost her fear of it. In 1929 it was installed in our home. 'Just look!' cried Mother excitedly, 'A little flick and we are flooded with light!'"[48] A 1929 advertisement featured a woman gazing into a hand mirror and proclaiming, "Pearl Mazda lamps certainly make me look my best."[49]

The conceit that light existed only as itself, and thus that electricity, in producing it, was germaine to an utterly discrete entity, had been given the lie by Hermann von Helmholtz in 1847, when to the Berlin Physical Society he proclaimed that "heat, light, and electricity are but one thing; energy," reports André Joffroy.[50] In 1888, Heinrich Hertz wrote in the Wiedmann Annals, "Light, heat rays and electro-dynamic motion are the same thing."[51] In marshaling the production and use of electric light for both domestic and universal purposes, then, it was to energy itself that women became allied, to a form of energy, indeed, that far superseded manpower. We need but think of the female hand turning the switch that awakened and released the current (or the female teacher lifting little Jimmy up for his ceremonial act) to understand how energy was not a thing but a movement, a fluctuation and decrease of potential, and how woman was damming and releasing it at will to enliven the home. Joffroy notes that Friedrich Engels observed that the multiple transformations of energy involved in electricity "doubtless contributed to a certain cultural evolution which tended to regard the world less as a complex of things than as a complex of processes."[52] The electric light, then, was a presence and a system, a motility and a happening, a capacity and an effect. If men designed electricity, if they mapped its possibilities and organized its manifestations, all this was done so that electricity could be woman's to possess, to use, to relish, and to identify with. Thus, it is no surprise that Peter Pan's electrically glowing fairy friend should have been a female one. Fairies came in both genders, after all.

The experience of fairies submits to a number of descriptions, according to geographical setting and cultural circumstance: "They were a small people dressed in green, and had dwellings underground in dry spots"[53] is one handy description, and, like Tinker Bell falling upon Peter Pan's glass, they are fond of milk: "Whatever milk falls on the ground in milking a cow is taken by the fairies, for fairies need a little milk."[54] They are sometimes seen as opalescent, and Evans-Wentz gives an Irish mystic's description (in 1911) strikingly evocative of an image that Herbert Brenon would conjure for Paramount in 1924:

There was at first a dazzle of light, and then I saw that this came from the heart of a tall figure with a body apparently shaped out of half-transparent or opalescent air, and throughout the body ran a radiant, electrical fire, to which the heart seemed the centre. Around the head of this being and through its waving luminous hair, which was blown all about the body like living strands of gold, there appeared flaming wing-like auras. From the being itself light seemed to stream outwards in every direction; and the effect left on me after the vision was one of extraordinary lightness, joyousness, or ecstasy.[55]

The fairy world, further, was a subject of more general invocation at the end of the nineteenth century in Europe. Walter Benjamin described the passages of Paris, for example, as similar to fairy caves[56] and quoted Adolphe Démy's comment that wandering in the Crystal Palace one might think oneself "in the crystal palace of a fairy" (*Arcades*, 162).[57] The sense of the fairy as embodying a "radiant, electrical fire" (of all possible fluids) and thus as being connected not only with beauty and nature and femininity but also with electricity, is a strong and important idea.

TINK ONSCREEN: 1924

Twenty years elapsed before Tinker Bell flitted onto the screen, with Barrie rejecting offers of several thousand pounds apiece on numerous occasions principally because he could find nothing that cinema could bring of freshness and inspiration to a subject that worked very well upon the stage. After a hundred and fifty performances in its opening production, indeed, the play migrated to America and was then restaged in Britain for years (even after 1912 when Charles Frohman, its stalwart producer, went down with the *Lusitania*). But Jesse Lasky prevailed upon Barrie, "the biggest literary game hunted by Paramount,"[58] with a promise of something new and bright, and Charles Chaplin, meeting Barrie at his flat in Adelphi Terrace in 1921, encouraged him, saying "It has even greater possibilities as a film than a play." Finally, the playwright agreed.[59] Barrie, who had full right of approval of any actor playing any role he had written, especially Peter, composed special scenes for the film, one of which, a football (soccer) game played high in the trees, was never used. In 1924, Paramount gave the project to one of its brightest and most promising directors, Herbert Brenon, who brought along a cinematographer with whom he had been working for some time, James Wong Howe.

The first screened Tink was produced through a combination of two separate processes imbricating all three central aspects of the character—her domestic femininity, her electrical potency, and her magical and spiritual charm. The first of these involved a technical lighting invention: a light bulb attached to a wire was powered through a rheostat, so that it could

1.1 As she hovers near Peter (Betty Bronson) on the mantel of the Darling nursery, the original screen Tinker Bell is, just as Barrie ordered, "a thousand times brighter" than the nightlights beside the children's bedsides in Herbert Brenon's *Peter Pan* (Paramount, 1924). Digital frame enlargement.

be dimmed and brightened on command and thus produce the dying and reviving qualities demanded in the poison scene:

> Howe uses his effect lighting to make Tinker Bell's [sic] death a poignant, real moment. Having created the tiny fairy by using a parking light on a dimmer switch, he could make the light appear to breathe by raising and lowering the voltage. After Tinker Bell sacrifices herself by drinking the poison meant for Pan, Howe gradually dims the light until it is extinguished. At "Tink's" miraculous recovery, the light returns to normal.[60]

The other was a camera process, involving the actress Virginia Browne Faire, who had been born in Brooklyn just months before the play's debut in London and was by now a veteran of twenty-six silent movies. Dressed in a long diaphanous gown to resemble the Yorkshire fairies that had been photographed in 1917 and shown to the world by Conan Doyle, Faire was posed tugging the handle of a dresser drawer and twisting shut the window lock in the nursery, "fighting the bedroom air currents."[61] James Card marvels that Brenon and Howe had "solved the magical riddle . . . not with ghostly transparencies but with real and solid images breaking new trails through stars and star wars to come."[62]

There are two distinct ways the "live-action" shots "miniaturizing" Faire could have been constructed: either through straight photography with giant sets, or through an in-camera matte process in which Faire, photographed separately, is printed over shots of the dresser and window. The work is of such a refined quality that it is impossible to tell with the naked eye which route was taken. Tom Gunning writes of spirit photography that it often provided an "extraordinary conjunction of uncanny themes," and that instead of revealing a visual discourse characterized by "apodictic clarity," the photographic encounter with spirits uncovers "a proliferating spiral of exchanges and productions of images, founded in a process of reproduction for which no original may ever be produced."[63]

With Brenon and Howe's film we have something of the same phenomenon, and in reference to images of a fairy! Whether we are looking at a photograph representing the "actual Faire" modeling upon a giant set, or at a photograph representing the photographic process itself—that is to say, representing a photograph of Faire layered into a complex image including a photograph of a set—is impossible to tell. In the lightbulb sequences as well as the process shots, Howe's low-key lighting (so typical of his work at the time that "Low-Key" came to be his nickname) helps establish a visual context for the special, magnified glow that is Tink, and indeed when she appears onscreen for the first time, in that children's nursery lit with candle-powered reading lights, the intensity of her illumination is so powerfully differentiated from the scene that she seems to symbolize electricity itself as it hurls gaslight and candlelight backward into history. She seems, for that matter, since her glow is so austerely, coldly white and powerful, to symbolize carbon arc light in its harsh, unremitting radiance. It was carbon arc light resembling the light of the sun that shone out in the earliest film projections, and that replaced direct sunlight as a source of illumination for shooting on set.

At the same time as it engenders special staging or lens effects, edited film makes possible both dissolves and the coherent use of close-ups—two visual possibilities that are impossible onstage; by dissolving into close-ups of the Tinker Bell light source and revealing Faire in her fairy gown, the film succinctly establishes the connection between technological progress, the new illumination, shocking brightness, domesticity, femininity, and graceful beauty, not to say wiles and motives Peter Pan might hardly comprehend. While Tink is dramatically linked to Peter as companion, helper, and protector, she belongs graphically in Wendy's world, equally female, equally domestically minded, equally brighter than her background. It is indeed into the sepia-tinted scene of the nursery that Tinker Bell makes her first cinematic appearance, zipping through the open window and hopping hither and thither before settling inside a vase upon the mantelpiece toward screen right. The light moves with exceptional rapidity, appearing occasionally to halt in mid-air and take stock of itself for a moment before jumping to a new position, all this to a musical accompaniment of sixteenth notes played upon a flute and punctuated now and then by delicate ringing sounds from a xylophone. We are treated to a close shot of one of the candle-powered reading lamps, its glow flickering upon the bedside wall. Then Tink hovers over Wendy's bed, shifting here and there while she examines the sleeping girl with scintillating strands dangling from her underside rather as though she is a sparkler. When Pan leaps into the room and beckons Tink to show him where his shadow is, we see her land upon the handle of the topmost dresser drawer and work at tugging it, stymied as she is by the fact that her feet have no purchase on any other surface; she first concentrates on her grip upon the handle and then turns back to flash a winning grin at Peter off-camera as her long gown flutters behind her. Later in the film, as, having drunk Peter's poisoned "medicine" to save his life, Tink lies in her tiny curtained, cavernous boudoir on the edge of death, we are again treated to a proportion effect, but this time through editing, as Peter gazes at Tink's little abode and a matching shot reveals what appears to be a wee theatrical proscenium, complete with dropped gauze curtain behind which we see Tink prostrating herself upon a rug, weakening by the moment. In the film's conclusion, when Peter and Tink have returned with the Darling children, Peter has Tink attempt to hold shut the nursery window to keep Wendy out, and once again an effects shot allows us to see her feisty personality as she turns to grin possessively at Peter off-camera.

While Brenon's film was the first explicit cinematic representation of Tinker Bell, it was not cinema's first venture into fairyland. Frank Kessler, who notes that "the fairy was quite often invoked as a metaphor to talk about the wonders of modernity," writes about earlier cinematic fairyworks, or "*féerie,*" in which a "fantastic subject" is presented through a method in which "the spectacular elements of the mise-en-scène, the sets, and the costumes are foregrounded, whereas the narrative serves largely as a pretext to introduce all sorts of marvelous effects."[64]

Kessler cites *La Biche au bois* of 1896, which included a fairy sequence of about a minute's duration, and goes on to discuss fairy-works in the films of Georges Méliès, who, because of a jam one day in his camera, discovered the "substitution stop-trick" and became able "to create effects similar to those presented on the stage with the aid of complex machinery."[65] *Le Royaume des fées* (1903) is a key example. In addition, between 1894 and 1897, numerous films were shot by W.K.L. Dickson, William Heise, or James White for the Edison Manufacturing Company and the American Mutoscope and Biograph Company, featuring Annabelle Whitford Moore and Crissie Sheridan moving voluptuously in front of the camera in long diaphanous gowns, the massive sleeves of which could be twirled rapidly to give a fluttering effect. These films, brilliantly hand-tinted, include at least one in which Annabelle is distinctly wearing fairy wings and a little fairy crown; the films were intended for projection in a Kinetoscope, which would make the dancing "fairy" both tiny and precious and also short-lived, evanescent, and thus miraculous. For his Tinker Bell, then, Herbert Brenon had a model that was luminous, artfully feminine, transformative, brilliantly illuminated, and notably theatrical, not only from the stage version of Barrie's play but also from early cinematographic renditions of fairies.

Through editing and camera techniques, and using both lighting effects and live acting, Tinker Bell and her fairy magic are interpreted in the Brenon film as a methodical alternation of electrical luminosity and female wiles. For it is unmistakable in the close-ups of Faire, as she works upon the dresser or upon the window handle, that she is female in the most fully embodied sense, a young woman with desire who acts spontaneously and with unpredictable flourish (like a light being turned on), and whose comportment is far less restrained than that of the other females in the story. Female comportment is a central issue in *Peter Pan*. In her lack of restraint and modesty, the Tinker Bell of this film reflects more general Hollywood trends of the time that are described by Elaine Tyler May:

> The twenties had witnessed a shift away from Victorian models of womanhood. Stars of the 1910s, such as Lillian Gish and Mary Pickford, with their childlike innocence, declined in popularity as new stars emerged. The more exciting women of the 1920s, like Clara Bow or Greta Garbo, experimented with new moral styles and sexual ethics. The plots of the most popular films in the 1920s centered on the romance between two young moderns leading to marriage, or on stagnant marriages that were revitalized through recreation, sensuality, and excitement.[66]

Tinker Bell and Peter may be presumed to be playing out a marriage of sorts, perhaps even a stagnant one here "revitalized" through the "excitement" of Peter's affair with Wendy. Wendy and Peter, of course, openly play at being married, with Tinker Bell as the lascivious, engaging, "exciting" other woman. Gilad Padva's observation that in European folklore fairies "are usually depicted as beautiful young women who help humans and even marry and reproduce with them"[67] may indicate a source of the erotic tension between the fairy and Wendy, a tension Barrie envisioned in 1903 as he wrote, "W has told P how T hates her—does things to her— changes her."[68]

While the antics of Tinker Bell were implicit in the 1904 stage play, that dramatization necessarily stopped short of actually presenting the fairy's notable lack of restraint in explicitly graphical terms; the brazenness of the fairy could thus have been confined happily to the willful imagination of the Duke of York's Theatre audience. By 1924, however, according to Walter Metz, "the flapper and other images of New Women were competing" with a nineteenth-century gender discourse of True Womanhood, under which "Victorian women stayed at home while their husbands went out to work. This arrangement was appropriate because women were morally pure and could regenerate their husbands upon their return home from the dirty, corrupt industrial world."[69] Barrie's Mrs. Darling is clearly a paragon of True Womanhood, and the explicitly naughty and lascivious Tinker Bell in Brenon's film is ideologically at war with her as the sort of model Wendy might profitably emulate as she grows into womanhood. While Tink's flirtatiousness had been part of the earliest conceptions of the character—

> Although that fairy had no existence beyond lightings and sounds, her flirtatious behaviour and appearance were referred to in the earliest scripts—"Tippy, if you don't get up and dress at once, I shall open the curtains and then we shall all see you in your negligee"[70]

it is embodied by Brenon in an unambiguously direct manner. Perhaps this is why Brenon's film was what William K. Everson calls a "freak success," since by 1924 "whimsy and fantasy were ingredients that materialistic jazz-age audiences just were not buying" in general.[71]

TINK ONSCREEN: THE 1950s

By the early 1950s, Simone de Beauvoir's *The Second Sex* (1949) had made waves in Europe but not yet found popularity in America, and Betty Friedan's revolutionary *The Feminine Mystique* was as yet a dream. Women's sexual and economic liberation during the Second World War was so intensive that popular culture was called upon to affirm "the project of domesticity."[72] "In the popular media," writes May, "women's sexuality became increasingly central to their identity. The promising as well as the troublesome potential of female eroticism found expression in the plots and genres of the decade."[73] But that sexuality was coiled in the war's noir aftermath with a certain stunned reserve—"In the wake of World War II . . . the short-lived affirmation of women's independence gave way to a pervasive endorsement of female subordination and domesticity."[74] Cultural practice and gender identification were directed in two contradictory ways at the same time. The libidinal freedom embodied in the pin-up and the femme fatale endured as the golden girl, specifically in the form of Marilyn Monroe in, for example, *Niagara*, Jayne Mansfield in *The Girl Can't Help It*, and Diana Dors in *An Alligator Named Daisy*. All three of these actresses made careers principally by displaying mammary prowess, blindingly bleached hair, genteel coyness, and generalized availability. Simultaneously, this caricature was held up for ridicule or criticism against popular models of the domesticated hausfrau that included, in early television, Harriet Nelson in *The Adventures of Ozzie & Harriet* and Loretta Young in "Letter to Loretta," and onscreen, Doris Day in *On Moonlight Bay*, June Allyson in *The Glenn Miller Story*, and Donna Reed in *The Last Time I Saw Paris*. As though the indecisive Wendy had retreated to a nunnery for an extended meditation upon her options, the explicit and implicit models of womanhood—presented respectively by Monroe and Day—competed with one another for girls,' and the world's, attention: New Womanhood and True Womanhood, as Metz calls them, in open battle.

It is not surprising that by the mid-1950s both the coordinated merchandising of home products from such megacorporations as General Electric (for instance color-matched kitchen appliances that appealed to the redomesticated housekeeper), and the shocking "wave" of juvenile delinquency, were happening, as it were, in light of one another. Monroe was thought by many (erroneously) to have been the model, in fact, for one particularly expressive and shameless Tinker Bell in 1953; while a much tamer, more modest, more bourgeois phantasm was presented on television only a short time later.

What Claude Coats, Eric Cleworth, Don Da Gradi, Joe Rinaldi, and the numerous other artists working at Walt Disney Studios achieved with their animation of Tinker Bell for the 1953 feature (directed by Clyde Geronimi, Wilfred Jackson, and Hamilton Luske) was a triple transformation of the character as envisioned originally by Barrie and then redramatized both in the Brenon film and the various stage presentations through the 1940s. First, the fairy creature whose sheath had been gossamer and whose abode had been a carpeted boudoir—she of the flashing grin and the long windblown hair, whose most ostensible quality had been an electric brilliance that in the end adapted her to the bourgeois interior as an illuminating, civilizing, cleansing presence—was now a vituperative pixie in a tight-fitting swimsuit. Two of the principal animators at the studio wrote that "Joe Rinaldi wanted Tinker Bell to look more like the popular bathing beauties of the time";[75] so it is that her beauty-contest body made a far more

1.2 Far beyond the postulates of spiritualism, Galvinism, and theosophy, and leaving the fairy image invoked by Arthur Conan Doyle far behind, the Walt Disney version of Tinker Bell is a narcissistic little flirt with a body shape designed to meet the needs of the 1950s consumer, in *Peter Pan* (Clyde Geronimi, Wilfred Jackson, and Hamilton Luske, Walt Disney Pictures, 1953). Digital frame enlargement.

lasting impression than did her spiritual capabilities. No mysterious inspiration for theosophists or Spiritualists, this!

And while Brenon's camera never moved in for a close-up of Tinker Bell that would have extended her body across the screen like the bodies of the other characters, the Disney team's tendency was to flesh out Tinker Bell and emphasize her curvy figure and cheeky personality with close-ups that made her as fully realized onscreen as any other (equally painted) character. In many ways, then, this production allowed Tinker Bell to become a legitimate rival of Wendy's for Peter's affection, since she partook of the same form as Wendy compositionally and, as a female, was drawn to be distinctly the shapelier of the two. The Disney project "might be said to follow the uncanny logic of *becoming* domestic," write Eleanor Byrne and Martin McQuillan of Disney's work in the 1950s in general.[76] Peter, further, in this and only this early rendition of the Pan story, is unequivocally a male figure.

Tink's nubile allure was sufficient pretext, secondly, for an important motivational sequence invented at Disney and inserted into the story, wherein she is captured, and then seduced, by Captain Hook, whose emotional manipulation results in her volunteering the location of Peter's hideaway by dancing across a map of Neverland to its secret coordinates. (Barrie's 1903 notebook contains a suggestion of Tippytoe "plotting with pirates" but goes no further.[77]) In this scene, Tink is jostled by Hook's chicanery into a jealous rage about Wendy. We might ask what sort of femininity she represents in this production. Sexual availability and desire are supplanted by the willingness to compete against another woman for possession of a male, which is a stark reaffirmation of masculinity—masculine embodiment and masculine presence—as a central and shared value; in short, the movie becomes an advertisement for patriarchy. At least as much as Mr. Darling or Captain Hook, Pan himself, in this cartoon, defines sexual identity in the field that surrounds him, and reduces both Wendy and Tinker Bell (and Tiger Lily) to subordinate positions, exactly by virtue of their willingness to do battle to win him as prize.

If the new womanhood demonstrated in earlier versions by Tinker Bell is coupled with her ability to illuminate her surroundings—her electrical charge linked to her magical spectacular potency—here it is interesting to see that although the pixie is still a source of light, nevertheless she does not radiate in her environment in the same outstanding way. The electrical Tinker Bell of the stage productions and the early film benighted her environment by her fierce luminous power, exactly in the way that the arc lamp in the Molteni lantern, used, for example, by the Lumière brothers for their first shows of 1895, astonished viewers with its clarity and intensity of illumination.[78] But here, all cells animated at Disney share a luminosity and a color saturation; all frames of the film are lit in the animation camera, not differentially on set. The world is entirely bright and colorful, Tinker quite as much as anyone or anything else. More embodied and fleshy, more randy, more sexually perverse than previous Tinker Bells— like many Disney characters, she delights in wagging her derrière in the viewer's face, as in the scene where she tries to open the dresser drawer— still she sheds less light.

The third transformation is the most marvelous, and has had the most long-lived effect in terms of its resonance in other Disney productions and in animation in general, and this is the so-called Disney dust, or fairy sparkle, that follows every twitch and gesture of Tinker Bell as a flutter of multicolored brilliant scintillations that wave off her body and then evaporate in a spangled trail behind her movement. This effect was not produced by the principal animators or cell painters but was added afterward by specialists called Color Model Advisors,[79] much in the way that nowadays a Foley track is laid in with decorative sounds after a picture is shot and edited. The scintillations of "fairy dust" are replacements for the intensity of illumination we see on film or onstage when actual electrical illumination can be used, and the effect is to accentuate not so much Tinker Bell's movement as the path she traces when she moves. The dust technique acts to map out her flight in a kind of evanescent highway system, replacing movement itself with a tracing of the perturbation in the territory that the movement has caused. Even before the poison scene, then, in which she must fade, Tinker's energy is always in a state of depletion and reduction in favor of a tracing of her curious vector. We see where she has been, instead of seeing her in fully dynamic action.

This motile Tinker Bell inhabiting the Disney *Peter Pan* was released to the world as of February 5, 1953. On March 7, 1955, NBC aired Fred Coe's production for television of the Richard Halliday/Jerome Robbins Broadway show, starring Mary Martin, a key example in the mid-1950s of what Pat Weaver, NBC's vice president in charge of programming, called a spectacular (and also of what Stacy Wolf considers lesbian performance).[80] This production, with music by Moose Charlap and lyrics by Carolyn Leigh, and additional songs by Betty Comden, Adolph Green, and Jule Styne, got a blockbuster overnight rating of 48 and moved the *New York Times*'s Jack Gould to rhapsodize upon it as "television's happiest hour."[81] The stage production had opened October 20, 1954, at the Winter Garden, and after this a special 1955 television airing; a reprise of it two years later; and an December 8, 1960, airing that was videotaped for release, it was mounted several more times on Broadway, commencing September 6, 1979, at the Lunt-Fontanne with Sandy Duncan and continuing with four productions to date that starred the ex-gymnast Cathy Rigby.

On 12 December 1976 another version of *Peter Pan* for television aired, with music by Anthony Newley and Leslie Bricusse and starring Mia Farrow and Danny Kaye. All stage productions of *Peter Pan* have nicely evidenced Adolph Klauber's claim that "there is no more difficult task for the theatrical producer than that involved in the task of suggesting a supernatural experience on the stage"; yet they have not, oddly enough, backed up his further claim that "as a rule, stage fairies, whether in Shakespearean play or modern pantomime, generally appear as pretty young ladies, chiefly conspicuous for the more than ordinary diaphanous nature of their apparel."[82] In these mid-twentieth-century New York stage and television productions, Tinker Bell was created by means of a shuttered follow-spot that was moved rapidly around the staging area, linked with small lights positioned in advance in certain stage props, such as, for example, the tree stump "boudoir" where Tink "lived" in Pan's underground hideout. The "voice" of the fairy was accomplished instrumentally in the Mary Martin production by a series of xylophone riffs. Reviewing the Duncan performance on 7 September 1979, Walter Kerr wrote in the *New York Times* of a "Tinker Bell who darts about like sky-writing, shimmers emerald-green, and can even spell," thus nicely conflating visions of the fairy as a kind of technical advancement (albeit one in the service of capitalism), an eerie, even mystical aesthetic manifestation, and a paradigm of literacy.[83] What is clearest about the staged Tinker Bell, however—and this includes the various stage productions I have mentioned above as well as the Eva Le Gallienne Civic Repertory production of 1928 and the 1950–1951 Leonard Bernstein musical—is that she is unembodied in all of them, to the extent, indeed, that she is included; she is configured in the narrative merely as a pure illumination. At the Empire Theater in New York, for example, in four productions starring Maude Adams between 1905 and 1916, Tinker Bell was played by Jane Wren, but it is difficult to know exactly what this means beyond the possibility of her playing music from offstage, since in at least the first of these productions the characterization was described in a Reuter's release to the *Times* of London as a "tintinnabulation" and "a will-o'-the-wisp gleam of light on the wall";[84] and the *New York Times* printed an anonymous review describing "a glancing flame of light and a musical tintinnabulation [sic], ephemeral witnesses that Tinker Bell (of the ilk of the fairies) is [Peter's] companion."[85]

Thus, while the Disney cartoon production is in many ways mawkish, to be sure, it does importantly revive one crucial aspect that is central to the earliest cinematic vision of Tinker Bell, her domestically positioned embodied femaleness. What the staged productions tended to do, at least after the 1924 Brenon film, was recapture and represent Tink as a source of vivid illumination, which is what we might call the "electric Tinker Bell." What Disney's animators did, however, was to retain her as a Little Woman.

SPECTACULAR TINK: SPIELBERG, LUHRMANN, HOGAN, FORSTER

However one summarizes the changing effect of Tinker Bell onstage and onscreen from her inception at the turn of the twentieth century through her manifestations in the 1950s, she remains consistently a concatenation of effects that conflate domestic femininity, electrical potency, and magical effusion. With her magic and her shine she cares for Peter and his household; or with feminine wiles she is jealous of Wendy and tries to use magic against her; or the intensity of her electrical glow is used as evidence of the vibrancy of her fairy life. But in *Hook* (1991), Steven Spielberg alters the equation, accentuating Tinker Bell's femaleness (through the casting of Julia Roberts), converting her magical potency to explicit special effects, and utterly expanding her electrical charge: she can carry Peter from London to Neverland; she can wish herself into human size, and then throw Peter into the air merely by reaching out and touching him. As a giant fairy, she can walk up and kiss him full on the lips, openly articulating that she

1.3 Effects rule. Neverland is Hollywood and Tinker Bell (Julia Roberts) is a movie star in Steven Spielberg's *Hook* (Amblin/TriStar, 1991). She can no more "die" than can Roberts's stardom, and the grown Peter (Robin Williams) is obliged to find her sexually attractive. Digital frame enlargement.

loves him and feeling mortified when he says he loves Moira and makes her realize that when this adventure is over he will leave Neverland and never come back. More than anything, then, Tinker Bell is here a contemporary movie star, female when she has expanded herself, in a way that summons images of a particular, rather than a generic, performer (even while, as a tiny fairy, she is as boyish as Pan is in all the other representations of this story); and transformational just as Pan himself is, through the agency of cinematic manipulation openly staged as such.

Schivelbusch suggests that "what Paul Lindau said in the 1880s about the impression made by electric arc lighting was equally true of the first gas lighting: 'The disproportionately strong and intense light . . . washes out all the surrounding colours and because theatrical devices become crudely apparent in the bright light, it destroys all illusion. Instead of a tree one sees a painted canvas.'"[86] In much the same way, there is a kind of intensity of "illumination" produced by sophisticated special effects, and they have a tendency to "wash out" the surrounding "color" of performance by creating a new standard of verisimilitude. Tinker Bell's fairy personality is entirely dissolved in the casting effect of using Roberts, and in the visual effects through which she changes size and moves through the air as a clearly visible miniature person.

Roberts came to the Spielberg shoot as a twenty-four-year-old actress whose performance in *Pretty Woman* had helped that film make 80 percent of its budget back on the opening weekend. She had also been seen in

Flatliners and *Sleeping with the Enemy*, films which did not do as well at the box office but certainly helped promote her name with audiences around the world. It was inconceivable that most viewers of *Hook* saw anything behind Tinker Bell but an extraordinarily well-known and much-celebrated star. The magic at her command, therefore, is nothing other than the magic of Hollywood. If the electricity of the earliest Tinker Bells was brilliant and cold, like the limelight of early staging and magic lantern projection or like the intense blue-white arc light of early cinema, the electricity effused by Roberts was, metaphorically, the emanation of film upon the screen itself, the illumination by which film was exposed. Her star quality infused every frame in which she was present, so that her screen appearance was at once a characterization and a self-reflection, a portrait of a fictional creature and a mirror image of Hollywood's most concentrated investment upon itself. Personification was of course a fundamental aspect of the character formula for this film, with Robin Williams playing a Peter Banning strikingly like a presumable offscreen super-sober Robin Williams, transformed into a Peter Pan strikingly like Robin Williams at his wackiest. In the rendition given by Roberts, Tinker Bell becomes the true love object for the transformed Peter, chthonic and female before she is anything else. To make her magical, Spielberg must utilize special effects of a sort more prominent and explosive than had been used before. When the Disney Tinker Bell has fairy dust follow her, that dust is as animated as she is, and so it seems no more an effect than she. And she can seem no more an effect than any other animated substance in the film. Spielberg's expanding and contracting Tink, on the other hand, seems to do things before our eyes that are ontologically impossible, since she also appears in the photography to be a real girl who cannot expand and contract in this way.

Tinker Bell is thus a kind of clef in the Spielberg film that allows us to read Neverland as Hollywood, the fairy as a movie star, the fairy magic as Hollywood's production machine to which she has been successfully subjected, and her femaleness as cultivated and industrialized and anything but domesticated. One effect of this reconstitution of the character is that the poison scene, now cleverly transposed, is made almost entirely unbelievable, since the stardom of Roberts is interminable for those who watch her fading as Tinker Bell: Tink cannot "die" anymore than Roberts can suddenly become ordinary. Peter Banning is in the nursery late at night, nursing a Scotch as he wanders past the crib and around a doll's house that rests on the floor. When Tinker Bell flies into the room she is fast-moving and coldly luminous, in what has become the tradition, though at first it is vaguely possible to discern a tiny female form inside the moving splotch of light; and soon afterward the light seems to be emanating from the little creature's heart. Peter at one point bats her into the doll's house, where we see her light flit around, illuminating this miniature domestic space room by room. He draws open the front of the house to speak to her and says he doesn't believe in fairies. She gags, falls down a staircase, and lies vitiating on a hall carpet until he "saves" her by clapping. It is only then that we see the Barbie and Ken dolls who "own" this house to which she has given light and spirit. It is not the viewer who needs to "believe," then, in order to "save" her, but the Peter who has forgotten Neverland and his role there as her consort. In this cinema of pure spectacle, what we are called upon to do is watch and watch only. Our credulity is of no concern, given the possibility that we can continuously be stunned.

A creature very akin to Tinker Bell (Marsha Kinder describes her as a "Tinker Bell–Ariel fairy"[87]), yet not Tinker Bell by designation appears as "The Green Fairy" (Kylie Minogue) in an absinthe-induced striptease parody of "The Sound of Music" in Baz Luhrmann's *Moulin Rouge!* (2001). Here, within a hazy green perfume, her wings fluttering hornily and her tight-fitting swimsuit nothing but a tease for the innocent lover Christian (Ewan McGregor), we see, in the context of "Bohemian Paris," a source of not only brilliant (electric-style) illumination, docile if energetic femininity, and evanescent spirit but also the illuminated word, since at a key moment, by speeding through the air with trails of fairydust sweeping behind her, she manages to spell out the words "Freedom . . . Beauty . . . Truth" upon the screen. "The hills are alive with the sound of music," she croons in a transport of green ecstasy, quickly multiplying herself until the starry sky is filled with a chorus line of "Tinker Bells."

While the character of Tink originates as language in the original play, the Luhrmann conception is the first to re-embody her as text in an explicit way. In this way, the doctrinaire femaleness represented by the character's appealing but conventional sexuality; her capacity to bring a new source of light, at least in the poetic sense, to the starving artist figure; and her magical potency are all conflated with her power to inscribe. Her brilliant flashing in the nocturnal sky is much more than a mere indication—it has become an outright statement or sign.

In P. J. Hogan's 2003 film *Peter Pan,* Tinker Bell is played in part by a vivid animation, in recollection of the Disney creation and with a copious sparkling fairy dust trail, and in part by the French actress Ludivine Sagnier, her blond hair bobbed quite fashionably, her torso clad in a tight-fitting gown of green leaves, and her flight enabled by giant translucent blue-green dragonfly wings. As she flies, she squeals merrily, posturing in her occasional pauses, which are often shown in close-up. There is something artificially boyish in the gesticulation and movement of this Tinker

Bell, exactly as there was something artificially boyish in the Peter Pans played by Boucicault and Adams, by Le Gallienne and Martin, by Duncan and Rigby. But in this film's Peter Pan, there is nothing girlish at all, since the role is performed by Jeremy Sumpter, a rather masculine boy of four-teen. Tinker Bell is his private spirit, to be sure, and one that moves with the speed of electricity if not with the coquetry or grace of a female, and without electricity's illuminating effect, since, as with the Disney cartoon, in this mixed animated and live-action feature there seems always to be sufficient illumination without Tink's contribution. Her lambency is in her twinkling, evident mostly in her movement, not in the simple intensity of the light she extrudes. When in the poison scene Peter is about to drink his "medicine" from a flowercup, Tink races through the woods, as only a computer-generated figuration can race onscreen, landing between the cup and Peter's lips just in time. She clamps his lips together with her hands, but he struggles free and tries again, so that she must position herself in front of his mouth with her own lips open to catch the liquid.

Two interesting features qualify a particular sequence in the Hogan film. First, since, unlike all other onscreen renditions of this story save the Dis-ney cartoon, the dramaturgy is not presented to an audience that is openly invoked (through characterizations that are two-dimensional and that fail entirely to connect with one another quite as much as they connect with those who observe), the plea to viewers to confirm their belief in fairies in order to make the dying Tinker Bell revive must be suspended entirely. The film is shot with a closed narrative, the characters fully engaging with one another in our invisible presence. Thus, we are not present in any sense and cannot be addressed. And yet some address must be made. Accordingly, the filmmaker reinvents from Spielberg, yet with a more direct and more chilling framing, the device of having Peter tearfully address to Tinker Bell herself the plaint, "I do believe in fairies!, I do!, I do!" over and over, as he bends over her cold blue body on the forest ground. The sky has rolled over with black clouds, and upon the *Jolly Roger,* Hook is celebrating the death of Pan. Back in the forest, it is snowing and Peter, as blue as Tink, drops a tear upon her and then looks up and proclaims his faith to the heavens, quite as though it were a manifesto; "I do believe in fairies! I do! I do!" Suddenly Wendy, lashed to the pirate ship's mast, looks up, too (in wide angle). Back to Peter: "I do believe in fairies," and then to Wendy, who echoes him. Peter: "I do believe in fairies," and then Wendy, "I do believe in fairies," and then John, "I do believe in fairies!," then Peter again, seen from high above as he looks up into the sky, "I do believe in fairies," with snowflakes tumbling into the forest around him; then all the Lost Boys on the pirate ship, in a rhythmic chant, "I do believe in fairies, I do, I do"; then one of the

pirates, unsheathing his sword, riotously and madly, "I do believe in fairies"; and Peter again, almost joyously; and in London, through her window,
a girl asleep in bed, "I do believe in fairies!," then a boy in his bed, then a
tiny girl in her bed, then Mrs. Darling in her reading chair; then triplets in
a single bed; then Mr. Darling to the board at his bank, expostulating in
some surprise and wonder, "I do believe in fairies! I do! I do!"; then Aunt
Millicent in her bathtub, and Peter in Neverland again, and a mad ballet
with all the pirates and the children, "I do believe in fairies!" as the sym-
phonic music builds extradiegetically, and Peter screaming "I do believe in
fairies!" and the warmth comes back into the light and Tinker Bell, soon,
soon, comes alive again. By now, everyone in the known universe—at least
the immediate dramatic universe—has bought into the mantra, everyone,
that is, of course, except the malicious Hook, who, as the chant is raised
to a heat, suddenly screams, "He's alive!" The first striking thing, then, is
that Tinker Bell is confirmed, and then saved, not by the audience but by
the characters of the story, who might very well be expected to believe in
Tinker Bell, since they share the "stage" with her and have no more reality
than she does if she expires.

The second feature is that the effect of the repetition of the mantra in
this musical, even thundering way, is to bring to our attention, quite explicitly, the idea of belief in fairies. Before the poison sequence, we encounter
a small aged male fairy on a tree in the woods, and Hook kills him merely
by whispering that there are no such things as fairies. It is interesting to
consider the effect of this ideological statement about the existence of fairies in light of the fact that this is clearly an early-twenty-first-century film
production—albeit one in which the London of 1904 is replicated—and
also one with a Tinker Bell who is not especially female, certainly not especially domestic, and whose electricity is used for locomotion more than for
illumination. By this point, in other words, the original configuration of
this character—as a conflation of femininity, electrical illumination, and
spiritualism—has entirely been converted to another sort of thing, a being
that fictional characters can substantiate as a "fairy" and who more clearly
inherits the explicit technologically assisted pedigree of the Julia Roberts
Tinker Bell. Our spiritualism is not invoked in the Hogan film. Nor is
our wonder at the illuminative powers of electricity, a wonder apparently
impossible to inspire in an age of computers and virtually universal electrical potency. Given our interest in gender-bending, gender reversal, gender
transformation, and gender play, we need not be sold a Tinker Bell who
can seduce Peter; and indeed, this Peter is a little young to be sexualized,
the part being played not only by a male but by an actual *boy*. His typical
response to her presence is a wide-eyed and dutifully attentive stare, as

though her technical capacity to dart through the air, to approach his face, to hover in front of his eyes, is in itself rather as astonishing as might be, say, a superimposition of an animated computer-generated character upon a straight piece of film. Watching Tinker Bell, Peter becomes any one of the many who are watching this film, a teeny-bopper smitten with "sexy" f/x.

FETISH

In two quite different ways, screen representations of Tinker Bell have elaborated a specific case of fetishism. First, an inorganic object, a spot of intense light, has been invested with spiritual, biological, and social characteristics exactly in the way that nature was transfigured by spiritualists, Galvinists, and theosophists early in the twentieth century. The projection of spirit into the object renders it a possession, a charm, and thus makes the world accord with our desire, as Bazin once said of film. The flitting, twinkling, speaking, conscious light becomes a spirit and then a character, at once a model of childish wish fulfillment and a paradigm for our adoption of technical material into the sphere of feelingful involvement. Nye reproduces in his *Electrifying America* a photograph made at the Golden Gate International Exposition of 1939 that shows the largest electric lamp ever made (50,000 watts). The giant bulb is being embraced by a little blonde female child with ringlets and a look of wonder on her face. Not only is electricity for women, in the feminist sense of freeing them from the drudgery of housework and importing to the domestic environment a permanent, clean, relatively safe slave; but it is *of* women, in that we directly associate its power of illumination and brightness with the female character. In this photograph, indeed, the female is tiny and wondrous, not unlike a fairy in many ways.[88] Nye also includes a photograph demonstrating "some early electrical appliances,"[89] in which the woman utilizing a silver electrical chafing dish is garbed in a long chiffon dress that vaguely resembles the diaphanous gown of the fairy in the Brenon film, the Doyle photographs, and the films of Spielberg and Hogan. Electricity becomes associated with domestic femininity through a linkage that invests it with spirit, embodiment, purpose, and human nature. But this linkage is not itself manifest as an object or connection between objects in the material world; it is conceived through the imagination spontaneously, and is thus spiritualist in and of itself.

The fetish of Tinker Bell is also centered upon a miniature version of the human form, a kind of moving doll, and this form is the subject of principal focus in the Disney, Spielberg, and Hogan film versions. Associated with intensive illumination only to the degree that she is a bright flash as she moves, and that she exudes scintillations, this Tinker Bell is most clearly a tangible sex object for Peter's imagination, reduced in size but not altered in shape. The Hogan Pan uses Tinker rather like a salt shaker at one point, when he tips her upside down and shakes fairy dust onto the Darling children. And when he deposits her dying body onto the forest floor, Tink is clearly for him a miniature substitute for a real full-sized being, a kind of sacred object. The fetishization by miniaturization is thus a way of sanctifying and objectifying the female, and the pronouncements of belief in fairies, however they are handled in any given production, speak to the investment of this fetish with the power to illuminate her world.

FULL CIRCLE

If she has lasted more than a hundred years—rumor has it that in the near future *Peter Pan* will appear again, over the signature of Larry Clark who will offer us, one might assume, a Tinker Bell characteristic of his distinctive tastes—Tinker Bell's power surely does not depend on the politics of femininity, since even as feminism has climbed and fallen she has endured. She attests to women's independence and power—power not only to illuminate but to control; yet at the same time she jealously fawns over Peter in a perfectly Victorian fashion; so there is something under or beyond her display of femininity that has made her perdure. That she was long associated with the electric universe imbued her with a capacity for motion, for brilliance, and for endlessly tappable reserves of potency, all of which seemed to transcend the more mundane power relations of everyday life; and allied her with a spiritual, unearthly self that promised to show the way out of the laborious confines of quotidian social arrangements. As energy, as movement, as brilliance, as fairy magic, she could be timeless. Indeed, our fascination with electricity in general, our conviction in its otherworldliness, and her link with it, trumped the domestic, servile associations that might just as well have characterized her. Her electric personality was, and remains, a signal of her high-tech character, making her passages across the boundary of rationality and presence and into the otherworldly part of a more general futuristic potency. She transcends the world we know and its temporal boundedness, in every way, while remaining for generation after generation a secure maidenhead of nourishment and love. She fuses mystery, mastery, mythmaking, and the sense of the marvelous. Yet, in all this, even as she moves forward through history, Tinker Bell may turn back upon herself and relive the past.

Marc Forster's *Finding Neverland*, a biographical tale of how James M. Barrie met the Llewelyn Davies children and came to write *Peter Pan*, treats us to a reconstruction of a few scenes of the December 27, 1904, opening night production, but Tinker Bell is entirely absent from the material on show. As Barrie's friend Sylvia Llewelyn Davies has taken very ill and missed this performance, however, a special presentation is arranged in her home, and during this sequence we do see the poisoning scene. Here the reconstruction does not follow history, but makes use of a reflection from a hand-held mirror accompanied by tinkling sounds a youth makes at the side of the staging area using a little silver bell. When Tink is about to die, she lands inside an electric lamp in the Llewelyn Davis drawing room, and here the illumination is gradually diminished using a dimmer. These maneuvers of staging have some importance, as Forster, the most contemporary director to produce a Tinker Bell for titillating an audience's credulity, foregoes direct electrical effects until the fairy is near death and instead makes use of reflection for the fairy's basic movement: it is true that what is reflected is also electrically produced light, although it need not have been. There is no direct physical manifestation of Tinker Bell in the Forster scene, and the audience's investment of belief is central for linking Peter Pan's dialogue addressed to the fairy and a conception of a fairy being who must be hearing that address.

Soon, a wall of the Llewelyn Davies house is raised to reveal an enchanted garden outside—"That," says Barrie, "is Neverland"—and here we find a number of fairy creatures dancing gently in the nocturnal half-light. These are full-sized female dancers, some airborne, with wings, but the effect produced by the filmic staging is to render them entirely believable in the phantasmal garden as fairy folk, at least insofar as the little audience onscreen—Sylvia, her mother, and her children—are concerned. There is also a male sprite, with huge purple dragonfly wings, moony eyes, and a purple pansy hat, hiding among ferns. Sylvia soon stands and walks into this scene, her train held from behind by two little fairies, and as she walks off into the distance the camera cranes up and the scene fades. We are next at her funeral, and thus aware that the fairy world she enters, her "Neverland," is the afterlife. In this production Tinker Bell's function is to signal the fairy domain of which she is a citizen, to introduce us to its precincts and make way for the more fully fleshed-out presentation of "living fairies" that are accessible to the vision of only the especially sweet and especially indoctrinated Llewelyn Davies clan. When Sylvia moves into the fairyland, she becomes a sort of fairy herself, the ultimate female figure in the center of a domestic scene now crossing the boundary of life in a moment that is utterly lambent. Her white gown radiates as she walks away, exactly like the blazing electric light that was in fact used to simulate Tinker Bell onstage in the first place.

So it is that Forster brings *Peter Pan* and its Tinker Bell full circle, round again to the place where she began. For a hundred years onstage and onscreen producers have enchanted the bourgeois imagination with a magical, electrical, feminine spirit, a fairy of electricity, just as for a hundred years, indeed, James M. Barrie's enchanting stratagem has worked as a brilliant triumph of theatrical staging (borrowed, of course, from *The Tempest*): to have the magical little female creature gulp Peter's medicine, dart into her little cove, and slowly, slowly fade; then to have Peter speak to her and, in a dazzling gesture, turn to ask the audience for its resuscitating faith. Clap, clap if you believe in fairies. Clap for the spirit of the woman of the house, she who has come from the fairy land—"Oh, thank you, thank you, thank you!"[90]—she who is transcendent. We were clapping, too, of course, since Tinker Bell, staged, was all a matter of wires and electrodes in fact, for the spirit of electricity, for electrons running through a wire. I mean by this not only that the scientific marvel of electricity was, for those ill equipped to understand it in scientific terms, something of a fairy spirit, but also, quite explicitly, that Barrie's dramaturgy converted a fairy spirit into a scientific one, that his character was little more than a light bulb, for the redemption of which audiences for a century have been willing to suspend their disbelief and give signal of this sacrifice through applause. At once the fairy of electricity has rite of passage across the border between life and death, between the domesticated and the raw; and a power of illumination finds its apotheosis in the one place all lost boys ever hope to find again, home.

NOTES

I am indebted to Thomas Doherty, Nathan Holmes, R. Barton Palmer, Nellie Perret, Natalie Rewa, Linda Robertson, Michael Sidnell, Steven Snyder, Matthew Solomon, and Fiona Whittington-Walsh.

1. Andrew Birkin, "Introduction," in James M. Barrie, *Peter Pan; or, The Boy Who Would Not Grow Up* (London: Folio Society, 1992), xxi.
2. Wolfgang Schivelbusch, *Disenchanted Night: The Industrialization of Light in the Nineteenth Century* (Berkeley: University of California Press, 1995), 50.
3. *Iolanthe* web page, http://homepages.ihug.co.nz/~melbear/iolanthe.htm, accessed March 23, 2006.
4. *Iolanthe* web page, http://homepages.ihug.co.nz/~melbear/iolanthe.htm, accessed March 23, 2006.
5. Untitled review of Peter Pan: Or, the Boy Who Wouldn't Grow Up , The London Times (December 28, 1904).
6. See Tom Gunning, "Phantom Images and Modern Manifestations: Spirit Photography, Magic Theater, Trick Films, and Photography's Uncanny," in Patrice Petro, ed., *Fugitive Visions: From Photography to Video* (Bloomington: Indiana University Press, 1994), 42–71.
7. See Patricia Fara, *An Entertainment for Angels: Electricity in the Enlightenment* (Cambridge: Icon, 2002).
8. Christoph Asendorf, *Batteries of Life: On the History of Things and Their Perception in Modernity*, trans. Don Reneau (Berkeley: University of California Press, 1993), 153.

9. Iwan Rhys Morus, *Frankenstein's Children: Electricity, Exhibition, and Experiment in Early-Nineteenth-Century London* (Princeton, NJ: Princeton University Press, 1998), 126.
10. Ibid.
11. Sir Arthur Conan Doyle, *The Coming of the Fairies* (London: Pavilion, 1997 [originally published 1922]), 32.
12. Sophie Schmit, "Conan Doyle: une etude en noir et blanc," in Clément Chéroux, Andreas Fischer, Pierre Apraxine, Denis Canguilhem, and Sophie Schmit, *Le Troisième oeil: la photographie et l'cculte* (Paris: Gallimard, 2004), 94.
13. Alexandre Fernandez, *Économie et Politique de l'Electricité Bordeaux (1887–1956)* (Talence: Presses Universitaire de Bordeaux, 1998).
14. Winfried Georg Sebald, *The Rings of Saturn*, trans. Michael Hulse (New York: New Directions, 1998), 281–282.
15. See Brian Bowers, *Lengthening the Day: A History of Lighting Technology* (Oxford: Oxford University Press, 1998).
16. Schivelbusch, *Night*, 64.
17. David Nye, *Electrifying America* (Cambridge, MA: The MIT Press, 1992), 243.
18. See "Work in the Home," unattributed documentary film, on view at The Franklin Institute, Philadelphia. © 1986 The Franklin Institute.
19. Tracy C. Davis, "'Do You Believe in Fairies?': The Hiss of Dramatic License," *Theatre Journal* 57 (2005), 68–69.
20. Sir James M. Barrie, *Peter Pan*, in *Peter Pan and Other Plays*, ed. Peter Hollindale (Oxford: Oxford University Press, 1995), 87.
21. Ibid.
22. Ibid.
23. Ibid., 97.
24. Sir James M. Barrie, *Peter Pan* (New York: Charles Scribner's Sons, 1911), 29.
25. H. M. Tomlinson, "Bed-Books and Night-Lights," in Christopher Morley, ed., *Modern Essays* (New York: Harcourt, Brace, 1921). Online at http://www.bartleby.com/237/19.html .
26. *Peter Pan*, in *Peter Pan and Other Plays*, ed. Hollindale, 87.
27. Barrie, *Peter Pan* , 29.
28. See Laurent Mannoni, *The Great Art of Light and Shadow: Archaeology of the Cinema*, trans. and ed. Richard Crangle (Exeter: University of Exeter Press, 2000), 136–175.
29. Anonymous, "The Story of Peter Pan," in Holland Thompson and Arthur Mee, eds., *The Book of Knowledge: The Children's Encyclopedia*, Vol. 13 (New York: The Grolier Society, 1926), 4659–4660.
30. Barrie, *Peter Pan*, 30.
31. Barrie, *Pan*, 97 (emphasis added).
32. Barrie, *Pan*, 99–100.
33. Quoted in Bowers, *Lengthening the Day*, 169; emphasis mine.
34. Barrie, *Pan*, 97.
35. Barrie, *Pan*, 99.
36. Barrie, *Pan*, 100.
37. Ibid.
38. Ibid.
39. Erving Goffman, *Frame Analysis: An Essay on the Organization of Experience* (Cambridge, MA: Harvard University Press, 1974), 534–537.
40. See Bowers, *Lengthening the Day*.
41. Schivelbusch, *Night*, 71.

42. Ibid.
43. I am indebted to Ariel Pomerance for this observation.
44. Nye, *Electrifying*, 239.
45. Karal Ann Marling, *As Seen on TV: The Visual Culture of Everyday Life in the 1950s* (Cambridge, MA: Harvard University Press, 1994), 255.
46. Nye, *Electrifying*, 245.
47. Ibid., 239.
48. Bowers, *Lengthening the Day*, 168.
49. Ibid., 163.
50. André Berne Joffroy, *Zigzag parmi les personages de "La Fée Électricité,"* trans. David Parris and Michael Walsh (Paris: Musée d'Art Moderne de la Ville de Paris, 1983), 44.
51. Ibid.
52. Ibid.
53. W. Y. Evans-Wentz, *The Fairy-Faith in Celtic Countries* (London: H. Froude, 1911; reprinted New York: Dover, 2002), 95.
54. Ibid., 37.
55. Ibid., 61.
56. See Frank Kessler, "On Fairies and Technologies," in John Fullerton and Astrid Söderbergh Widding, eds., *Moving Images: From Edison to the Webcam* (Sydney: John Libbey & Company, 2000), 41.
57. Walter Benjamin, *The Arcades Project*, trans. Howard Eiland and Kevin McLaughlin (Cambridge MA: Harvard University Press, 1999), 162.
58. James Card, *Seductive Cinema: The Art of Silent Film* (Minneapolis: University of Minnesota Press, 1994), 83.
59. R.D.S. Jack, "From Drama to Silent Film: The Case of Sir James Barrie," *International Journal of Scottish Theatre* 2, no. 2 (December 2001): n.p.
60. Todd Rainsberger, *James Wong Howe Cinematographer* (San Diego: A. S. Barnes, 1981), 154.
61. Card, *Seductive*, 87.
62. Ibid.
63. Gunning, "Images," 68.
64. Kessler, "Technologies," 41; 39.
65. Ibid., 40.
66. Elaine Tyler May, *Homeward Bound: American Families in the Cold War Era* (New York: Basic Books, 1988), 41–42.
67. Gilad Padva, "Radical Sissies and Stereotyped Fairies in Laurie Lynd's *The Fairy Who Didn't Want to Be a Fairy Anymore*," *Cinema Journal* 45, no. 1 (2005): 69.
68. Birkin, "Introduction," xxi.
69. Walter Metz, "Modernity and the Crisis in Truth: Alfred Hitchcock and Fritz Lang," in Murray Pomerance, ed., *Cinema and Modernity* (New Brunswick, NJ: Rutgers University Press, 2006), 78–79.
70. Jack, "From Drama to Silent Film," n.p.
71. Quoted in Jack, "From Drama to Silent Film," n.p.
72. May, *Homeward Bound*, 61–62.
73. Ibid., 63.
74. Ibid., 89.
75. Frank Thomas and Ollie Johnston, *Disney Animation: The Illusion of Life* (New York: Abbeville Press, 1981), 199.
76. Eleanor Byrne and Martin McQuillan, *Deconstructing Disney* (London: Pluto Press, 1999), 63.
77. Birkin, "Introduction," xxi.

78. See Mannoni, *Great Art*, 287; 461.

79. Thomas and Johnston, *Disney Animation*, 278.

80. See Stacy Wolf, "'Never Gonna Be a Man/Catch Me if You Can/I Won't Grow Up': A Lesbian Account of Mary Martin as Peter Pan," *Theatre Journal* 49: 4 (1997), 493–509.

81. See website of the Museum of Broadcast Communications, http://www.museum.tv/archives/etv/P/htmlP/peterpan/peterpan.htm.

82. Adolph Klauber, "Bringing the Fairies to Time Square," *New York Times* (January 12, 1913), VII, 7: 1.

83. Walter Kerr, "Soaring in 'Peter Pan': Up, Up and Away," *New York Times* (September 7, 1979), C3.

84. "Duke of York's Theatre: 'Peter Pan,'" *Times* (December 28, 1904), 4.

85. "A Joyous Night with 'Peter Pan': Maude Adams Triumphs as 'The Boy Who Wouldn't Grow Up,'" *New York Times* (November 7, 1905), 9.

86. Schivelbusch, *Disenchanted Night*, 199.

87. Marsha Kinder, "Moulin Rouge," *Film Quarterly* 55, no. 3 (Spring 2002): 57.

88. Nye, *Electrifying*, 376.

89. Ibid., 251.

90. Barrie, *Pan*, 137.

CHAPTER 2

"To die will be an awfully big adventure"

PETER PAN IN WORLD WAR I

Linda Robertson

ON MAY 7, 1915, a first-class passenger stood on a deck of a sinking ship. He held hands with two other men and one woman. Both he and one of his male companions had given away their lifebelts to women. As the first of two powerful green waves overwhelmed the four people clinging to each other, the man who holds our immediate attention said, "Why fear death? It is the greatest adventure in life." The first wave subsided and the four drenched passengers continued to cling together. As the second wave crested to overtake them, the man was heard to say, "Why fear death . . . ?" The rest of his sentence was cut off. Of the four, only the woman survived. She was Rita Jolivet, an actress. Her companion who greeted death as the "greatest adventure" was the "Napoleon of the American Stage," the producer and manager Charles Frohman. The ship was the British Cunard Line *Lusitania*. It sank off the southwestern coast of Ireland only eighteen minutes after a torpedo from a German U-boat struck it just ahead of midship. Of the 1,959 passengers and crew, 1,198 either drowned or died after being rescued. Among those killed were 128 Americans. There was no mistaking that his last words were a slightly altered quotation—an error forgivable under the circumstances—from the play *Peter Pan*.

Peter Pan is a floating signifier, a construction of social meaning. Popular American culture has given him a dark and indeed very selfish side, in which the desire for adventure and pleasure trumps all other motivations. Dr. Dan Kiley invented the popular term the Peter Pan Syndrome to describe men who are narcissistic, emotionally immature, irresponsible, aggressive, and dependent. Other critics interested in psychology have concluded that Peter

Pan reflects the emotional numbness of his creator. But the cultural legacy of Peter Pan argues for a very different understanding of what he represents.[1] Prior to World War I, he signified an eternal boyhood of youth and joy and heartlessness. With the advent of the war, he signified the seductive lure of combat as the "great adventure," promising death for a glorious cause as preferable to the prosaic indignities of adulthood and aging.

The Great War at the outset made answering the call of Mars the necessary foundation for a vigorous civilization and the defining characteristic of vigorous manhood. The war effort appropriated Peter Pan in a variety of ways. Understanding them sheds light on how a particular conception of human nature was naturalized and used to legitimate protracted war on a scale that beggars the imagination. But, the transformation of Peter Pan into an emblem of the Great Adventure did not end with the war. The particular legacy linking Peter Pan with the Great War reappears in Stephen Spielberg's *Hook* (1991).

Peter Pan before the War

In one of the scenes added to the 1906 theatrical production, Peter Pan and Wendy are stranded on Marooner's Rock. The tide is slowly rising and will soon cover the island completely. Peter Pan has been wounded by Captain Hook so that he can neither swim nor fly. A friendly kite comes along and offers to fly Wendy to safety, but it cannot bear the weight of two children. Wendy escapes at Peter's insistence while Peter stays behind, certain he will die but exclaiming, "to die will be an awfully big adventure." Fortunately, the Neverland bird paddles her nest to the fast-disappearing island. Peter climbs into it and sails to safety. Barrie's notes, included in the 1911 published version of the play, renders Peter as something other than the gallant victim. Peter seems to want to die. He tells Wendy he can neither swim nor fly to safety because "Hook has wounded me twice." Barrie comments in his notes: "(He believes it. He is so good at pretend that he feels the pain, his arms hang limp.)" When the kite comes along, Peter tells Wendy that she will have to go on alone because the kite cannot lift two people, which he knows because he saw two of the boys try. Barrie's note reads:

(She [Wendy] knows very well that if it can lift her it can lift him also, for she has been told by the boys as a deadly secret that one of the queer things about him is that he is no weight at all. But it is a forbidden subject.)Wendy wants to draw lots to see who departs on the kite, but Peter knows that would not be the gentlemanly thing to do.Wendy, as she drifts off on the kite's tail, tries to give Peter a kiss, but again Barrie's note: (Peter knows he cannot do that.)

2.1 Peter Pan on Marooner's Rock. J. M. Barrie, *Peter and Wendy*, illustrated by Francis Bedford (Charles Scribner and Sons, 1911), 143.

Peter is alone on the rock. Night falls, and the melancholy singing of the mermaids is heard as the waters rise. Barrie writes the stage note:

(PETER is afraid at last, and a tremor runs through him, like a shudder passing over the lagoon; but on the lagoon one shudder follows another till there are hundreds of them, and he feels just the one.)

PETER: (with a drum beating in his breast as if he were a real boy at last.) To die would be an awfully big adventure.[2]

What makes Peter almost a "real boy" is that his heart is beating in fear of his own mortality. He is, in short, capable of feeling—at least of feeling fear. But to be Peter Pan is to be "heartless"—incapable of emotional range. When children play war, or pirates, or cowboys and Indians, or Ninja, or space alien invasion, it is part of the fun to kill one another, but it is only make-believe. After a brief moment playing dead, the child springs back to life. Peter cannot determine to stay so young that one can enjoy the heartlessness of pretend killing, and at the same time accept a kiss—the innocent initiation into adult relationship—from Wendy; but he can accept the sacrifice of a mother: in this case, the Neverbird, who risks her own eggs to rescue Peter.

The novel *Peter and Wendy* includes the scene without Barrie's commentary. Peter asserts his courage using the same words as the playscript:

> Peter was not quite like other boys; but he was afraid at last. A tremor ran through him, like a shudder passing over the sea; but on the sea one shudder follows another till there are hundreds of them, and Peter felt just the one. Next moment he was standing erect on the rock again, with that smile on his face and a drum beating within him. It was saying, "To die will be an awfully big adventure."[3]

Of the two versions, Frohman's last words most reflect the intimations of a death wish found in the script notes. This impression is all the greater since Frohman took off the flotation belt another passenger had helped him put on. In other words, he refused any opportunity to save himself and linked himself to the character whose fame, he hoped, would be the thing for which he was best remembered. Frohman's final words hooked Peter Pan into one of the pervasive expressions of zealotry associated with World War I—that facing death in warfare was the great adventure.

Charles Frohman, Peter Pan, and the *Lusitania*

An understanding of the prewar cultural definitions attached to manliness and nationalism sheds light on the impact Frohman's final words were to have on those who read the accounts of the last minutes of the *Lusitania*. One of the primary reasons his words made an impact was his own fame. Frohman rose from obscurity to become the major theatrical entrepreneur of his era. His parents were German Jews who lived on the margins of poverty. Frohman's early interest in the theater led him to his first success as a manager, arranging bookings in the United States and London for a traveling minstrel show, one of the major sources of entertainment in the United States at that time. As there were few theaters available outside major cities, the performances for this show (and other, less successful shows that Frohman toured with) often played in barns.

Frohman was one of the most important producers responsible for developing theater in the Broadway district. He built the Empire Theatre at Fortieth and Broadway and purchased controlling interest in the Garrick, Criterion, the Savoy, and the Garden theaters, and a part interest in the Knickerbocker. He ultimately controlled the theater district in Boston. He held interests in the Columbia, Hollis Street, and Park theaters, built the Colonial Theater, and acquired the Boston and Tremont theaters. In addition, he owned two theaters in Chicago and was a member of a theatrical booking group called The Syndicate, a chain of theaters established in 1898 that controlled bookings and contracts coast-to-coast. Frohman sent many of his most popular New York productions, including *Peter Pan*, on tour to theaters controlled by the Syndicate. In England, he produced 125 plays. He held a long-term lease on the York Theatre in London, and was responsible for producing numerous plays in the Adelphi, Vaudeville, and Garrick theaters and ultimately had an interest in a dozen London playhouses.[4]

Frohman created the "star system" for actors and actresses in New York, providing them with exclusive contracts and generous salaries in exchange for guarantees of performances in plays he produced. The actors he developed into stars included John Drew, Maude Adams, Ethel Barrymore, Annie Russell, William Faversham, Clara Bloodgood, Julia Marlowe, Virginia Harned, Leo Ditrichstein, Billie Burke, Marie Doro, Julia Sanderson, and Ann Murdock. Frohman also engaged playwrights in long-term contracts to develop vehicles for the stars he developed. While his penchant was always for spectacle and melodrama, Frohman also brought the work of serious and important playwrights to the American stage. These included, in addition to Barrie, Oscar Wilde, Henry Miller, Haddon Chambers, Paul Potter, William Gillette, Arthur Wing Pinero, and Augustus Thomas. He established the Repertory Company at the Duke of York to bring new productions by new playwrights to the stage. The Company, which never made a profit, produced plays by John Galsworthy, Bernard Shaw, James Barrie, George Meredith, Granville Barker, Elizabeth Baker, Lawrence Housman, and Arthur Pinero.[5]

The connection between Barrie, Frohman, and the actress Maude Adams illustrates how well this collaboration worked. Barrie's novel *The Little Minister* (1891) had been such an enormous success that many pirated dramatizations were produced. Frohman urged Barrie to write a dramatic version, but Barrie declined because he could not envision any actress who could play the part of Babbie. *The Little Minister* is the story of the sober and serious new minister, the Reverend Gavin Dishart, in a small Scottish village. When Barrie visited the United States, Frohman made sure he saw Maude Adams in *Rosemary* (1896), which was playing in the Empire

Theatre, because Frohman felt certain that Adams's acting would inspire Barrie. His intuition proved correct. After the play, Barrie rushed upstairs to Frohman's office and declared excitedly that he was now confident he could dramatize *The Little Minister* because "I have found the woman to play Babbie." *The Little Minister* (1897) was a tremendous success, with three hundred performances at the Empire. Two-hundred-eighty-nine were to standing-room-only. The total gross was a record at that time: $370,000.[6]

A dozen years later, Barrie met Frohman at the Garrick Club in London. Barrie owed Frohman a play, and he opened the subject nervously:

> You know I have an agreement to deliver you the manuscript of a play? Well, I have it all right, but I am sure it will not be a commercial success. But it is a dream-child of mine, and I am so anxious to see it on the stage that I have written another play which I will be glad to give you and which will compensate you for any loss on the one I am so eager to see produced.

Frohman told Barrie he would produce both plays. Barrie's "dream-child" was *Peter Pan*, and his anxiety was understandable since the play had already been rejected by other producers. With Frohman's help, *Peter Pan* would become an epic theatrical success. The other play, *Alice-Sit-by-the-Fire* (1905), lasted only a season.[7]

Peter Pan debuted in London with Nina Boucicault in the title role to highly enthusiastic reviews. That spring, Barrie wrote to Maude Adams asking her to be in his "play for children, which I don't suppose would be much use in America." He wrote that he wanted her to play all the parts: the mother, Wendy, Peter Pan, Hook, and the Lost Boys. When Adams read the play, she recounted that she "fell in love with him [Peter] at once."[8] The play opened on November 6, 1905, and enjoyed the longest run in the history of the Empire Theatre, closing June 9, 1906; it was revived in New York in 1912 and again in 1915. New York was not the only town to meet Peter: the play successfully toured the United States for decades with several actresses in the lead. *Peter Pan* created its own vogue: the Peter Pan collar was named after the costume Adams wore, babies were named after Peter, and Peter Pan was transfigured from a character in a play into a cultural icon.[9]

Similarly in London, the play created its own craze. The name Wendy came into vogue for baby girls, and the term Wendy House for a little playhouse is still used there today. Frohman produced Peter Pan annually in London, and as noted above, the character of Peter Pan became widely known through many media, including the statue Barrie commissioned and had placed in Kensington Gardens.

2.2 Maude Adams as Peter Pan in the 1905 New York production. Photographer: Napoleon Sarony. Personal collection of Linda Robertson.

Between 1883 and 1915, Frohman produced five hundred plays in the United States, England, and Europe. His record far outpaced that of any other American theatrical producer. For all intents and purposes, he was the driving force behind the emergence of American legitimate and commercial theater. But of all of his achievements, the one that gave him both the most pleasure and pride was having brought *Peter Pan* to the stage. From the moment he read the play, Frohman had been enchanted with it, sometimes stopping his friends in the street to act out bits of the play before it was produced.[10] Frohman believed in the play, and it was his intuition and commitment that brought it into the hearts of countless theater audiences, and ultimately, to film and television as well.

A member of the public in either Great Britain or the United States would have had to make a great effort to remain ignorant of Charles Frohman's death and his last words. A picture of Frohman taken aboard the *Lusitania's* sister ship, the *Mauritania,* a year earlier was often reproduced (without identifying that it was taken aboard the *Mauritania*) with a caption with his last words—or related variants. The May 22 issue of the popular American periodical *Literary Digest* carried the picture with the caption: "Death's Adventurer: On the tilting deck of the *Lusitania,* Charles Frohman's last words were: 'Why fear death? It is the most beautiful adventure life gives us.'"

Frohman's public funeral service was held at Temple Emanu-El in New York, which filled to its capacity of 2,000. John Barrymore was one of his pallbearers. Rabbi Joseph Silverman based his eulogy on Frohman's question, "Why fear death?" Confident that the words helped to calm his fellow passengers, Rabbi Silverman drew the lesson of manly virtue as the source of courage in the face of death:

> Charles Frohman was not afraid to die because he had not been afraid to live—to live in the real sense, to live for an ideal, to struggle, to battle for a principle, to love the right, to do justice, practice mercy, and walk humbly before God and man.[11]

Memorial services organized by the actors and actresses he had promoted to stardom were also held in Los Angeles, San Francisco, Tacoma, and Providence. The subdeacon of Saint Paul's Cathedral (apparently unconcerned that Frohman was Jewish) conducted a memorial service at St.-Martin's-in-the-Fields, chosen because of its proximity to the Duke of York's theater.[12]

Rita Jolivet's account of his last moments are given in his biography (1916), and include the biographer's observation: "smilingly and with the highest heroism, he met his fate." Elaborating on the point, the biographers assert that Frohman's last words will "join the category of the great farewells of all time" and "will give humanity a fresher faith with which to meet the inevitable."[13] The tributes to Frohman appealed to the idealized image of a gentleman: gallant, self-sacrificing, fearless, competitive, and welcoming Death as but one more test of virtue and manhood. The accounts of his death forged a link between conceptualizing Germany as exemplary of an

2.3 Charles Frohman on the deck of the *Mauritania,* in an article about his loss on the *Lusitania. Literary Digest,* May 22, 1915, 1214.

absolute barbarism (in light of the *Lusitania* sinking), death in warfare as a great adventure, and the play *Peter Pan.*

PETER PAN IN THE NAME OF WAR

The English needed an event around which to center their concerted effort to finally convince the Americans to enter World War I. Provoking American outrage over German audacity on the high seas was very much on the minds of British leaders in the hours just prior to the sinking of the *Lusitania.* Colonel Edward House, President Woodrow Wilson's closest advisor, was in London promoting an American peace initiative. Sir Edward Grey, the British foreign secretary, invited House on a walk through Kew Gardens on the morning of May 7 and asked him, "What would the United States do if the Germans sink an ocean liner with American passengers on board?" House replied, "I believe that a flame of indignation would sweep the United States and that by itself would be sufficient to carry us into the war." At noon, House met with King George V. After some small talk, King George, standing with his back to House and looking out the window, asked House: "Colonel, what would the Americans do if the Germans sank the *Lusitania?*" At 2:10 P.M., Kapitan-Leutnant Schwieger gave the order to launch a torpedo at the *Lusitania.*[14]

There is still vehement debate over the sinking of the *Lusitania.* Was it the result of intentional planning by the English, or the result of their military miscalculation, or was it, inter alia, hoped for, sadly acknowledged as likely, or understood as highly probable? One thing is certain: the British used it for propaganda, intending to make an ally out of the United States. While the sinking of the *Lusitania* did not bring America immediately into the war, it did provoke President Wilson sufficiently to change from his earlier policy of strict neutrality to a policy of "preparedness" (getting ready for war), and threw the balance of American opinion toward the Allies and against Germany. The American reaction led the Germans to temporarily stop their policy of unconditional submarine warfare. When they renewed the policy in 1917, it became one of the decisive factors in America's entry into World War I.

The public would not have known Peter Pan as a beloved icon of naïve courage without the vision directed and propagated by Frohman; conversely, Frohman's last words might have had only a short life without the English government's commitment that these words would ring in the public's— especially the American public's—ears. It committed significant energy and ingenuity to transform the event into a centerpiece in the burgeoning propaganda effort designed to bring America into the war.

Among the writers who served Great Britain in this effort before the sinking of the *Lusitania* was J. M. Barrie. Initially, he proposed a series of lectures in the United States, but the British asked him to cancel his plans because they did not wish to be accused of overtly attempting to influence American neutrality. The proposed tour seems entirely out of character for Barrie, who was extremely shy and avoided any contact with the press if he could help it. But he felt he must do something to contribute to the war effort, and so he arrived in New York (ironically, on the *Lusitania)* in September 1914. To the reporters who greeted him on deck he denied that he was in the country to promote the British view of the war, a position greeted with general skepticism because it had been seventeen years since Barrie had set foot on American soil.

Barrie did not pursue a public tour, but he did adopt the approach favored by Wellington House—engaging in conversations about the war with close friends and powerful people. During this time, Barrie stayed with—and undoubtedly discussed the war with—Theodore Roosevelt. Upon his return to Great Britain, he reported that the only Americans likely to join in World War I were Roosevelt and his four sons. Roosevelt had long admired Barrie, and one can only surmise what they discussed. But a clue is provided by an interview in the *New York Herald*. A persistent reporter managed to see the reclusive Barrie in his room at the Plaza Hotel shortly after he arrived in New York. According to the published account, Barrie grew comfortable only when talking of children. In his conversation, he referred to Peter Davies, one of the five children of the Llewelyn Davies family who had become his wards following the deaths of their parents:

> It's funny . . . that the real Peter Pan—I call him that—is off to the war now. He grew tired of the stories I told him, and his younger brother became interested. It was such fun telling these two about themselves. I would say, "Then you came along and killed the pirate" and they would accept every word as truth. That's how Peter Pan came to be written. It is made up of only a few stories I told them.[15]

There is a sad irony here, a pride and nostalgia mixed with regret: the fantasy of killing and derring-do has become the reality for the Peter who did grow up. Roosevelt and Barrie must have talked of the war and of their sons—or wards, in Barrie's case. And as we can see, for Barrie, the fantasy of childhood he had conjured mixed uneasily with the reality that Peter was facing along the Western Front.

The propaganda that Barrie helped to spread worked, or perhaps the sinking of a pleasure liner was simply too much for Wilson to ignore. America joined with Britain to send its sons to war. Once again, Peter Pan's words were part of the chorus—this time, as filtered through Frohman and his acquaintance, former president Theodore Roosevelt. Three years after the sinking of the *Lusitania*, Frohman's last words echoed in a collection of articles Roosevelt published under the title *The Great Adventure*. He dedicated it to all those Americans who died in the war. Conceptualizing war as a "great adventure" did not originate with Roosevelt, nor was its genesis derived from *Peter Pan*. But clearly, Frohman's use of Peter Pan's familiar words contributed significantly to the uncanny condensation of meaning behind the "great adventure." It celebrated the romance, if not desirability of, dying in warfare. In the popular imagination, a soldier's death on the battlefield or a pilot's death in the skies became, quite literally, "the great adventure" and was linked in an ironic and grisly way with the innocent, romanticized seductiveness of "The Boy Who Would Not Grow Up."

PETER PAN AND THE GREAT ADVENTURE

Peter Pan captivated the prewar popular consciousness in both Britain and America because he rebelled against the idea of becoming an adult with a professional career. He refused to be trapped in the straitjacket of civilized life. His rebellion against modernity, urbanity, and domesticity reflected a dominant strain in both American and British cultural criticism; he offered a fantasy that allowed adults a release from lives constrained by "getting and spending" and into an imaginary world of adventure. With the onset of World War I, that ideal of remaining eternally youthful—of never having to take on the emasculating drudgeries of adulthood or the physical insults of old age—was transmogrified into the image of the youthful soldier off on the Great Adventure.

Social critics in the years before the war noted that the society was becoming increasingly decadent and destructive. Thomas Carlyle, the nineteenth-century man of letters, was the first to use "condition of England" to observe that the advent of industrialization and capitalism had a weakening effect on morality, particularly of those males who gained privilege without effort through inherited wealth or investment. He was one of a number of significant intellectuals and politicians who saw the danger to England of the advent of a decadent plutocracy whose greed created an increasing number of workers reduced to poverty by the new economic order. C. F. Masterman was a member of Parliament in 1909 when he published his best known work, *The Condition of England*. He identified the upper classes as greedy, exploitative of the working class, and lacking in moral responsibility. The middle classes were materialistic and lacking in moral values, while the working class and the poor were deprived of legitimate participation. He worked closely with both Winston Churchill and David Lloyd George to produce The People's Budget (1909), the first budget intended to redistribute wealth in England.

To some social critics, war seemed the desirable cure for the materialism, indolence, and indifference of the moneyed classes. It offered the contrary moral condition—self-sacrifice in the name of a higher ideal. Edmund Gosse, a formidable writer and critic, enjoyed considerable social and political influence, particularly after he was appointed librarian of the House of Lords (1904). In a 1914 essay, Gosse extolled war as the necessary purgative to English decadence. "War," he asserted, "is the sovereign disinfectant, and its red stream of blood is the Condy's Fluid that cleans out the stagnant pools and clotted channels of the intellect." The reddish-purple color of Condy's Fluid—a disinfectant and deodorant (similar to Lysol or Pine Sol, for example)—suggested the sanguinary comparison between war and cleaning. Speaking to and about the upper classes, Gosse expanded on his thesis that war was a positive benefit to a decadent society:

> Our wish for indulgence of every sort, our laxity of manners, our wretched sensitiveness to personal inconvenience, these are suddenly lifted before us in their true guise as the spectres of national decay; and we have risen from the lethargy of our dilettantism to lay them, before it is too late, by the flashing of the unsheathed sword.[16]

Males of the privileged classes were considered automatically suited by breeding and education to merit rank as commissioned officers.

England entered the war without a draft, relying upon volunteers to meet the first quota of 500,000 soldiers in August 1914, and the call for an additional 3.5 million by January 1915. The officers for this military force came from the very class Gosse describes, and they volunteered in large numbers. Among the wealthy young men who were first to enlist was the poet Rupert Brooke (1887–1915). The son of a comfortably wealthy academic—his father was the headmaster at Rugby School, one of Britain's exclusive public schools—Brooke attended Cambridge, and after gradua-tion, was heralded as a promising young poet. When war came to Great Britain, Brooke applied for and received a commission in the Royal Naval Division. He saw one day of action—the retreat from Antwerp in October 1914. In February 1915, Brooke sailed for the Dardanelles. In April, his ship was stationed off Skyros, Greece. He developed blood poisoning and died on April 23. His friends buried him there.

In his remarkable sonnet "Peace," written while in England after the retreat from Antwerp, Brooke subscribed to Gosse's vision of war as the sovereign cure for decadence—his own as well as England's:

> Now, God be thanked Who has matched us with His hour,
> And caught our youth, and wakened us from sleeping,
> With hand made sure, clear eye, and sharpened power,
> To turn, as swimmers into cleanness leaping,
> Glad from a world grown old and cold and weary,
> Leave the sick hearts that honour could not move,
> And half-men, and their dirty songs and dreary,
> And all the little emptiness of love!
> Oh! we, who have known shame, we have found release there,
> Where there's no ill, no grief, but sleep has mending,

Naught broken save this body, lost but breath;
Nothing to shake the laughing heart's long peace there
But only agony, and that has ending;
And the worst friend and enemy is but Death.[17]

Brooke, like Peter Pan, associates death with water. And like Peter Pan, Brooke would clearly prefer an eternity of youth enflamed with the purity of warfare—the "laughing heart's long peace"—to a world of "half-men." While death is the enemy of life, it is also the "worst friend," because ironically it is a salvation from the "world grown old and cold and weary."

Brooke agreed that to become middle-aged was an appalling tragedy. "Is there a greater tragedy than for a boy to die, except for him to grow old, to live!" Brooke wrote to a friend. A. S. Byatt comments on Brooke's love of *Peter Pan*:

> Brooke was addicted to the play *Peter Pan* (which opened in 1904). He saw it at least 10 times, and fantasised about it when he was a Cambridge undergraduate: "As I stroll through Cambridge, Trinity Street fades and I find myself walking by the shore of the Mermaid's Lagoon, King's Chapel often shrinks before my eyes, and rises, and is suddenly the House in the Tree-tops." In a letter to his friend Lyton Strachey, Brooke wrote: "I suppose you know a play called *Peter Pan*? I saw it last year & fell so much in love with it that I am going up to see its revival again in a few days. I found it enchanting, adorable, and entirely beautiful."[18]

Brooke draws upon an imagined war imbued with the coloration of values that had shaped him—and of which Peter Pan was a part. His enthusiasm for war was echoed by thousands of others who answered the call to enlist. An eager volunteer sent a message of farewell to his girlfriend in a personal ad in the *Times* of London: "Pauline—Alas, it cannot be. But I will dash into the great venture with all that pride and spirit an ancient race has given me."[19] His heady rush to war succinctly captures a shrinking from the entanglements of love, marriage, offspring, and adult responsibilities justified by the ultimate test of manhood. Both Brooke and the careless lover of the *Times* advertisement reject Freud's Pleasure Principle in favor of the Death Wish—or the drive for oblivion. Psychologists writing after Freud reinterpreted this duality as the conflict between Eros (the desire for procreation, and hence, continuity, life, family, and community) and Thanatos (the drive for oblivion, which when sublimated is projected as destructiveness and aggression).

Freud's invention of the Death Wish to explain the effect of the war was anticipated by prewar poets and writers. The phenomenal eagerness of men who volunteered for World War I has pushed scholars to make serious inquiries into the literature of the prewar period. The imaginations of boys and men on both sides of the Atlantic had been fired by the romantic adventure literature of the late nineteenth and early twentieth centuries, including stories by Sir Walter Scott, George Alfred Henty, Rider Haggard, Lord Alfred Tennyson, and William Morris—and notably, J. M. Barrie's *Peter Pan*.

In *The Great Adventure: Male Desire and the Coming of World War I*, Michael C. C. Adams pays particular attention to what *Peter Pan* reveals about Edwardian dreams of how the world ought to be. Adams joins others in characterizing the masculinity of the period in negative terms, as one of "virulent anti-intellectualism, obsession with sports, stultifying conformity to team and social rules, callousness to the less fortunate." Mr. Darling illustrates the stifling version of masculinity performed by the professional classes in the name of civilized domesticity. "Better to be Captain James Hook," Adams points out. Hook "somewhat represents the Englishman freed from the claustrophobic atmosphere of career and home which have stunted Darling."

As for the female figures in Pan's life who either dominate him or whom he has reason to fear—Tinker Bell and Tiger Lily—their portrayal certainly owes a great deal to Barrie's own sexual reticence. But Peter's rejection of Wendy's proffered kiss on Marooner's Island also reflects the spirit of the times. Men were cut out not to enter domesticity, but to face competition, and the ultimate risk of death. Commenting on Peter Pan awaiting the adventure of death by drowning, Adams says: "In an age which wanted exciting exploits, the big adventure would be the formative experience for a generation which experienced the trenches." Love, marriage, children were stultifying; what men yearned for in their imaginations was the ultimate challenge of facing death.[20]

Women were given the role of ensuring their male offspring understood that following this drive was the ultimate test of both patriotism and manhood. Wendy articulates the hopes of English women. Asked by Hook if she has any last words to the Lost Boys as they are about to walk the plank, she says:

> I feel that I have a message from your real mothers, and it is this: 'We hope our sons will die like English gentlemen.' (Barrie, 78)

Wendy's charge to the little warriors who must walk the plank is an amalgamation of a number of statements well-known in England among the educated classes, and made by adults about how men—and gentleman—should face death. The Lost Boys would have recognized the reference because every English child would have learned in school the signal sent by Admiral Lord Nelson to the British fleet before the decisive sea battle at Trafalgar: "England expects that every man will do his duty."

The tradition of raising young men who would be prepared to die for Mother and Country was entrenched in Britain by the late nineteenth century. To it was added the cultural codification of dying like a gentleman. Nothing exemplifies this more clearly than Robert Scott at the end of his ill-fated expedition to the South Pole. As he lay dying, he wrote messages in his journal; his last words were particularly concerned with assuring that the crew's surviving families, including his own, were provided for, because these men had died as Englishmen ought. Among those to whom he wrote was his friend Barrie, who was godfather to Scott's son: "We are showing that Englishmen can still die with a bold spirit, fighting it out to the end. It will be known that we have accomplished our object in reaching the Pole, and that we have done everything possible, even to sacrificing ourselves in order to save sick companions. I think this makes an example for Englishmen of the future, and that the country ought to help those who are left behind to mourn us." In a statement intended for the public, he wrote: "I do not regret this journey, which has shown that Englishmen can endure hardships, help one another, and meet death with as great a fortitude as ever in the past. We took risks, we knew we took them; things have come out against us, and therefore we have no cause for complaint, but bow to the will of providence, determined still to do our best to the last."[21]

Barrie was naturally devastated by the news of Scott's death. While his words did not inspire Barrie when he wrote the script for Wendy's roles, it may have been that Barrie's words inspired Scott. Both Barrie and Scott reflected the ethos of their era. Scott's rhetoric indicates his firm confidence that his English readers will understand and admire his bravery and honor in the face of death. Both Barrie and Scott reflect the Edwardian ideal of the Gentleman, who faces both life and death "with great fortitude," without complaint, and with a willingness to sacrifice everything, including one's own life, in the name of a greater cause.

The ideal conduct for a gentleman soldier—that is, an officer—was to never take advantage of an opponent, to have respect for the enemy, and, if necessary, to die in face-to-face combat, knowing that whoever lived was the better man.[22] The reticence about physical love and courtship, the eagerness for adventure, the feeling that masculinity was linked with national identity, the demand for fearlessness in the face of danger—all of these were reflective of a much broader set of social and political tendencies associated with the revival of interest, particularly among the professional and upper classes, in the Age of Chivalry. The popularity of the medievalism of

William Morris, Sir Walter Scott, and Alfred Lord Tennyson, along with
the revival of Gothic architecture and design, were part of a nostalgic look
back, past the disruptions of economic liberalism and industrialization, to an
idealized time when it was good to be an aristocrat, imagined as a knight-
errant. The flavor of this nostalgia is captured in Hook's interest in the
costuming of the Restoration (he idealizes the golden age of the pirate, not
the knight-errant). One characteristic of the gentleman knight-errant was
a sense of fair play. Thus the nostalgic idealization of masculinity merged
with the identification of field sports as the best way to shape a young man
for the future. Hook's sense of "good form" and Peter Pan's outrage when
Hook does not play fair are indicative of this sense that, even in combat, one
had to remain civilized.

To say that *Peter Pan* reflects the dominant idealizations of Edwardian
gender roles and fantasies of adventure does not detract from the unique,
delightful, and bittersweet charm of the play; rather it contextualizes it in
the cultural matrix and demonstrates the creativity Barrie brought to these
pervasive social values. Many of the same influences shaped the conception of ideal masculinity during the American Progressive Era (1890–1913),
which followed upon—and was a reaction to—the excesses of the Gilded
Age (1878–1889).

President Theodore Roosevelt was highly influential in promoting
the image of masculinity associated with fairness, ruggedness, and violent
adventure, whether through hunting big game or going to war. He not
only led volunteer forces in Cuba, he also sought to develop the United
States Navy as the primary force for American imperial expansion. He
wrote many popular books, quite a few detailing his own adventures. In
1900, Roosevelt published *The Strenuous Life*, a collection of his essays and
speeches. The speech that gives the collection its title was given in Chicago in 1899. In it, he argued that the man of "timid peace" could not be
admired, but the man of "victorious effort" is one who "never wrongs his
neighbor, who is prompt to help a friend, but who has those virile qualities
necessary to win in the stern strife of actual life." The nation depends upon
men and women instilled with the proper moral fiber and physical stamina,
and weakness, fear, and fragility are fatal to America's success.

Roosevelt saw to it that his sons fought in World War I, three of them
initially for Great Britain, transferring to the United States forces after
America entered the war. His youngest son, Quentin, became a combat
pilot for the United States. He was shot down and died on July 14, 1918.
He was twenty years old, and the only one of Roosevelt's four sons who
served in the war not to survive. His death hit Roosevelt very hard. He paid
tribute to his son in *The Great Adventure*, which he dedicated to "those who

paid with their bodies for their souls' desire." The first essay, which gives its name to the book, acknowledges the loss of Quentin indirectly. He quotes from a letter his wife had received, describing it as a letter sent by the "wife of a fighting soldier at the front" who wrote to the "mother of a gallant boy, who at the front had fought in the high air like an eagle, and like an eagle, fighting, had died." Unmistakably, the reference is to Quentin. The correspondent wrote: "I hope my two sons will live as worthily and die as greatly as yours."[23]

Roosevelt approves of this seemingly callous sentiment, first, because he believed that women were required to have children, as a kind of sacred duty, and to prepare their sons for war; and second, because he saw the willingness of the young to die for their country as essential to the future of the nation. "Both life and death are parts of the same Great Adventure. . . . Therefore it is that the man who is not willing to die, and the woman who is not willing to send her man to die, in a war for a great cause, are not worthy to live."[24] The "Great Adventure" thus becomes the willingness to die for "a great cause." The gentle fantasy of the little boy who refused to grow up now becomes praise for young men who will not live past twenty. A fairy tale about being able to fly by thinking happy thoughts and laughing under a sprinkling of fairy dust becomes the military reality of learning to fly a plane fueled by gasoline into the skies, and, if fate calls for it, going down in flames. And, above all, it underscores the willingness to undertake The Great Adventure as the very foundation upon which Civilization must rest.

Clearly Roosevelt would have found much to admire in Wendy's admonition (as he must have admired those of the mothers of Sparta) that all mothers expect their sons to die nobly and without complaint for a righteous cause. While America did not enter World War I until 1917, many Americans volunteered for service in the Canadian, British, or French services after the war broke out in Europe in 1914. Among them was Alan Seeger (1888–1916), who was lauded in America as the poet-soldier equivalent of Rupert Brooke. Like Brooke, he was born into a wealthy family, attended private school, and graduated from a top university—Harvard. Between 1910 and 1912, he lived a bohemian life in Greenwich Village as part of a group of social radicals. In 1912, he moved to the Left Bank in Paris, again associating with artists and radical writers. When the war broke out in 1914, Seeger joined the French Foreign Legion and fought along the Western Front. He was killed in 1916. His poem "The Rendezvous," published in 1916, was the best known and most popular poem of the war in the United States. Seeger expresses his reasons for volunteering using the conventional dichotomies of rejecting sexual love in favor of rushing into the arms of Death:

God knows 'twere better to be deep
Pillowed in silk and scented down,
Where love throbs out in blissful sleep,
Pulse nigh to pulse, and breath to breath,
Where hushed awakenings are dear . . .
But I've a rendezvous with Death
At midnight in some flaming town,
When Spring trips north again this year,
And I to my pledged word am true,
I shall not fail that rendezvous.[25]

The conception of masculinity that rejects love in favor of the siren song of death in warfare is far more explicit in Seeger than in Brooke; but the underlying duality—the rejection of love and sexuality in favor of facing certain death is clearly present in both and reflects the values of their immediate cultural contexts.

FLIGHT AND THE GREAT ADVENTURE

The application of "The Great Adventure" to flight was noticeable among Americans who wrote about flying in the war, whether for the Lafayette Escadrille prior to America's entry, or for the Americans after 1917. Normal Hall wrote highly popular accounts of his life in the Lafayette Escadrille that were serialized before they were published together under the title *High Adventure* (1917). The bit of doggerel titled "The Great Adventure" by Major Kendall Banning (Signal Reserve Corps, Aviation Section, U.S. Army) is interesting not simply as an example of conventional sentiments badly expressed, but because Banning, who was a minor poet prior to the war, was assigned along with other writers and artists to the "Division of Pictorial Publicity": in short, he was part of the division producing domestic propaganda.

Whatever fates ye send me,
Whatever cast the sky,
Grant me the grace to live a man
And as a man to die!
    . . .
So this my life, become the great
Adventure of my soul![26]

The seductiveness of imagining one's own death while battling in the sky outlasted the war. Cecil Lewis, a pilot in World War I, published his autobiography, *Sagittarius Rising*, in 1936, as he anticipated the coming of World War II. Here is how Lewis explains the seductiveness of combat:

Besides, there is, as everybody who has fought knows, a strong magnetic attraction between two men who are matched against one another.... For what have I been spared? to die, diseased, in a bed! Sometimes it seems a pity.[27]

Lewis more than any other writer confesses the eroticism of pursuing *Thanatos*—one's own oblivion—by challenging another to combat. If tempting death does not result in one's own oblivion, one is condemned to the indignities of living to a ripe old age.[28]

HOOKED ON THE GREAT ADVENTURE

The link Frohman forged on May 7, 1915, between Peter Pan, death as the great adventure, and World War I did not sink into historical oblivion. Steven Spielberg's *Hook* (1991) reprises the fantasy of a boy who never wanted to grow up by presenting Peter Pan (Robin Williams) as an adult—Peter Banning—who has forgotten he ever was Peter Pan. He is the man trapped by civilization, a family man who cannot spend time with his children because his obsession with his career as a cutthroat real-estate lawyer occupies his attention. When Captain Hook kidnaps his two children, he is drawn back to Neverland to discover his true inner child as well as his responsibilities as a parent. Only when he becomes Peter Pan again can he be the person both he and his son can admire: he can fly, he can fight, and he can crow.

Hook has not been treated particularly well by film critics, and Spielberg admits that he lost the energy for the Neverland scenes because he had become a father—and therefore, no longer felt like "Peter Pan."[29] But the film is called *Hook*, and whatever else might be said about Robin Williams playing the spontaneous and manic Robin-Williams-as-Peter-Pan, the role of Captain Hook is flawlessly realized by Dustin Hoffman.

The scene is Captain Hook's ornate Restoration cum Louis IV–style cabin. Hook has fallen into despair. He did not kill the adult Peter Pan when he had the chance because it would have been "bad form." He allowed the out-of-shape "Peter Pan" three days to get into fighting trim for an all-out war. Upon reflection, Hook sadly realizes that the "fat, old" adult Peter Pan will never be a worthy enemy, even if Hook waits three decades. He discovers himself trapped in a disappointment that arouses his hatred: of his own "flawed body," of Neverland, and especially of Peter Pan. Staring at the hooked hand (which replaces the one he lost in a fight with Peter Pan the younger), Hook decides his life has lost all purpose and resolves to commit suicide. He holds a cocked gun to his head. Dissuaded by his own cowardice, he orders Smee (Bob Hoskins) to stop him. Smee grabs the gun, which fires. It sinks the model of Hook's boat, which is floating in a pool, surrounded by a diorama of Neverland.

HOOK: There's no adventure here.
SMEE: (holding up the pistol) You call this no adventure?
HOOK: Death is the only great adventure I have left to me. It's all over. I'm so tired. I want to go beddy bye. My career is over.
SMEE: Don't say it Cap'n. You're still you, I'm still me. There's things you haven't even thought of yet.
HOOK: I must get to bed. This was supposed to be the war to end all wars.
SMEE: (tucking Hook into bed) And it will be.
HOOK: The ultimate war.[30]

Hook wants his war with Peter Pan to avenge the loss of his hand. He imagines his war with Peter Pan as "the war to end all wars"—an allusion to World War I. The phrase was originally coined by H. G. Wells as the title to a collection of his prowar essays first published between September and the end of 1914: *The War That Will End War* (1914).

The scene with Hook brings together the same elements that originally tied *Peter Pan* to the sinking of the *Lusitania*: Hook is the villainous captain of a ship, seeks death as the great adventure, and welcomes a "war to end all wars." Hook thus represents not only the captain of the U-boat, but the Allied leaders who led millions of soldiers to their deaths in the ludicrous ambition to end all war. He also reflects the Public School morality of showing good form in all things, including and especially warfare. Once Peter Banning is restored as Peter Pan, he also recalls the seductive call of death. In the final battle scene, he says to Hook: "Death is a great adventure," to which Hook replies, "It's the only adventure you have left." Pan would now be a worthy son to Theodore Roosevelt; that is, the reborn Peter Pan is the embodiment of that version of masculinity that would assure the building of a great nation. When he returns happily restored as a man-child to his family and his great grandmother (who is also his childhood companion) Wendy (Maggie Smith), she says to him sadly, "No more adventures for you." To which Peter replies with the last line of the play, "Life, life will be the great adventure."

Spielberg, unlike Barrie, wants to foster the illusion that a man can have it both ways. Both vitality and virility return to the driven, workaholic father upon rediscovering the Peter Pan within, while Hook's masculine characteristics are predicated on the Peter Pan who was hooked into signifying World War I—that is, as validating masculine desire for death as the great adventure. The battle scene is fought in part with harmless weapons—tomatoes, eggs, and paint fired from a variety of weapons by the Lost

Boys—but partly with real weapons, and there is a real death. Rufio (Dante Basco), who has led the Lost Boys in Peter's absence, is really killed by Hook. There is also the hapless soul Hook casually shoots for trying to steal third base in the baseball game Hook arranges to flatter Peter Banning's disaffected son. It is because Peter Pan's spirit returns in the body of a middle-aged man that Peter Banning is able to return to his family fully engaged as a parent and husband, but it is possible only because he has led the Lost Boys in a real war against the pirates and fought and defeated Hook. Proving that real, true innocence cannot be attained because the taint of grown-up war accompanies it.

For Barrie's Peter Pan, the line that could not be crossed included love—that is, submitting to the principle of Eros, and seeking to create new life. He could seek a mother to nursemaid him, yes, but nothing beyond that in the way of emotional maturation, or of a grasp of the future he might create. For Spielberg, as for Theodore Roosevelt, tapping the life-giving wellspring of Eros depends upon acting upon Thanatos. The redemption of the middle aged Peter Pan depends upon putting aside sublimated aggression—as a cutthroat modern-day pirate raping the land he buys and develops—and facing actual physical annihilation to save those he loves. The adult Peter Pan finds that he wants nothing more than to be an engaged father and husband, but to achieve that identity, he must be willing to destroy what stands in his way—his own drives—as well as the threat from without, the threat posed by Hook.

Spielberg ultimately extends pity to Hook, who is revealed to be that worst of all possible things—old. Still, everyone is quite cheered when a large stuffed alligator clock falls on Hook. This unconvincing—and poorly directed—scene points to the weakness of Spielberg's attempt to have it both ways: Peter Pan cannot really kill Hook in front of his children if the ending is to be comedic; if Peter Banning's conflict with his children is to be resolved through a restoration of love untainted by the guilt of blood on his hands. Yet he cannot leave Hook on the loose to pursue him and his children. So, while he fights him presumably to the death, ultimately the conflict is clumsily resolved *crocodilus ex machina*.

Barrie, in his wisdom, presents the case that the make-believe world of fighting and dying has to remain just that: the killing is only imaginary, one is always a hero, and one never dies. That distinction between the imaginary world of childhood and the dangers of acting it out in the real world must have enforced itself upon Barrie's imagination. The changed referent of Marooner's Island during the war was too painfully clear: during the war years, the scene was omitted from the play and from children's versions of the story used in British classrooms.

J. M. Barrie suffered painful losses during the war. In addition to the loss of Frohman, two losses devastated his adopted family, the Llewelyn-Davies. One of the children's uncles on their mother's side was killed in the war. A few days later, the family suffered an even more crushing blow: the death of one of Barrie's wards—George Llewelyn-Davies—on March 15, 1915. He was shot in the head at St. Eloi in Flanders. One of the children, Nico, was in bed asleep when the telegram came to the house: "Voices soon came up the stairs but stopped at the landing. Then I heard Uncle Jim's voice, an eerie Banshee wail—"Ah-h-h! They'll all go, Mary [Nico's sister, who had gotten out of bed and gone downstairs]—Jack, Peter, Michael—even little Nico—This dreadful war will get them all in the end!"[31]

Barrie's disillusionment and sorrow can be traced not only in his private life, but in his plays. The first play he wrote during the war, *The New Word* (1915), examined the reconciling effect between an estranged father and son when the otherwise dull and nondescript son joins up for the war and inspires his father's pride. Plays written later in the war—*The Old Lady Shows Her Medals* (1917) and *The Well Remembered Voice* (1918)—are about the dreadful effects of the dead young men on the women left behind to mourn them.

THE WORLD WAR I PETER PAN TODAY

Chris Hedges in *War Is a Force That Gives Us Meaning* (2002) recounts his emotional and intellectual fifteen-year journey as a war correspondent. Acknowledging the addictive power of the adrenaline rush that comes with being exposed to danger, Hedges argues the seductive power of the *mythos* of war: "The enduring attraction of war is this: Even with its destruction and carnage it can give us what we long for in life. It can give us purpose, meaning, a reason for living."[32] We hear in this striking confession the echoes of Gosse, Brooke, Seeger, and Theodore Roosevelt. The struggle for civilization, argues Hedges, is what Freud set out as the essential struggle between the impulse for Eros and Thanatos. Hedges ruefully acknowledges he was drawn into the mythic realm of war. He wishes to redeem both himself and us by arguing that the sensory reality of warfare is the only reality, and that it is only about brutality, destruction, and death. For Hedges, there is no way through Thanatos to Eros except via disillusionment, guilt, and hope for redemption. The two are incompatible.

The First World War (1914–1918) yielded 15 million dead; World War II (1939–1945), 55 million; the Korean War (1950–1953), almost three million; the Vietnam War (1960–1975), three and a half million; Bosnia and Herzegovina (1992–1995), 175,000. There are no accurate casualty counts for the U.S. participation in Lebanon (1993), Grenada (1983), Panama

(1989), the Gulf War (1990 to 1991), Kosovo (1998), Afghanistan (2001–), and Iraq (2003–). The body count for Americans in Afghanistan is about 300; Iraq, 4,000; Gulf War, 148. The ratio of civilian to American soldier death in Afghanistan and Iraq is estimated to be eighteen to twenty civilians for every one American soldier.

Since the war in Vietnam, American forces have had to rely on volunteers. This means that the mythos of war has to be sustained in order to attract young men and women into the armed forces. Maintaining the seductive vision of war requires, as we have seen, the mobilization of powerful cultural as well as political forces. Today, the military does not rely upon appealing to the desire to sacrifice oneself as an example of patriotism; rather, the appeal is to the individual's desire for self-fulfillment, as it was for Brooke and Seeger. Potential soldiers are appealed to less in terms of a sense of duty to nation than through the promise of special training, money for college tuition, or to become "Army strong"—that is, a manly man. Sophisticated video games are available for free download on U.S. Armed Services sites to any curious youngster who wants to see what warfare is "really like." Only it is make-believe. These games, developed in cooperation with Hollywood special effects production companies, knowingly shred the distinction between fighting Hook in Neverland and adding to the toll of dead in the bloodiest one century and eight years the world has ever seen. The video games play upon sublimated Thanatos—the aesthetics of destruction. And that desire becomes the chief virtue of manhood without invoking any consequences. Make-believe carelessly applied makes a vice of virtue. Pan, the goat-footed god, is a seductive pipe player who in mythology causes panic especially in the hearts of men in battle. The impulses of his mischievous namesake Peter Pan, who steals away little children, are best sequestered in the imaginary little boy who never wanted to grow up and was carried off to Neverland, and not idealized as the spirit that makes a man a man.

NOTES

1. Dan Kiley, *The Peter Pan Syndrome: Men Who Have Never Grown Up* (New York: Dodd Mead, 1983).
2. J. M. Barrie, *The Plays of J. M. Barrie* (1911; New York: Charles Scribner's Sons, 1956), 60–61. All subsequent quotations from *Peter Pan* are from this edition.
3. J. M. Barrie, *Peter and Wendy and Margaret Ogilvy* (1911; New York: Charles Scriber's Sons, 1912), 118.
4. Isaac F. Marcosson and Daniel Frohman, *Charles Frohman: Manager and Man* (New York and London: Harper & Bros., 1916), 187–191; 247; Mary C. Henderson, *Theatre in America* (New York: Abrams, 1986), 29.
5. Marcosson and Frohman, *Charles Frohman,* 250, 260–289.
6. Ibid., 160, 163.

7. Ibid., 369.

8. Bruce K. Hanson, *The Peter Pan Chronicles* (New York: Birch Lane Press, 1993), 53.

9. Marcosson and Frohman, *Charles Frohman,* 171.

10. Ibid., 169.

11. Rabbi Silverman, "Stage Pays Final Tribute to Frohman," *New York Times* (May 26, 1915), 13.

12. Marcosson and Frohman, *Charles Frohman,* 389.

13. Ibid.

14. Colin Simpson, *The Lusitania* (Boston: Little, Brown, 1972), 147–151.

15. Andrew Birkin, *J. M. Barrie and the Lost Boys: The Real Story Behind Peter Pan* (New Haven, CT: Yale University Press, 2003), 225.

16. Quoted in Samuel Hynes, *A War Imagined: The First World War and English Culture* (New York: Macmillan, 1990), 12.

17. Rupert Brooke, *The Collected Poems of Rupert Brooke* (New York: Dodd, Mead, 1959), 101.

18. A. S. Byatt, "A Child in Time," *The Guardian* (October 23, 2004).

19. Quoted in Paul Fussel, *The Great War in Modern Memory* (New York: Oxford University Press, 1975), 11.

20. Michael C. C. Adams, *The Great Adventure: Male Desire and the Coming of World War I* (Bloomington and Indianapolis: Indiana University Press, 1990), 85–88.

21. Robert Falcon Scott. *Scott's Last Expedition*, Vol. I. Arranged by Leonard Huxley (1913; London: John Murray, 1927) 467, 468, 472.

22. Linda R. Robertson, *The Dream of Civilized Warfare: World War I Flying Aces and the American Imagination* (Minneapolis and London: University of Minnesota Press, 2003), 164–170.

23. Theodore Roosevelt, *The Foes of Our Own Household, The Great Adventure, Letters to His Children* (New York: Charles Scribner's Sons, 1926), 243–244.

24. Ibid., 243

25. Alan Seeger, *Poems* (New York: Charles Scribner Sons, 1917); "The Rendezvous," http://net.lib.byu.edu/~rdh7/wwi/memoir/Seeger/intro.htm.

26. Kendall Banning, "The Great Adventure," in W. D. Eaton, ed., *Great Poems of the World War: Electronic Edition.* http://beck.library.emory.edu/greatwar/poetry/contents.php?id=eaton.xml.

27. Cecil Lewis, *Saggitarius Rising* (Peter Davies, 1936), 399.

28. Ibid.

29. Lester D. Friedman, *Citizen Spielberg* (Urbana and Chicago: University of Illinois Press, 2006), 18, 25–26.

30. Steven Spielberg, dir., *Hook.* Sony Pictures Home Entertainment, 2001.

31. Birkin, *J. M. Barrie and the Lost Boys,* 243.

32. Chris Hedges, *War Is a Force That Gives Us Meaning* (2002; New York, Anchor Books, 2003), 3.

CHAPTER 3

"I do believe in fairies, I do, I do"

THE HISTORY AND EPISTEMOLOGY
OF PETER PAN

Allison B. Kavey

JAMES M. BARRIE'S *Peter Pan* has provided the landscape for children's imaginations for over a century, and it was first presented in literary form in *Peter in Kensington Gardens*. This short book provides crucial background information about the boy who chooses an eternity of childhood and independence rather than consenting to accept the privileges and obligations attached to growing up and living a middle-class life in early twentieth-century England. The concept of a world that exists alongside the everyday one has deep roots in British culture, in which fairies, elves, and changelings were regularly believed to share fields and woods with human beings. Barrie borrowed heavily from that familiar and popular tradition when he created the landscape and inhabitants of Neverland.

One of the most significant folk traditions behind Peter Pan's story is the myth of changelings: elves who stole human children and brought them to live in their world, leaving behind replacements in the shape of old or sickly elves. Though Barrie's figures are not perfect exemplars of changelings, most notably because no child (elven or otherwise) is left behind to take their place in the nursery, the characters of Peter and the Lost Boys are intertwined with ideas about lost children. Prevailing ideas about fairies and changelings in early twentieth-century British culture provide a means for uncovering two of the most important dichotomies in Barrie's writing, the conflict between imagination/belief and knowledge/fact. These dichotomies, like the characters and the landscapes, developed and changed as Barrie reconsidered and consistently reedited his story about the boy who refused to grow up. Thus, a close analysis of the fairy traditions in British folk and literary culture uncovers some of the cultural background for

Barrie's construction of fairies and other preternatural creatures in the Peter Pan narratives, as well as providing a more sophisticated understanding of Peter Pan himself.

WHAT'S IN A NAME? THE DIVIDED NATURE OF PETER PAN

The name Peter Pan links super- and preternatural beings such as gods and fairies with Barrie's main character. The god Pan is a product of Greek mythology, a half-man and half-goat, known for lusting after women, playing the pipes, and serving as the god of shepherds and herders. Due to his libidinous and sensual nature, Pan is also the god associated most closely with the pagan tradition and its death at the hands of Christianity. An early Christian story recounts that: "when the heavenly host told the shepherds at Bethlehem of the birth of Christ, a deep groan, heard throughout all the isles of Greece, told that the great Pan was dead."[1] But for all the reputation Pan gained as the paragon of wantonness and lust, his story reveals a stable existence defined more frequently by sexual rejection than conquest. We first hear of him in the forest Arcadia as the god of flocks and shepherds, where he led a responsible, if solipsistic, existence. His pipes are the product of frustrated lust: they were what the nymph Syrinx put in his way so that she could escape his attempt to rape her. They also represent his easily distracted nature, since upon hearing the reeds make music of his sighs, he threw over his pursuit of Syrinx in favor of fashioning an instrument of reeds that he named after her.[2] Finally, they represent one of his greatest weaknesses: his love for himself and his need for adoring followers. Pan was so proud of his music that he compared his playing with that of Apollo and challenged the sun god to a contest to determine the better musician. He played first, "and with his rustic melody gave great pleasure to himself and his faithful follower, Midas." But Pan lost the contest, and Midas suffered for defending Pan's playing against Apollo, while Pan himself escaped entirely unscathed.[3]

Peter in Kensington Gardens, the story that explains how Peter left his nursery and embarked on his newfound existence in the park, makes explicit links between the boy Peter Pan and the god Pan and points to the ways in which Barrie exploited the mythological tradition to develop his character. The first similarity between the two figures is their bodies, both of which have animal and human aspects; while Pan the god is half-man and half-goat, Peter Pan is half-bird and half-child. In Barrie's story, all children begin as birds and many believe, especially in their first few weeks of life, that they still are. Peter believed this so intensely that he flew right out of his nursery window and back to Kensington Gardens, where the birds and the fairies rule the night. But his sudden sensitivity to cold, a constantly stuffy nose, several awkward run-ins with fairies, and a final encounter with the wise Solomon force him to realize that he is not a bird any longer. That encounter so unmoored him from his identity that he began to doubt his ability to fly, which immediately resulted in his losing it. Solomon explains to Peter that he will be stuck on the bird's island forever, and that he is now "a Betwixt-and-Between," neither fully human nor fully avian.[4]

Being both human and animal has its advantages for both Pan and Peter, and it is fundamental to their identities. The god's body symbolizes his sexuality, perhaps his best-known characteristic, and links him to the animals for whom he has responsibility. In much the same way, Peter's physically mixed body represents his divided nature. Although he looks like a child, he weighs almost nothing and can hover in the air, being borne by the wind. The other children, even with the help of fairy dust, cannot manage such a feat: "He could sleep in the air without falling, by merely lying on his back and floating, but this was, partly at least, because he was so light that if you got behind him and blew, he went faster" (Barrie, 103). Peter's lack of physical mass harkens back to his days as a bird, and it represents his fundamentally divided identity. Barrie's description of the birds as domestic, perseverant, and cautious, adjectives that no one would apply to Peter, demonstrates that, whatever birdlike physical characteristics he may possess, his nature is perfectly childish, and represents both the most charming and most anxiety-provoking aspects of that state. Much like the solipsistic Pan, he is almost entirely self-referential, and his interactions with other characters, from the Lost Boys to the Darlings to his own mother, reflect this. When he is flying to Neverland, Michael keeps falling asleep and succumbing to gravity; Peter does rescue the little boy, but only at the last second, "and you felt that it was his cleverness that interested him, not the saving of human life" (Barrie, 103). In fact, he is rather cavalier about death, dealing it to pirates on a regular basis and consistently losing Lost Boys. Much like a toddler, he has no memory of anything that has happened before, so his imagination drives both his narratives of the past and his expectations for the future. This results in an elegantly disconnected text, which frustrates the other children because his explanations rarely match his physical condition and they, unlike their leader, are already connecting narrative to evidence to assess its validity. "He often went out alone, and when he came back you were never absolutely certain whether he had had an adventure or not. He might have forgotten it so completely that he said nothing about it; and then when you went out you found the body; and, on the other hand, he might say a great deal about it and you could not find the body" (Barrie, 137).

But Peter is not just a combination of entirely birdlike and entirely childish characteristics; he also contains some traits that mark him as being between existing categories, or at least fundamentally different from both birds and children. Like Pan, Peter is perceived by other beings as containing both sides of his mixed nature. The fairies, for example, accept him in Kensington Gardens at night, though they drive out or attack other children; the birds are constantly amused by his vagaries; and the mermaids, who actively loathe the Darling children and the Lost Boys, spend hours chatting with Peter (Barrie, 17, 27, 140). His behavior is especially reflective of his divided nature, since he has to intentionally mimic the behavior of either children or birds. He sometimes remembers that he was once just a child, and this memory, which is one of very few he has retained, shapes his behavior in the Gardens. "But he has still a vague memory that he was a human once, and it makes him especially kind to the house-swallows when they visit the island, for house-swallows are the spirits of little children who have died. They always build in the eaves of the houses in which they lived when they were humans, and sometimes they try to fly in at a nursery window, and perhaps that is why Peter loves them best of all the birds" (Barrie, 64).

While Peter may love the house swallows for what they represent, he must also envy them their freedom from his in-between state. These children managed to die and move on into new existences, while Peter will spend eternity caught between the landscapes and desires of two very different natures. Although he does not consistently yearn for the nursery or his mother, he sometimes misses both and his epic nightmares acknowledge that he cannot regain the human life that he abandoned when he left the nursery. "Sometimes, though not often, he had dreams, and they were more painful than the dreams of other boys. For hours he could not be separated from these dreams, though he wailed piteously in them. They had to do, I think, with the riddle of his existence" (Barrie, 181).

Peter is fully aware, when he chooses to acknowledge such mundane details, that he is not like the Lost Boys, the Darling children, or the fairies with whom he spends his time. While his mixed nature has the potential to torture him, it also gives him extraordinary strength that exceeds any held by either part of his character. This is most evident when he is under duress, such as when he is wounded and facing death by drowning in the lagoon: "Peter was not quite like other boys; but he was afraid at last. A tremor ran through him, like a shudder passing through the sea; but on the sea one shudder follows another until there are hundreds of them, and Peter felt just the one. Next moment he was standing erect on the rock again, with that smile on his face and a drum beating within him. It was saying, 'To die will be an awfully big adventure'" (Barrie, 152).

Fear of death is not only a human characteristic; the prospect of impending doom will raise anxiety levels in everything from mice to horses. But the ability to move beyond it and reimagine death as an adventure, and even a potential escape from Neverland and eternity in-between, is essentially human and remarkably boyish. Like the god Pan, Peter's mixed nature and body link him to his landscape and represent his dominant characteristics, but Barrie does not simply rely on their "betweenness" to link them; he intentionally gives Peter Pan the god's most notable accessories, his goat and his pipes.

The goat, for Peter, is a result of his beguilement of a little girl, and the story surrounding it is integral to Peter's history. In *Peter in Kensington Gardens*, Barrie asserts that there was a story about Pan before the goat, and an equally well-known one that came after he attained one:

> If you ask your mother whether or not she knew about Peter Pan when she was a little girl, she will say, "Why, of course I did, child;" and if you ask her whether he rode on a goat in those days, she will say, "What a foolish question to ask; certainly he did." Then if you ask your grandmother whether she knew about Peter Pan when she was a little girl, she also says, "Why, of course I did, child," but if you ask her whether he rode on a goat in those days, she says she never heard of him having a goat. (Barrie, 12)

And then he explains how Peter got his goat. It was the gift of a little girl, Maimie, who broke the rules and spent the night in Kensington Gardens. She had great adventures with the fairies and was nearly seduced into marrying Peter before she realized that she would not be happy if she could not regularly see her mother. While she chose to leave him in the garden and return to her mother, on Easter, she gave him a gift of the imaginary goat she had used to terrorize her brother in the nursery at night. She left the goat in a fairy circle with a note to Peter explaining the gift and urging him to ask the fairies for help in making it rideable (Barrie, 62–64).

This story and the appearance of the goat represent Peter's first failure at full-fledged seduction. Like the god Pan, he is within inches of completing his conquest—though this one is undoubtedly more honorable, since rather than attempting to rape his object of affection he covers her with kisses then asks her to marry him—when he is abandoned in favor of Maimie's mother. Left behind in the garden like the abandoned and forgotten toys he adopts as his playthings, Peter mopes for a bit, hoping that his love will return to him, but he then reflects a child's, and the god Pan's, talent for moving on from past failures: "Though Peter still remembers Maimie he is become as gay as ever, and often in sheer happiness he jumps off his goat and lies kicking merrily in the grass" (Barrie, 64). The goat turns out to be an excellent present, since it allows Peter to pursue his new routine of scanning the

Gardens for other children who, like his lost love, have crossed the boundary between the pleasant daytime park and the dangerous one that emerges after nightfall. Much like Pan with his flocks, Peter is a herder and tender of children, responsible for protecting them from the dangers posed by fairies and weather and keeping them happy and peaceful until the morning, when they can escape.

Peter's pipes are crucial for this task and he uses them to alert lost children to his presence. His musical skill also earns him the respect of the fairies, and a job playing for their regular dances that will eventually result in their granting his wish to return to his nursery and his mother. The pipes are a more consistent accessory to Pan's character than the goat, which has no role at all in *Peter and Wendy*. They function as his ticket to acceptance among the birds and fairies, and they also serve as an excellent means for seducing women and girls. *Peter Pan in Kensington Gardens* explains that Peter's pipes are a means for him to express in his human form his birdlike glee: "Peter's heart was so glad that he felt he must sing all day long, just as the birds sing for joy, but, being partly human, he needed an instrument, so he made a pipe of reeds" (Barrie, 18). This first mention of the pipes points to the ways in which the instrument allowed him entrance into the very land—the world of the birds—that his human birth had caused him to leave. They also signal the ways in which he is not like fully human children, who find constantly glad hearts impossible to maintain and waste their time and energy being "mad-dog and Mary-Annish" instead of playing all the time (Barrie, 29). Peter Pan straddles the divide between birds and humans, and the instrument is a human invention that allows him to express his birdlike joy.

His pipes also become a means for bridging the much larger gap between the world of Kensington Gardens and the world of the nursery. Upon arriving in Kensington Gardens for the first time after his birth, he still believes himself to be a bird. But increasingly his environment and its inhabitants nudge him into realizing that something is terribly wrong. Solomon, the old wise bird in charge of changing birds into children and sending them out to the human world, tells Peter the truth; he is neither fully human nor fully bird, and his in-between status strands him without any of the conveniences of being either wholly human or bird. He has no mother to care for him, and he can't fly, which means he can never leave the island again. Peter manages, through clever manipulation of the birds, to have a boat built that allows him to cross between the island and Kensington Gardens; but without the power of flight he is absolutely unable to return home to his mother. His pipes provide that chance when, after many nights of perfect playing at fairy balls, Queen Mab offers him two wishes as a reward. He wished to fly home to his mother, and the fairies tickled him on his shoulders until he rose into the air and flew away (Barrie, 36–37).

The results of this homeward return are fateful and dramatically emphasize how Peter's conflicting desires trap him between the fairy-tale world of Kensington Gardens and the human one of the nursery. The first indication of this is that he did not go straight back to the nursery, but instead had a lovely cruise around London because he was so enchanted by the experience of flying. By the time he did make it to the nursery window, "he had quite made up his mind that his second wish should be to become a bird" (Barrie, 37). Upon his first visit home, the window through which he escaped his nursery was open, his mother was sleeping, and he knew that she longed to have him back; but he was not able to commit himself to life as a human. The fun he had enjoyed with the fairies and the birds, combined with his recent regaining of flight, rendered him reluctant to return to full-time childhood: "I quite shrink from the truth, which is that he sat there in two minds. Sometimes he looked longingly at his mother and sometimes he looked longingly at the window" (Barrie, 38). Instead, he played a tune on his pipes woven from the way she said his name to console her, and then left for Kensington Gardens believing that he would always be able to come back using the second wish granted to him by Queen Mab. But time moves very differently in the Gardens and it took Peter a long time to decide that he was ready to "go back to mother for ever and always" (40). After flying home, convinced that he was finally ready to make his mother eternally happy, he found that she had betrayed him: the window was shut and another little boy was asleep in his bed (40).

While this was the end of Peter's tolerance for mothers, it was certainly not the end of his using pipes to beguile women. Peter attracted the attention of Mrs. Darling with the leaves he had left beneath the nursery window, which drew Wendy's explanation that: "Peter sometimes came to the nursery in the night and sat on the foot of her bed and played on his pipes to her" (Barrie, 76). The pipes offered him entrée into Wendy's imagination, as they had provided him entrée into the world of the fairies and flight. He did not need them again, either to beguile a woman or to express joy, until the night the Darlings and the Lost Boys try to leave Neverland to return to the world. That night, he "continued, for a little time, to play gaily on the pipes," but they had lost their sirens' tongues and become instead cold comfort. His playing, in this case, was nothing but "a rather forlorn attempt to prove to himself that he did not care" (Barrie, 180).

The pipes play different roles in the two novels because Peter's character becomes more fully developed over time. In particular he moves from a poignant character stuck between two worlds to a leader whose endless energy and imagination shape his geography and the adventures of his merry band while at the same time trapping him. The frustrated nature of his existence, as represented by the pipes that allow him to seduce women into his world but never to keep them with him or join them in theirs, consistently links Peter to the god Pan, who also fashioned his pipes out of need, was responsible for shepherding lost things, and became a symbol for freedom and licentiousness that Pan himself could not enjoy.

Peter's crow is the most extreme extension of Pan's pipes. It best represents his personality, which can be understood, like the character himself, to be "betwixt and between" the self-indulgent hedonism of Pan and the naïve egotism of childhood. Notably, Peter does not crow at all in *Peter Pan in Kensington Gardens*. This story reveals the saddest parts of his history and the bittersweet aspects of being both child and preternatural being. While Peter is often joyful, he is never so pleased with himself that he literally trills with happiness. The closest he comes happens during his first visit to his mother, when the first traces of his remarkable self-regard nearly cause him to wake her so she can appreciate his cleverness. After piping for her a lullaby based on the way she said his name, the narrator remarks: "He thought this so clever of him that he could scarcely resist waking her to hear her say, 'Oh Peter, how exquisitely you play!'" (Barrie, 38). He does resist and returns to Kensington Gardens, convinced that his next visit to his mother will be "the greatest treat a woman can have" (Barrie, 38). The devastation of the locked window he finds upon finally returning to his mother establishes the emotional nadir that Peter will reach repeatedly in *Peter and Wendy*. But it is the necessary ingredient to set him free from the belief that there are people other than himself to whom he might owe attention and obligation. That freedom allowed Peter to emerge fully as himself and to note that rebirth with a resounding crow.

Crowing and crying represent Peter's emotional highs and lows, respectively. And while he is happy to claim the former, he refuses to even remember that he is capable of the latter—even when there are witnesses. Peter's first encounter with Wendy begins when he wakes her with his sobs because his shadow refuses to be rejoined to his body. The girl courteously asks the strange boy on her bedroom floor why he is crying. He initially refuses to answer, and then does so only because she attacks the core of his existence when she attributes his tears to the lack of a mother: "'I wasn't crying about mothers,' he said indignantly. 'I was crying because I can't get my shadow to stick on. Besides, I wasn't crying'" (Barrie, 90). Wendy, charmed by his tears, sews his shadow back on, only to discover his crow and the solipsistic, timeless sense of self it represents: "Alas, he had forgotten that he owed his happiness to Wendy. He thought that he had attached the shadow himself. 'How clever I am,' he crowed rapturously, 'Oh the cleverness of me!'" (Barrie, 91).

Peter's crow is so clearly his trademark that it sounds again to mark his reappearance in Neverland—"it was always thus that he signaled his return" (Barrie, 125). It also signals his triumphs, especially over his archenemy, Hook. But because his great sense of self is not matched with an equally rich sense of patience, he has a tendency to crow too early. This happens when he first imitates Hook in order to make Smee and Starkey release Tiger Lily from the rock on which she is sentenced to drown (Barrie, 144). In that case, the crow turns into a whistle when he realizes that Hook is in the area and can easily catch him in the game. An individual with less Pan in him would have given up, but with complete confidence in his own cleverness, Peter leaps back into the game of imitating Hook with even more enthusiasm now that his nemesis is the butt of his efforts. The joy of the game rests, for Peter, in triumphing under the worst possible conditions and in a way that asserts his own superiority while reducing his enemy to a selfless mass of insecurity. Their exchange, in which Hook is outwitted and left considering his similarities to a codfish and Peter pronounces himself wonderful, ends with a crow that announces Peter's identity as surely as the declaration of his name (Barrie, 148).

The crow breaks forth most powerfully in the epic battle scene on the pirate ship between Peter Pan and Hook. Peter, who has come to rescue the Lost Boys and Wendy, boards the ship and kills two pirates, then crows. Hook, too distracted by Peter's initial strategy of ticking his way onto the ship, fails to recognize his archenemy's trademark sound and instead identifies it, with the help of the other pirates, as the mark of a new enemy that is both ticking crocodile and rooster. Even if Hook is convinced that he had poisoned Peter and freed himself from the former's imagination, any character who believes so wholeheartedly in the power of an enemy to determine his fate would surely believe that enemy possessed the potential for resurrection and further interference with his plans. It is hard to believe that Hook imagines himself, even for a moment, to be truly free of Peter. This is reflected in the nature of the "new enemy" he creates to explain the ticking and the crowing and the deaths on his ship, all of which point to Peter in no uncertain terms. This fantasy of freedom splinters in the loudest crow yet, followed by Peter's announcement that the great enemy on the ship is, "Peter Pan the avenger" (Barrie, 201).

Peter's final crows appear in the melancholy last pages, when he escapes the boundaries of the stories that Wendy tells her daughter Jane and emerges again in the nursery. He signals his reappearance in Wendy's life with an echoed crow. As Wendy tells the story of her adventures in Neverland, Jane asks for Peter's last words. Wendy replies: "The last thing he ever said to me was, 'Just always be waiting for me, and then some night you will hear me crowing'" (Barrie, 222). It is Jane, this time, who imitates the crow to perfection—Wendy has forgotten how. And then, on cue, the boy himself appears, young and cocky and as unburdened by memory as ever. He escapes through the window with Jane, and then Jane's daughter Margaret, with the cocksure joy of a lady's man who knows his effect on women (Barrie, 222–226). But he also knows, even as he slips away into the darkness with a new little girl playing mother on his arm, exactly what he has lost, just as Pan the god took up the reeds with a last sad glance at the nymph who would always be just out of his reach. For Pan, the loss was a sexual one, just as his conquests were sexual. For Peter, both loss and joy involve the maternal, just as all the females he encountered, from the Darling girls to Tinker Bell and Tiger Lily, he understood only as mothers (Barrie, 162).[5] The joyful crow and the belief that girls and women will always be charmed by him comes directly from the fact that Peter, unlike his adult namesake Pan, is an eternal child, who interprets the world from the perspective of a boy enthralled with his own cleverness and devastated by his original mother's apparent rejection of him. His thoughtlessness, which allowed him to fly away from his mother after his first visit with the blithe belief that she would wait forever while he had his adventures, reflects his youth—for children, mothers will always be waiting, and time does move differently. For children, fairies are just as real as the nurseries in which they reside. For Peter, both fairies and nurseries hold their own appeal, but the former, not the latter, promises both familiarity and a timeless eternity in which to play.

PETER AND THE FAIRIES

In order to understand the cast of characters who appear alongside Peter, both in Kensington Gardens and in Neverland, one must first understand the place of fairies and other preternatural creatures in British culture and the British imagination. Evidence suggests that fairy stories played a significant part in the oral cultures of medieval and Renaissance England, Ireland, and Scotland, and their preeminence is reflected in the proliferation of fairies, elves, sprites, and changelings in sixteenth- and seventeenth-century print, both fictional and dramatic.[6] Scholars such as Jack Zipes and Richard Darnton have focused on fairy tales as highly flexible pieces of narrative that reflected prevailing cultural anxieties and emphases and were capable of changing to suit shifts in social structure and ideology.[7] They have also argued that the culture of imagination and the culture of oral storytelling were tightly intertwined, a relationship that continued to shape print culture even after the printing press made silent reading and established texts more available.

The arguments of adaptability offered by scholars such as Darnton and Zipes are more compelling than the interpretations of the cultural place of fairies and other aspects of the preternatural in early modern Europe offered by many historians of science.[8] This latter approach, which emphasizes the sociological bases of belief in fairies, does little to answer the question of why they occupied equally significant if slightly different parts in the British imagination in the long-separated sixteenth and early twentieth centuries. This chapter takes these creatures, and the intellectual traditions that surrounded them, more seriously, following the more fruitful approach demonstrated by scholars such as Darnton and Zipes.

Even if we take the belief in fairies, elves, and their ilk seriously in the sixteenth and early seventeenth centuries, we are still left with two hundred years in which these characters serve more as background scenery than major performers. It is not until the nineteenth century that we again see fairies emerging as among the major preoccupations of the British imagination. During the intervening years, fairies were certainly a part of Scottish, Irish, and English folklore, but they did not draw the attention of many authors at the time. It was in the nineteenth century, particularly with the English publication of the Grimm brothers' fairy tales, that British writers from Charles Dickens to John Keats and Oscar Wilde included fairies, elves, and ogres among the characters in their literary works.[9] And it was during this period that the two great English children's authors, James Barrie and Lewis Carroll, wrote their exceptional stories of children and the imagined worlds into which they could disappear.

The worlds into which these fictional children escaped often mirror the most bizarre aspects of the culture that they left behind, especially the obsessions with manners, performance, consumption, and work. Recent scholars have linked literary fairies, beginning in the late sixteenth century, to a critique of court culture that reflected popular anxieties about the materialism of the Tudor and Stuart monarchs and growing unease about the place of consumption in early modern British culture. In the early modern literature that Marjorie Swann reviews, fairies' courts are decorated with rotted, discarded, or hideous things, such as mouse corpses, moths' wings, and nutshells, which reflect the decadent and over-ripe aspects of consumer culture.[10] In *Peter Pan and Kensington Gardens*, however, the fairies use fresh natural products, such as berries, leaves, and branches, to enhance a palace of glass that is already exceptional for its beauty and its chameleon-like ability to stay hidden during the day by matching the colors of the Gardens.

3.1 The fairies make their summer curtains from skeleton leaves. Arthur Rackham illustration from *Peter Pan in Kensington Gardens,* 1906.

> Their blues and reds and greens are like ours with a light behind them. The palace is entirely built of many-coloured glasses, and it is quite the loveliest of all royal residences, but the queen sometimes complains because the common people will peep in to see what she is doing. (Barrie, 33)

Rather than showing an anxiety about the decadent aspects of court culture, Barrie's fairy court reflects a respect for monarchy and its power, a belief that its place in British society is rooted in the natural, and the hope that even such an august institution could be improved upon by imagination and fairy magic.

Instead of scorning the rampant consumption of the monarchy, Barrie's fairies and Peter Pan himself are critical of the ideas about work and productivity espoused by the middle class and the limitations placed on children's imaginations by toys with directions that say they can only be played with one way. Barrie is quick to note that the fairies "do nothing useful" though they appear to work all the time, and that education and productive labor, the primary occupations of the human world, have no place in fairy land (Barrie, 32). Furthermore, he empowers the youngest fairies, noting that they are generally ignored in human culture, to lead their families in daily activities. Of course, Peter's very existence is the product of resisting bourgeois male identity, since he claims that he ran away when he heard his parents "talking about what I was to be when I became a man" (Barrie, 92). His existence in Kensington Gardens offers insight into the ways in which toys, when played with only according to cultural rules, are inherently frustrating, while their entertainment value, when unhampered by expectations and developed by the imagination, can be endless. Peter finds abandoned toys in the Gardens, and in combination with the few stories he hears from the birds about how children play, he creates his own ways of playing with them that bear only a vague resemblance to the original. The narrator is quick to establish, however, that Peter's approach is superior.

> Do you pity Peter Pan for making these mistakes? If so, I think it rather silly of you. What I mean is that, of course, one must pity him now and then, but to pity him all the time would be impertinence. He thought he had the most splendid time in the Gardens, and to think you have it is almost quite as good as really to have it. He played without ceasing, while you often waste time being mad-dog or Mary-Annish. He could be neither of these things, because he had never heard of them, but do you think he is to be pitied for that? Oh, he was merry! (Barrie, 29)

The effort to turn upside down the chronological and professional hierarchy of nineteenth-century life is not unique to Barrie (though he and Carroll are its best-known representatives), and it reflects the ways in which fairies were used to poke fun at the Victorian obsession with work and provide imagination and enjoyment as alternatives to productive labor.

Enjoyment is, in fact, a mild term for the pleasures sought by Barrie's fairies. From all-night balls filled with dancing and impromptu weddings to orgies, the fairies in Kensington Gardens and Neverland devote themselves wholeheartedly to self-indulgence, if not downright hedonism. They seek nothing more than a good time, claiming their nights in the Gardens as a safe space and time to explore music and desire. During the day, the Gardens are reserved for childish pursuits, such as cricket, sailing paper boats, and fabulous imagined adventures. But Barrie's fairies, who are inextricably linked to children in their existence and their landscapes, manage to shed light on the shared aspects of these two cultures—the passionate quest for pleasure, even at the expense of others. Peter Pan may be the best example of a child who follows his own desires with full knowledge that his doing so tortures his mother, but the Darling children are also demonstrably reckless with their parents' feelings. The fairies, like Peter and his band, are fully devoted to accumulating and maintaining their sources of pleasure, and they are as willing as their childish counterparts to use force to do so.

When children stumble into the Gardens at night, for example, they are more often met with fairy armies than gossamer wings.

The fairies are different from Barrie's depictions of children in one very significant way: the fairies will use trickery to get what they want. Peter and his band are notable for their rejection of tricks and manipulations in battle as violations of the principles of fair play; Peter scorns John for his suggestion that they kill a pirate without first waking him and even gives Hook a hand up during their battle in the lagoon (Barrie, 107, 150). The fairies, on the other hand, consistently try to trick the children into doing what they want. In *Peter Pan in Kensington Gardens*, for example, they repeatedly attempt to trick Peter into wasting his second wish so he cannot go home for good and deprive them of their best musician (Barrie, 40). In *Peter and Wendy*, Tinker Bell famously tricks the Lost Boys into shooting Wendy, claiming that Peter has asked her to do so (Barrie, 122). She also authors an elaborate plot to remove Wendy from Neverland by floating her away on the lagoon and is foiled only by Wendy's untimely awakening (Barrie, 139).

In this way, the fairies combine the self-indulgence of children with the wiles of adults, just like Captain Hook and his pirates, who break the rules for fighting with the Indians and manage to defeat their noble opponents, who will refuse even to bend the rules, though they know it will mean their horrible defeat (Barrie, 173–174). It is only under extreme duress—when the rules of fair play have been rudely violated—that Peter experiments with dissimulation. He does so first by imitating Hook in the lagoon in order to get the pirates to free Tiger Lily, a tactic he adopts because he does not approve of her being ganged up on by two adult pirates and has no other options to save her. Notably, this first flirtation with trickery ends with his near death by drowning, suggesting that lying poses a threat to his very existence. The second time is when he imitates the crocodile to distract Hook and the pirates while he boards the boat and frees the children. Again in this scene, he is trying to even the playing field and, once his friends are free, he chooses to face Hook completely alone. In both instances, he is horrified when Hook violates the principles of fair play, and his shock proves nearly disastrous during his first fight with the pirate when Hook bites Peter after the boy has helped him up onto the rock: "It made him quite helpless. He could only stare, horrified. Every child is affected thus the first time he is treated unfairly" (Barrie, 150). Since Peter has no memory, every time he is treated unfairly is the first time, so the shock is always great, and in this case, nearly fatal because it gives Hook the upper hand in their fight. The fairies represent a more cunning, if not a more heartless, population than the children, and thus they reflect, like the pirates, the wiles of adulthood combined with the selfish pursuit of pleasure at any cost.

The fairies in the Peter Pan stories also develop the links among children, fairies, and Britishness. "It is frightfully difficult to know much about the fairies, and almost the only thing known for certain is that there are fairies wherever there are children" (Barrie, 30). This idea has been developed by literature scholars such as Katharine Briggs and Carole Silver, who have argued that the proliferation of fairies in late-nineteenth-century British culture reflected an effort to relocate Britain in a historical tradition that included consistent interactions with the preternatural, that those interactions most frequently occurred around children, and that they provided nineteenth-century Britons a unique cultural identity.[11] A review of fairy tales written by eminent authors in the nineteenth century reflects the importance of fairies and the preternatural in Victorian morality and intellectual culture.[12] This thesis is well reflected in Barrie's work, which tightly intertwines fairies, children, and the British landscape, even carrying them into the urban wilderness of Kensington Gardens: "There are also numbers of them [fairies] along the Baby Walk, which is a famous gentle place, as spots frequented by fairies are called" (Barrie, 31). This clearly connects Barrie's ideas about fairies to existing ones in the United Kingdom that fancied some places—particularly hills and fields—to be especially conducive to fairy settlement. Those areas had traditionally, however, been in rural and wooded areas far from dense human occupation, so Barrie's extension of the fairy domain into an urban landscape, even one left intentionally "wild," reflected an adjustment of fairy mythology to the realities of the increasingly urban landscape of the early twentieth century. As children moved into urban landscapes, fairies had to follow them. Since they could not thrive on rooftops, they found their way to the groves and meadows of Kensington Gardens, a centerpiece of the English romantic gardening tradition that had been built to allow Londoners to reconnect with nature and the pastoral.[13] But over time, children joined adults in the Gardens, and the Gardens' purpose shifted from an adult attempt to reestablish a lost pastoral world to a place where middle-class children escaped the bricks and smoke of industrial London. "Long ago, children were forbidden in the Gardens, and at that time there was not a fairy in the place; then the children were admitted, and the fairies came trooping in that very evening" (Barrie, 30). Barrie cannot imagine the Gardens, once they had been claimed by children, without their dark shadows, the fairies. This link depends upon their shared history and the fairies' belief-based existence, which relied predominantly on children to continue believing in things they could not see. Leaving the fairies in the hands of most adults would have doomed the population in a matter of weeks.

There are two distinct pieces to the shared history of children and fairies in Barrie's works. The first reveals the longstanding tie between the two groups: "When the first baby laughed for the first time, his laugh broke into a million pieces and they all went skipping about. That was the beginning of fairies" (Barrie, 32). There is, then, no significant history of human existence without fairy accompaniment, and notably, the humans that prompted the appearance of fairies were babies. This connection relies on the story of prebirth existence explained in *Peter Pan in Kensington Gardens*, which imagines all children before birth living as birds in the park and regularly interacting with the fairies. Fairies and prehuman birds are able to communicate and regularly interact in a friendly manner. But once a bird is transformed into a human and sent from the park into a nursery, the process of separation between humans and fairies begins. Children, who were once able to converse with fairies, lose their ability to understand them once they are able to speak to other human beings (Barrie, 33). Under the influence of adults and especially of school, they stop trusting things they cannot see and insist on worldly evidence.

The transfer from imagination and belief to fact-based knowledge comes with a high price, not just for children, who run the risk of becoming boring adults, but also for the fairies, who depend upon children's belief for their continued existence. As Barrie tells us in the original staging of the play and again in *Peter and Wendy*: "You see, children know such a lot now, they soon don't believe in fairies, and every time a child says, 'I don't believe in fairies,' there is a fairy somewhere that falls down dead" (Barrie, 93). Even though audiences have been clapping Tinker Bell back to life with consistent vigor for over one hundred years, the narrator in *Peter and Wendy* takes note of the cynics among England's children: "Many clapped. Some didn't. A few little beasts hissed" (Barrie, 185). This suggests that some children had shifted their allegiance from the things they encountered in stories and their imaginations to things they could see and touch. Barrie tries to provide fact-based evidence for the existence of fairies in *Peter Pan in Kensington Gardens* based on their favorite activity; dancing. Because their balls leave rings in the grass long after the dancers have retired, children who happen into the park during the day and know what they are looking at will be able to identify circles of trodden grass as proof of fairies' existence. The fairies also change the Gardens' closing time on ball nights to give themselves more time for dancing, which provides attentive children with an explanation for why their time in the park is longer some days than others (Barrie, 34).

But the fact that fairies are dependent on children for their existence and share a history with them does not mean that they are friendly to young human beings. Like the fairies abounding in the British tradition, Barrie's fairies can be quite malicious.[14] Their nastiness seems to come in two forms,

3.2 The fairies are distinctly nasty to a child in the Gardens. Arthur Rackham, illustration from *Peter Pan in Kensington Gardens*, 1906.

one that is straight out of fairy lore and entirely independent of children's behavior, and a second that is Barrie's creation and is the consequence of children breaking the rules that separate the two realms by threatening to or actually invading the fairies' kingdom.

Bad things that happen during the day when children inhabit the park can be chalked up to the second reason for fairy malevolence. The fact that fairies abound in Kensington Gardens during the day, when the park is supposed to belong to the children, makes it easy for them to overhear any wish a child might have to interfere with their plans and to punish him for any wayward desires. "Nearly all the nasty accidents that you meet with in the Gardens occur because the fairies have taken an ill-will to you, and so it behooves you to be careful what you say about them" (Barrie, 43). The fairies devote a great deal of energy to avoiding children during the day, but those children who lurk in the Gardens after dark can incite their fear as well as their wrath. Peter Pan, upon his first return to the Gardens after his birth as a child, causes the fairies he encounters to flee because he is invading the park after dark (Barrie, 15). When he first successfully crosses in his boat from the birds' island to the park mainland, necessarily after dark, he encounters a horde of armed fairies. He wins them over by insisting that "he was not an ordinary human" and by charming the fairy women with the baby's nightshirt he used as a sail for his boat (Barrie, 27). The trees warn wayward children of the risk they run if they encounter the fairies, and the stories they tell Maimie, a child who stayed in the Gardens after closing time, are straight out of British fairy lore: "'If the fairies see you,' they warned her, 'they will mischief you—stab you to death, or compel you to nurse their children, or turn you into something tedious like an evergreen oak'" (Barrie, 47). While Maimie's first encounter with an individual fairy does not bear this out, she is nearly killed by the entire fairy kingdom when she interrupts their ball—only the favor she did for the first fairy she encountered saves her from certain death (Barrie, 52).

CHANGELINGS AND SICK CHILDREN

One of the most hostile interactions between children and magical beings is reflected in the changeling myth, in which fairies intentionally seek to steal human children. Changelings were understood to be old, weak fairies who were left in place of healthy children to take advantage of human hospitality while the original children were turned into slaves in the fairy kingdom.[15] Some historians have interpreted this myth as a cultural explanation for frightening and unfamiliar illnesses in children that made them look prematurely aged or enfeebled.[16] The changeling myth and this explanation have some significant connections with Peter Pan. Peter, like the fairies, takes children away from their families. The children he chooses seem to be healthy—the Darling children, for example, are in perfect form when he charms them from their nursery. Some of the other children with whom he is associated, however, are less well. As noted earlier, he searches Kensington Gardens for children who have remained there after dark and whose chance of surviving the fairies' vicious tempers is slight. While he is supposed to save them, he does not always make it in time: "He has been too late several times, and when he sees he is too late he runs back to the Thrush's Nest for his paddle, of which Maimie had told him the true use, and he digs a grave for the child and erects a little tombstone, and carves the poor thing's initials on it" (Barrie, 65). While this image is equally tragic and touching, its heartwarming qualities are undermined by the narrator's musing, "I do hope that Peter is not too ready with his spade" (Barrie, 65).

The chilling possibility that Peter kills the very children he is supposed to protect is not present in *Peter and Wendy*, but there continues to be an association between Peter and dead children. Mrs. Darling's first recollection of Peter Pan was that, "There were odd stories about him, as that when children died he went part of the way with them, so that they should not be frightened" (Barrie, 75). But the children who inhabit Neverland are not yet dead, as indicated by Peter's role in maintaining their numbers by sending some away when they start growing. "The boys on the island vary, of course, in numbers, according as they get killed and so on; and when they seem to be growing up, which is against the rules, Peter thins them out" (Barrie, 112). Thinning them out has a violent ring, but they could as easily be sent back to their parents as killed, especially since growing up implies a breach of the children's contract with Neverland and thus signals the time for their expulsion. This offers a more compelling explanation than the one Peter offers for why there are Lost Boys. Child morbidity was very high and tended to be a drawn-out ordeal in nineteenth- and early-twentieth-century Britain, and sick children had the time to indulge in their imagination without intrusions from real-world, fact-centered institutions like school. Those imaginations would, as I will subsequently argue, include Neverland. Since fairies were very popular in Victorian England and strongly associated with sickness and death, such imaginings were also likely to include fairies.[17]

Unlike fairies, however, Peter Pan leaves nothing in place of the children he takes, and while the original story of Peter and its continuation with the Darlings suggests that all of the lost children are really gone from their homes, I would like to offer another possibility. The Lost Boys, who happen into Peter's world, unlike the Darlings, who he intentionally seduced into Neverland, don't need to have fully disappeared—or fallen out of their prams, as Peter claims. They could just be sick and unavailable to the human world, and thus able to indulge fully in their imaginations. Illness could have provided one of the most frequent routes to Neverland, since while all children have maps of Neverland in their heads and devote mental energy to maintaining them, only sick children can live there. Neverland thus operates as a halfway point for sick children between the material world and wherever they go if they die. Mothers like Maisie's and Mrs. Darling, because of their obligation to love and protect their children, have more access to the fairyland and the Neverland than other adults and know the risk Peter and his kingdom pose to their families.

IN AND OUT OF NEVERLAND

Peter Pan and the world he commands operate as exemplifiers of imagination-driven knowledge systems, and the appeal he has for children comes partially from his familiarity: he already occupies a place in their minds. Wendy, among the Darling children, is the first to comment on Peter in a conversation with her mother about some strange leaves found underneath the nursery window. "She explained in quite a matter-of-fact way that she thought Peter sometimes came to the nursery in the night and sat on the foot of her bed and played on his pipes. Unfortunately, she never woke, so she never knew how she knew, she just knew" (Barrie, 76). Notably, it is not Wendy's story that pushes Mrs. Darling to believe that Peter is frequenting the nursery, but rather the physical evidence of the leaves on the carpet, which look nothing like leaves found anywhere in London and must, therefore, be explained. Despite Mrs. Darling's vague memories of Peter and his band, she cannot have faith in him; he defies belief, provides no evidence, proving beyond all doubt that, despite some characteristics that make her less adult than her husband, she has grown up and left Neverland forever.

Neverland is the place that all children share, and it exists in multiple dimensions. It operates first as a unique location for each child, inhabited by her favorite characters and their conflicts. It provides a place for them to live other than the material world, and it serves as the backdrop for their best adventures. It also operates as Peter's realm, where his presence determines the action. The landscape of Neverland and the characters who live there, including the Lost Boys, are playing out Peter's scripts and keeping him occupied as he spends eternity in this space.

> In his absence, things are usually quiet on the island. The fairies take an hour longer in the morning, the beasts attend to their young, the redskins feed heavily for six days and nights, and when pirates and lost boys meet they merely bite their thumbs at each other. But with the coming of Peter, who hates lethargy, they are all under way again: if you put your

ear to the ground now, you would hear the whole island seething with life. (Barrie, 112)

Only Peter stays in Neverland forever—he is an anomaly, permanently evading the most basic human necessities of growing up or dying.

The multiplicity of Neverlands is introduced before Peter appears in person when Barrie describes the maps of children's minds. This section of the text introduces the concept of mental landscapes, placing children's mental landscapes outside the ken of adult experts such as physicians. Physicians are especially singled out here as the people most accustomed to mapping and reading children's bodies. "I don't know whether you have ever seen a map of a person's mind. Doctors sometimes draw maps of other parts of you, and your own map can be intensely interesting, but catch them trying to draw a map of a child's mind, which is not only confused, but keeps going round all the time" (Barrie, 73). Physicians, who command so much power over children's bodies and whose knowledge can be both interesting and dangerous (resulting in nasty-tasting and fate-determining medicine), are singularly unqualified however to cope with the complexities of their pediatric patients' minds. This may explain why they are so inaccurate at predicting when a child will escape the disease that has sent her to Neverland or when she will die and slip through the circle of adults and stories that tie her to the earth. The fact-based knowledge systems used by adults are too linear to chart the multidimensional fabric of Neverland and they crumble in the face of the determinedly nonlinear and highly varied quality of children's thoughts.

The complicated thing about children's Neverlands is their variability and nonlinear motion; their basic geography is rather simple and inherently similar:

> There are zigzag lines on it, just like your temperature on a card, and there are probably roads in the island, for the Neverland is always more or less an island, with astonishing splashes of colour here and there, and coral reefs and rakish-looking craft in the offing, and savages and lonely lairs, and gnomes who are mostly tailors, and caves through which a river runs, and princes with six elder brothers, and a hut fast going to decay, and one very small old lady with a hooked nose. (Barrie, 73)

The island is a useful metaphor for children's minds, which exist well away from the more predictable geographies of the mainland. Like those minds, an island cannot be breached without alerting the natives, and any attempt would broadcast the prospect of invasion. Adults cannot trespass into children's minds without getting caught, but because of the shared geography of Neverland, children can cross into and impact each other's minds. More interesting is the fact that Neverlands are highly variable, changing according to children's understandings of what exactly makes an island and the fictional narratives that have influenced those understandings. Finally, islands represent the gap between the material world and its occurrences, which play such dominant roles in the minds of adults, and the imagined geography and adventures that occupy children. The ocean between the minds of children and adults is largely uncharted, and while some adults (like Mrs. Darling) retain a sense of having lost something in the process of growing up, they lose sight of the distance between their realities and those of their children. This is why the individual Neverlands are always available to children and hardly accessible to even the most diligent mothers, and why the meta-Neverland, the combination of all of those individual imaginings, cannot be found unless it invites you in, as it drew in the Darling children when they first left their nursery with Peter:

> So with occasional tiffs but on the whole rollicking, they drew near the Neverland; for after many moons they did reach it, and what is more, they had been going pretty straight all the time, not perhaps so much owing to the guidance of Peter or Tink as because the island was out looking for them. It is only thus that anyone may sight those magic shores. (Barrie, 105)

Children's fairy tales, fantasies, and adventure stories also determine the nature of each particular Neverland. The cast of characters peopling Neverlands represents the iconic figures of children's literature who, from gnomes to hags, join the children in adventures and manipulate their outcomes. It might be most useful to think of the Neverland at the time of a child's birth—before the stories, before contact with parents or nursery expectations or school—as the outlines of a landscape waiting to be filled in with the experiences, desires, narratives, and expectations that occupy children's minds. Each Neverland incorporates the characters and adventures that most entertain the child, but they vary, despite the relative similarities of children's literature in the early twentieth century, according to the stories that most interest each child and their own ideas about those stories: "Of course the Neverlands vary a good deal, John's for instance, had a lagoon with flamingoes flying over it at which John was shooting, while Michael, who was very small, had a flamingo with lagoons flying over it" (Barrie, 74). The characters and adventures of Neverland will change as children age and encounter new stories and interests, but their basic geography will remain the same.

As children leave their nurseries and their nannies for schools, playgrounds, and each other's company, their Neverlands evolve to incorporate the things they learn under the tutelage of adults and in their explorations of the material world. "It would be an easy map if that were all; but there is also first day of school, religion, fathers, the round pond, needlework, murders, hangings, verbs that take the dative, chocolate-pudding day, getting into braces, say ninety-nine, three pence for pulling out your tooth yourself, and so on" (Barrie, 73–74). School, parents, and the surrounding culture begin to make their marks on the Neverlands as they increasingly intrude upon children's lives, and children cope with these intrusions in different ways. Most children allow the two worlds to coexist, incorporating bits of the real world into Neverland or creating another map for them: "either these are part of the island or they are another map showing through, and it is all rather confusing, especially as nothing will stand still" (Barrie, 74). Children who remain faithful to the imagination will keep their Neverlands as pure as possible, shunting "real world" information to another map, while less dreamy children, or those with more interest in what they encounter in the nursery or at school, will allow the real world to contaminate the imagined landscapes of their Neverlands. Children consigned by illness to their beds will of necessity keep their Neverlands pristine of material interference, and they will elaborate them into landscapes for the adventures they cannot play out in real life. All children who survive are fated to lose their places on their islands; the process of growing up separates them from the imagined landscapes and ties them more tightly to the material world. The narrator laments the loss of the Neverland as among the more painful experiences of growing up, and he points out that adults' lack of access to it is made more painful by the realization that it still exists but has no place for them, "We too have been there; we can still hear the sound of the surf, though we shall land no more" (Barrie, 74).

As children become more engaged by facts they need to remember and are increasingly integrated into the material world, they spend more intellectual time in their "real world" maps and less time in their Neverlands. They allow the real world to eclipse the earlier fantasy constructs, overwhelming the imagined with the empirical. The world of the imagination strikes back, though—Peter kills or banishes the imagined self that has played on the magical island, and the child is afterwards consigned to remain in the material world. We call this growing up, and "all children, except one," are fated to do it (Barrie, 69). But the process is time consuming, and Neverland remains an active part of children's minds for a long time. It is most real in the minutes children spend awake in the dark, waiting to fall asleep. That is when Peter can reintegrate the individual Neverlands with the darker whole and break through from the realm of the imagined to the realm of the material.

Neverland and Peter Pan are inextricably intertwined. His refusal to grow up keeps him a permanent resident of Neverland—he will never return to the world of parental expectations and responsibilities, but nor can he slip the bonds that tie him to that world: "Wendy, I ran away the day I was born. It was because I heard father and mother talking about what I was to be when I became a man. I don't want ever to be a man. I want always to be a little boy and to have fun. So I ran away to Kensington Gardens and lived a long long time among the fairies" (Barrie, 93). This story is compelling, and like most of Peter's early stories, it is entirely made up in response to an inappropriate intrusion of the real world into Neverland and the riddle of his existence. He invented it when Wendy asked him something that all children know about themselves and that constitutes an integral part of childhood relations and conversations: his age (Barrie, 92). Knowing your age requires both chronological continuity and predictable markers, the very things that are missing from Neverland. Instead of knowing, Peter relies on imagination and invests it with the same level of belief that adults invest in the things that they "know" and that children invest in both knowledge and imagination. By consistently allowing the world he escaped to shape his behaviors and expectations for others, however, Peter remains trapped by it. Despite his integral role in Neverland, he always comes back to the real world, looking for stories to bring back to the Lost Boys so they can learn what the world will expect of them should they return to it, and searching, always, for his next mother. Other children, however, find that Neverland, and imagination, are not as pleasant as they seemed in the real world. Once you live there and engage in battles and high-risk adventures, you quickly find that you can also die there. Death is, in fact, a regular occurrence in Neverland, where pirates, redskins, and lost boys often meet that fate. The Darling children learn that the island does not play games with mortality before they even set foot on it—Hook sees them returning with Pan and begins to shoot cannonballs at them, "Thus sharply did the terrified three learn the difference between an island of make-believe and the same island come true" (Barrie, 110). The children's imaginations brought them to the island, but when they left their nursery they had no expectation of the dangers that awaited them there. Even though their daydreamed adventures were full of violence, as indicated by the ongoing battle on the island among the pirates, the redskins, and the Lost Boys, their imaginations had no place for their own deaths. That, perhaps, comes with growing up, and so the children face death for the first time, not in safety of their minds, but in the action-packed and highly dangerous atmosphere of Neverland.

While children are expected, in fact forced, to leave Neverland as they grow up, they are also expected to value it and its inhabitants as real. Very few older children and even fewer adults are capable of doing this, and Peter reminds them of the price Neverland pays when they become too grounded in empirical knowledge and the material world. Peter explains this threat to Wendy when he describes the fatal effect on fairies of people's announcements of their disbelief. Abdicating faith has painfully real consequences for those in Neverland, while at the same time, a willingness to believe has equally real, and vivifying, effects on the inhabitants of this imaginary landscape. Neverland would become a blank landscape again if all children were to disappear from the world, or if children were born with minds that preferred evidence to imagination. The conflict between imagination and knowledge, however, does not just take place in Peter's kingdom. A privileging of rich imaginations poses a threat to those who, in the name of growing up, replace their investment in the imagined with dependence on empirical knowledge.

Growing Up Is Hard to Do

Mr. Darling paid that price, and his life is defined by what he thinks he knows and the expectations other people have for him because he is an adult, educated man. Mr. Darling wants to earn the respect of his family, but they seem remarkably unimpressed by his command of stocks and bonds. Moreover, he raises the stakes against himself, especially in his attempt to make Michael take his medicine without complaint, which he affiliates with both masculinity and adulthood: "Strong man though he was, there is no doubt that he had behaved rather foolishly over the medicine. If he had a weakness, it was for thinking that all his life he had taken medicine boldly; and so now, when Michael dodged the spoon in Nana's mouth, he had said reprovingly, 'Be a man, Michael'" (Barrie, 82). It is that very masculinity that Mr. Darling worries that he lacks. While he has a highly desirable wife and a good job that provides for his family, he wonders whether the neighbors scoff because he has a dog for his children's nurse, and he frets that this very dog does not respect him: "No nursery could have been conducted more correctly, and Mr. Darling knew it, yet he sometimes wondered uneasily whether the neighbors talked. He had his position in the City to consider. Nana also troubled him in another way. He had sometimes a feeling that she did not admire him" (Barrie, 72).

The problem with Nana and his children, and even, to a lesser extent, his wife, is that none of them valued the knowledge and skills that made Mr. Darling a desirable commodity as a banker. Nana remains rooted in timeless traditions of child-rearing that respect intrinsic knowledge and have no respect for innovations derived from medical research nor admiration for the men who conduct it: "She had a genius for knowing when a cough is a thing to have no patience with, and when it needs a stocking round your throat. She believed to her last day in old-fashioned remedies like rhubarb leaf, and made sounds of contempt over all this new-fangled talk about germs, and so on" (Barrie, 72). Mr. Darling, who fears that his education and authority might, in fact, not be the only answers to life's persistent questions, greatly fears Nana's dedication to her own approach to the world, especially since it so clearly rejects his own. His children pose the same problem for him, since they value above all else bravery and fortitude, neither one of which is immediately evident in his daily life. Worse still, when given the chance to display both characteristics by taking his medicine without complaint, he utterly fails. After tricking Michael into taking the medicine and refusing to take his own, Mr. Darling is faced with his disappointed children, "It was dreadful the way all three were looking at him, just as if they did not admire him" (Barrie, 84).

Even Mrs. Darling causes him to fret, since she fails to react to the crises in his life the way he would like her to do. When he cannot tie his tie, for example, he produces an operatic string of consequences that will stem from the wardrobe failure simply because, "he thought that Mrs. Darling was not sufficiently impressed" (Barrie, 81). And then there is the matter of the kiss at the corner of her mouth that he simply cannot get, though he knows that is there and tries until the disappointment causes him to give up (Barrie, 69). It is no surprise, perhaps, that Mr. Darling, after losing his children because he banished Nana to the nursery, retreats to the dog kennel, a drastic departure from the world of acquired knowledge and evidence. This retreat represents a return for the character to the world of the imagined, rather than simply an expression of regret and shame. By choosing the kennel, he is abandoning his role as a man, a role that he cannot inhabit as long as his children are missing, in itself a consequence of his own failure of self-confidence.

Mrs. Darling, on the other hand, manages to inhabit the real world while keeping part of her mind so deeply in the imaginary that her husband never knows that it is missing, and a part of her body so removed from the world that neither her children nor her husband can get the kiss at the corner of her mouth.

She was a lovely lady, with a romantic mind and such a sweet, mocking mouth. Her romantic mind was like the tiny boxes, one within the other, that come from the puzzling East, however many you discover, there is always one more; and her sweet mocking mouth had one kiss on it that

Wendy could never get, though there it was, perfectly conspicuous in the right-hand corner. (Barrie, 69)

Mrs. Darling's missing pieces belong, not to the real world, but to the imagined one that she inhabits while performing as a wife to her husband and mother to her children. Ironically, that imagination, at least at the beginning of the story, is entirely dominated by the storylines of weddings and maternity. She begins the story as the most desirable girl of her generation, and she enters into her marriage with remarkable enthusiasm for her new job of managing the household: "Mrs. Darling was married in white, and at first she kept the books perfectly, almost gleefully, as if it were a game, not so much as a Brussels sprout was missing; but by and by whole cauliflowers dropped out, and instead of them there were pictures of babies without faces. She drew them when she should have been totting up" (Barrie, 70). The future she imagines for herself is entirely defined by the role of motherhood, and instead of spending her afternoons in Neverland, she spends them imagining the children she wants to have. This version of imagination is shaped by cultural expectations for women of her social class and thus is different from the Neverlands crafted by children. It is significant that all of the female characters in *Peter Pan,* from the nameless fairies in Kensington Gardens to Tinker Bell to Mrs. Darling and her daughter and granddaughter, share the desire to become wives and mothers. In the case of the human females, that desire is so all-encompassing that their experiences in Neverland are entirely defined by it.

It is Mrs. Darling, the adult most sympathetic to imagination and Peter Pan, who discovers that he is intruding upon the minds of her children. She does so in the course of her motherly duties, sorting through the thoughts in her sleeping children's minds: "Occasionally in her travels through her children's minds Mrs. Darling found things she could not understand, and of these quite the most perplexing was the word Peter" (Barrie, 74). After this discovery, she recalls that she does know the name and the boy, though she finds it hard to believe the half-remembered stories she digs up from her memory: "She had believed in him at the time, but now that she was married and full of sense she quite doubted whether there was any such person" (Barrie, 75). It will require the evidence of the skeleton leaves on the nursery floor to make her question whether Peter might indeed be real, since no dream can leave dirty footprints on a carpet.

It is not the evidence alone that brings him back to the front of her mind, but a dream she has one night in the nursery, followed by his sudden appearance right in front of her. Peter leaves his mark on mothers, but he especially affects those who have lost children or who cannot have any at all. The grief he leaves behind ties them inextricably to Neverland, though the tie is not sufficiently tight to allow them to join their children, touch them, or hear anything but the echoes of their voices. That grief is familiar to all of Barrie's mothers. They recognize in each other the countless small wounds inflicted by living children in their struggles to escape the proscribed routines of childhood, and in a few the stark despair of a lost child. Mrs. Darling is no different: "He did not alarm her, for she thought she had seen him in the faces of many women who have lost children. Perhaps he is to be found in the faces of some mothers also" (Barrie, 77). He never left Mrs. Darling's face, even after her children returned, remaining stubbornly in the corner of her mouth as the kiss; "If you or I or Wendy had been there, we should have seen that he was very like Mrs. Darling's kiss" (Barrie, 77). Peter did not, however, recognize himself in her, seeing her instead as the worst thing he could find in a nursery—an adult. And while she should have realized, since she still had her memories of Peter absconding with lost children, that he posed a significant threat to her children, she put off mentioning him to Mr. Darling because of the more immediate concern of keeping him happy, and instead locks Peter's severed shadow in the nursery wardrobe rather than leaving it hanging out the window because "it looked so like the washing and lowered the whole tone of the house" (Barrie, 78). This represents a significant failure of her imagination at a time when a little trust in the unbelievable would have stood her in good stead, but even the most imaginative mother is intrinsically limited because she is an adult, is defined by her role as a woman, a wife, a mother, and can never return to Neverland, even while her children are playing there and Peter Pan is standing on the nursery windowsill.

CONCLUSION

From the god Pan to fairy tradition in Britain and the epistemological divide between imagination and knowledge, Barrie's Peter Pan stories produce a complex landscape in which children play. Peter himself is a composite of bodies and characteristics borrowed from Pan, birds, fairies, and children that cannot fit into a single world but fits perfectly into neither the world of the living or the dead, the material or the natural, the real or the imagined, the human or the nonhuman (preternatural or animal). Because he cannot fit into existing categories, he straddles the worlds from which those categories derive their meanings, pressing hardest on the divide between the real and the imagined to create a space that can intrude into both places, the Neverland. The Neverland is literally Peter's creation, responding to his presence and representing his desires and imagined adventures, most of which center around a rejection of adult roles and responsibilities in the real world, but it does not belong only to him. All children are born with Neverlands of their own that are connected to the one Peter inhabits, and they spend a great deal of their time in their Neverlands until the real world intrudes, takes them away, and makes it impossible for them to return. Peter's consistent association with sick children suggests that illness, because of its high frequency in childhood and the long periods of rest and isolation with which it is correlated, is one of the most frequent causes of children spending more time than usual in Neverland. Children who are sick and then recovering for a long period of time will have less real-world intrusion into their Neverlands, and children who are very sick, especially with high fevers, may see the divide between the real and the imagined disappear and enter Neverland as their dominant world. Sickness is not the only route to Neverland, as evidenced by the entrance of the hale and hearty Darlings, but it is a compelling explanation for the ever-changing population of the Lost Boys and the fact that the crew of six that Wendy brings back with her can return to the real world simply because they wish to do so, a wish that reflects a return to health and renewed attention to the demands of growing up. Only Peter is left behind—trapped by his divided nature and his conflicting desires, but most of all by the children who need him and all of us who believe in him.

Notes

1. Bryan Holme, comp., *Bullfinch's Mythology* (New York: Viking Penguin Press, 1979), 206.
2. Ibid., 60.
3. Ibid., 74.
4. James M. Barrie, *Peter Pan in Kensington Gardens* (Oxford: Oxford University Press, 1991), 16. Subsequent references to this work appear parenthetically in the text.
5. There is an extremely revealing exchange between Peter and Wendy on exactly this subject in which he rejects the potential for females to be anything but his mother, saying, "'You are so queer,' he said looking frankly puzzled, 'and Tiger Lily is just the same. There is something that she wants to be to me, but she says it is not my mother. . . . Perhaps Tinker Bell will tell me. . . . Perhaps Tink wants to be my mother?'" Barrie, *Peter and Wendy*, 162.
6. Adam Fox, *Oral and Literate Culture in England, 1500–1700* (Oxford: Oxford University Press, 2000).
7. Robert Darnton, *The Great Cat Massacre and Other Episodes in French Cultural History* (New York: Penguin, 1985); Jack Zipes, *Breaking the Magic Spell: Radical Theories of Folk and Fairy Tales* (Austin: University of Texas Press, 1979).
8. Keith Thomas, *Religion and the Decline of Magic: Studies in Popular Beliefs in Sixteenth and Seventeenth Century England* (New York: Oxford University Press, 1993).
9. Charles Dickens, *The Cricket on the Hearth: A Fairy Tale of Home* (New York: Classic Books, 2000); Oscar Wilde, *The Happy Prince and Other Fairy Tales* (New York: Dover Juvenile Classics, 2001).

10. Marjorie Swann, "The Politics of Fairylore in Early Modern English Literature," *Renaissance Quarterly* 53(2) (2000): 449–473.

11. Katharine Briggs, *The Fairies in Tradition and Literature* (London: Routledge, 1967). Carole G. Silver, *Strange and Secret Peoples: Fairies and Victorian Consciousness* (Oxford: Oxford University Press, 1998).

12. Briggs, *The Fairies in Tradition and Literature*, 3–13; Jack Zipes, *Victorian Fairy Tales: The Revolt of the Fairies and Elves* (New York: Methuen, 1987).

13. Andrea Woodner made this excellent observation.

14. For a quick example, see Charlotte Brontë's *Jane Eyre*, in which Rochester, upon finding out that Jane has no parents, explains his fall on the ice that caused her to come to his aid by saying that she must have been, "waiting for her people" and asking, "Did I break one of your rings, that you spread the damned ice on the causeway?" Charlotte Brontë, *Jane Eyre* (New York: Penguin Classics, 2003), ch. 13.

15. Briggs, *The Fairies in Tradition and Literature*, 136–141.

16. Silver, *Strange and Secret Peoples*, 75–77.

17. Briggs, *The Fairies in Tradition and Literature*, 18.

CHAPTER 4

"Shadow of [a] girl"

AN EXAMINATION OF *PETER PAN* IN PERFORMANCE

Patrick B. Tuite

SINCE *PETER PAN* OPENED, the play has enjoyed a long and prosperous life, and as Anthony Lane notes, "it gives freakishly little sign of growing old."[1] However, the longevity and apparent stability of J. M. Barrie's narrative, especially in its musical form, masks how different productions have altered the style and content of the original script. Barrie revised the play on more than one occasion, adding scenes to meet the technical demands of the early productions and modifying dialogue with the input of important cast members. In addition to the changes that the author made, other artists have adapted the play's plot, characters, and dialogue for subsequent productions, over a period that now span more than a century. Most importantly, the ways in which different artists have enacted *Peter Pan* and its characters have evolved substantially over that period. The play's production history from 1904 to 1933 reflected an intimate collaboration between Barrie and the women who first embodied his main character in England and America. These theater artists contributed to the development of Barrie's original play, transforming both its form and meaning in the process of making its characters come alive for different audience members in diverse locations.

With the popularity of the musical and the ubiquity of the animated film, it is difficult for contemporary audiences to overcome these dominant and conventional iterations of Barrie's play and recapture the wonder and danger that its early theatrical productions inspired. Other authors have described the dynamic Peter that Mary Martin created for the 1954 musical, a performance still available in the 1960 video.[2] The sophistication and complexity of the play's early productions detail how specific actresses made

Barrie's character more than simply a boy played by a woman. The cryptic phrase, "Shadow of girl," appears in the notes Barrie created while working on a draft of his play in 1903.[3] It provides an early description of Wendy, but it calls to mind the women who helped create Peter's complicated identity. Barrie capitalized on the popularity of these actresses, appropriating their beauty, fame, talent, and tastes to develop and market his work. Barrie's phrase expands the complicated notion of authorship to include more than just the playwright.

The play's early production history highlights the contributions that powerful and pioneering actresses made toward its development. How did specific actresses interact with Barrie and other theater artists to craft the elfin boy? What did these women hope to achieve when they played Peter Pan between 1904 and 1932? Were they trapped in a representation of their own creation, locked into the confines of a commercial enterprise, or did their desires, abilities, and agency give them the power to move beyond the intentions of the playwright and the expectations of their audience to redefine Barrie's character?

OF ACTRESSES, AGENCY, AND SHADOW PUPPETS

Barrie enjoyed working with a variety of theater artists to develop his plays. This was especially true for the early productions of *Peter Pan*. He did not finalize the script until after the 1904 production had opened in London. He even inserted an additional scene for the 1905 revival and made changes to accommodate the needs of specific actors and actresses while he controlled the rights to the play. With this interactive approach to developing the production's script, talented and imaginative actresses created different Peters and Neverlands according to their readings of Barrie's work. Therefore, it is important to understand the play not as poetry or a well-constructed narrative, but as a blueprint for performance. In this regard, the success of a given theatrical production depends in large part upon the collaboration of theater artists and the willingness of audience members to accept their work as engaging and meaningful. The process that has dominated theatrical production since the end of the nineteenth century often begins with an individual playwright composing a play, but that material is not realized as a theatrical event until it is performed by various artists before an audience. According to Steven Orgel, through much of theater history "the playwright has only a very small role in the creation of the theatrical event." The theater artists that constitute a production's creative team and the audience members who attend a given performance determine whether or not a production is successful or not, and the members of these groups deserve recognition for their share in the creative process.[4]

During Barrie's lifetime, a small group of actresses that he approved were responsible for recreating Peter in new productions. The different productions of Barrie's play bring into sharp relief the changing outline of Peter's shadow when different actresses embodied the elfin boy for various audiences. Examining productions of the same play in different cultures and historical periods inevitably brings a "fresh perspective on inherited expression."[5] Shifting contexts makes the production and reception of meaning between two individuals complicated, and it is much more difficult to trace the development of language and its means of communication among larger groups. To understand the constructed nature of a theatrical performance in a given place and time, one must first understand that those artists responsible for the production of the play's meanings do not have an equal share in the construction of its representations, but by varying degrees each person involved in a given performance participates in the social interactions that constitute that event.[6] Orgel argues that when one studies the theatrical event as the sum of these interactions, what the audience sees is more important than what the playwright wrote. This shift in focus assigns to directors, designers, actors, actresses, and audience members greater responsibility for the success of a theatrical production.[7]

To illustrate my point, let me begin with a recent adaptation of *Peter Pan* that included, among other powerful images, shadow puppets. In 1996, Mabou Mines, an avant-garde theater company based in New York, used Barrie's *Peter and Wendy* to create an original theatrical production featuring one narrator, live musicians, puppets, and their puppeteers. I was fortunate enough to attend one of the last performances of the play in which Karen Kandel played the narrator.[8] Kandel developed the role in collaboration with Liza Lorwin, Julie Archer, Lee Breuer, and Johnny Cunningham when they first conceived of the play.[9] The narrator supplies the voices for all of the play's characters, giving each a distinct quality, while also maintaining a separate persona as the play's storyteller. These responsibilities are physically taxing and artistically demanding. The narrator manipulates her voice and body to create sounds and images that help the puppeteers animate the characters, making them responsive to one another and the audience. The production's choreography combines the narrator's movements with those of the puppeteers, weaving their actions and gestures into a seamless whole. For the 2007 production at Arena Stage in Washington, D.C., the set provided an appropriately simple backdrop for the striking visuals that the narrator and puppeteers crafted, and the production's music and lighting made the world of the play appear beautiful and charming while also communicating a sadness and longing that other theatrical productions of the Peter Pan story often lack.

Mabou Mines's *Peter and Wendy* exemplifies the complex nature of theatrical production. The company's members foster a shared collaborative process and create "new work either from original texts or through the adaptation of existing (often classic) texts staged from a reimagined point of view."[10] This alternative perspective is apparent in *Peter and Wendy*; among other possible readings of Barrie's play and its novelized 1911 publication, the Arena Stage production offered a postcolonial interpretation in which the narrator appropriates the function of the author and conjures living characters from simple objects using her vivid imagination and physical virtuosity. The narrator's vocalizations and movements combine with the production's design elements including Celtic music and bunraku and wayang kulit puppets, traditions that originated in Japan and Java, to manifest the shadows that haunt Barrie's 1911 publication. When I saw *Peter and Wendy* at Arena Stage I had already begun this essay, and I was anxious to examine how the production's design, score, and acting style reshaped the iconic images established by past iterations of Barrie's play. This analytical approach both enhanced my experience and limited my enjoyment of the performance at Arena.

I brought my youngest son, Colm, to the performance. He watched it intently, asked questions, and wanted to talk about it afterward.[11] We attended the same show, but we had very different experiences. While I analyzed the performance text and attempted to map the various voices, gestures, and sounds to identify what specific elements constituted the production's hybridity and contributed to its postcolonial pastiche, Colm concentrated on the events of the play as they unfolded before him. He did not have to understand the significance of every detail found in the performance's rich semiotics in order to enjoy the show and recognize its themes. I was surprised to find that while I looked for representations of empire in decline, my son saw haunting images of death. I noted how the production's white sets and the white costumes of the puppeteers contrasted with the color of the narrator, an African American actress. The white Edwardian costumes included veils that covered the faces of the puppeteers, and my son thought that they were ghosts. He also feared that the puppet for Hook was a skeleton. The performance text, the stage picture that the director, designers, and actors created in the performance, inspired these readings, and reviewers have praised the adaptation for being able to capture "the humor and adventure [of Barrie's play] without skirting the more adult themes of the pain of abandonment, the hovering shadow of aging and death."[12]

Colm interpreted the performance's images in a more immediate and phenomenological manner, seeing its objects and actions and listening to its sounds without having to compare them to other representations from the long tradition of *Peter Pan* in performance. By doing so, he understood the performance as the source of a new narrative, and his enthusiasm for its form helped me to see the silent ghosts that stand behind and haunt many of Barrie's characters. Writing about the performance at Arena Stage with Colm's perspective in mind made the experience much more engaging and relevant. This is the way in which I want to approach the earliest productions of *Peter Pan*. I recognize the impossibility of bringing to life what were ephemeral representations that relied in part upon their cultural, political, and historical circumstances to communicate meaning. In order to make those meanings more relevant, I do not analyze past productions of *Peter Pan* based on the author's intentions or try to ascertain the play's significance at the time of its first performances. Instead, I want to capture the excitement that productions of *Peter Pan* generated between 1904 and 1933 by identifying the women who helped to popularize Barrie's play during that period and by examining their contributions to the character's identity in the hope of restoring to past performances the wonder, awe, confusion, and delight that they inspired in their original audiences.

NINA BOUCICAULT, PAULINE CHASE, AND ENGLISH BOYISHNESS

Nina Boucicault, the first actress to play Peter Pan, was not Barrie's first choice for the part. He wanted a young boy to play the role. However, labor laws prevented anyone under fourteen from appearing on stage, and Barrie's producer, Charles Frohman, wanted one of his leading actresses to play Peter.[13] Frohman was an important figure in England as well as America. He was the first American theater manager to establish an office in London and lease a playhouse in the heart of its theater district.[14] When Barrie visited his theater in New York, they quickly became friends and established a powerful transatlantic partnership that linked professional theater artists in London and New York from the end of the nineteenth century to the beginning of World War I.[15] Barrie asked Frohman to read *Peter Pan* in 1904, and the producer fell in love with the play. He was eager to stage it in New York in order to showcase his leading actress, Maude Adams. However, Frohman was a shrewd businessman, and he wanted to test the reception of Barrie's play in England before he brought the production to America. Barrie agreed with Frohman's plan, but he had originally hoped that Adams would play the part of Wendy in London. Commercial interests prevented Adams from appearing in the London production—Frohman decided that she would remain in New York in order to continue playing in a revival of Barrie's *The Little Minister*.

Without Maude Adams, Frohman and Barrie had to find an actress capable of playing the most important part in what initially appeared to be a risky venture. At this time, Dion Boucicault, Jr. was the manager of Frohman's theater in London.[16] When the manager learned that Adams would not play the lead role in the London premier of *Peter Pan*, he suggested that Frohman and Barrie cast his sister in the part. This was not a simple case of nepotism. Dion served as the resident director for Frohman's London theater. His sister, Nina, was an accomplished actress in her own right, and Barrie knew her work well. She had appeared as the lead character in the London productions of two of his plays. She played Susan Throssel in the 1902 production of *Quality Street* at the Vaudeville Theatre and Moira Loney in the 1903 production of *Little Mary* at Wyndham's Theatre. Though *Little Mary* was not a hit, Nina proved her versatility by playing the same character in two stages of life, as a child and an adult.[17] To support Boucicault, Barrie turned to other actresses who had appeared in productions of his plays. Hilda Trevelyan, one of Barrie's character actresses, played Wendy, and Dorothea Baird, another actress who had worked with Barrie, got the part of Mrs. Darling.[18]

The 1904 production at the Duke of York's had a six-week rehearsal period.[19] Dion ran the rehearsals in an authoritarian manner, picking on young members of the cast and making even seasoned professionals afraid of his tirades.[20] Though the director was her brother, Nina struggled to build her character. Barrie often attended rehearsals, and, in a moment of anxiety, she asked him to define Peter Pan. "How much is he human and how much fairy?" Barrie did not offer much guidance. He told Nina that Peter "was a bird a day old"; yet he wanted the cast to move and speak as if each character existed in ordinary life.[21] Despite these difficult rehearsal conditions, the cast helped to clarify the play's action and develop their characters. For example, instead of doubling Dorothea Baird as Mrs. Darling and Hook, which Barrie had originally established in an early version of the play that he entitled, "The Boy Who Hates Mothers," Gerald du Maurier asked to play the pirate. Du Maurier was already cast as Mr. Darling, and his doubling as the father and pirate has had an important impact on contemporary readings of the play. Like Nina Boucicault and Hilda Trevelyan, Du Maurier had worked with Barrie before he appeared in *Peter Pan*, appearing in productions of *The Admirable Crighton* and *Little Mary*.[22] He was also the uncle of the Llewelyn Davies boys, the children who had inspired much of Barrie's narrative.[23] Du Maurier's Hook was not a burlesque of storybook pirates or a dashing swashbuckler. On the contrary, Du Maurier's pirate was a tragic and sinister royalist living in painful exile.

Though she was not Barrie's first choice, casting Nina Boucicault to play Peter for the London production turned out to be a fortunate decision.

4.1 Nina Boucicault as Peter Pan in the 1904 London production. Credit: Photograph of Nina Boucicault used with kind permission of Great Ormond Street Hospital for Children, London.

A review of the opening night declared that the production was lucky in its casting and praised Nina for her performance, stating that, "Miss Nina Boucicault, as Peter Pan, knows well how to blend pathos with frolicsomeness."[24] It appears that Dion had been correct when he claimed that no man could play the adolescent boy with authority.[25] Nina played the role with the energy and spirit of a boy, while reaching beyond a conventionalized and sentimental depiction of British boyishness. Frohman believed that she played Peter with "wistfulness and charm."[26] *The Times* found that Nina portrayed the elfin boy as a modern version of Shakespeare's feisty spirits. She was, "a prose Puck, a twentieth century Ariel, who has come to the nursery to recover his shadow."[27] Contemporary accounts also indicate that her character was more than a playful little boy. One audience member who saw Boucicault in the original London production described her performance as unearthly but real. Her Peter Pan "obtruded neither sex nor sexlessness," and captured the tragic elements of Barrie's character.[28] Many critics later claimed she was one of the few actresses capable of displaying the darkness found in Barrie's play. No other actress who played Peter Pan in England during Barrie's lifetime matched the complexity of Boucicault's characterization; she found Peter's shadow and made it her own.

The Peter that first appeared at the Duke of York's Theatre in 1904 was no "chirping Disney figure wrenched from the unsettling landscapes where he originally appeared."[29] Boucicault created a mythical character, an avenger who loved a good fight but remained aloof and sad at the end of the performance.[30] There are many reasons why Boucicault had the license to craft Peter in her own fashion, including that she knew Barrie and was the sister of the production's director. But it was her own radical alterity, both as an Irish actress on an English stage and a woman playing a boy, that allowed her to develop her darker, ultimately divided Pan.

Her father's Irish ancestry and celebrated career may have contributed to the strength of her performance.[31] Dion Boucicault was born in Dublin to a French Huguenot father and an Irish mother. He was a wealthy theater manager and actor, but he did not shirk from inserting social commentary into his plays. Critics associated Nina Boucicault's work with her father's many productions. When Barrie added the scene in which Peter fights Hook at the "Marooner's Rock" to the 1905 production in London, the *New York Times* compared its setting to Dion Boucicault's *Colleen Bawn*, a play set in rural Ireland.[32] The younger Boucicault had left Barrie's play before 1905, but critics still found parallels between the revival and the imagery found in Dion Boucicault's earlier productions. The most popular of these productions attacked slavery in America and the harsh conditions of poor subjects living in England and Ireland.[33]

Some of Barrie's plays share similar concerns about industrialization and alienation, and Nina Boucicault's interpretation of Peter appears to have highlighted these concerns. Barrie's later plays, especially *Mary Rose* and *A Well Remembered Voice*, elaborate on themes of innocence and loss that also appear in *Peter Pan*. All three plays reveal the tensions between the center of the empire, with its urban and industrialized setting, and more remote and pristine locations along its periphery, in which local customs and the spirituality that they maintain resist the center's dominant ideology. Boucicault embodied these tensions in her performance of Peter. Hook, a character who was educated in the center of the empire and then drifted to its periphery, cannot identify Peter as a legitimate subject. Troubled by Peter's ability to fight him, he asks, "Pan who and what art thou?" a question that gets more complicated when you realize there is a woman inside the boy's costume.

Boucicault was a woman playing a boy. She was an English actress of Irish ancestry cast as a defiant trickster. In addition to her father's ancestry and his penchant for political drama, Boucicault's character was clad in green, living on a green island populated by savages and pirates. Though the savages are "Redskins," they have many of the characteristics that early modern historians used to identify the native Irish. This makes the fight between Peter and Hook more than a battle between a little boy and an evil pirate. Peter defends a native population living along the edges of the empire against a character that represents the worst qualities of the English aristocracy. In addition, he defends the young and innocent who cannot defend themselves against the forces of imperial progress and takes them from its industrial center. Barrie voiced similar concerns in other plays. He was a Scot who was concerned with preserving the dialect and customs of his country, and he may have encouraged Boucicault to play Peter as a wild spirit who defends the island's natives against imperialist forces.

Critics and audiences recognized her Irish ancestry and were aware of the social commentary in her father's plays, especially those set in Ireland. By concentrating on Peter's pathos and her association with her father's earlier plays, audience members and critics could read her character as a rebellious figure living on the edges of the empire. Boucicault brought this character to life on the London stage. She also celebrated Peter's marginality in the center of the British Empire when she mimed the defeat of Hook. In 1904, these actions may have suggested to the audience the creation of a new British family, one that recognized the presence of its hybrid subjects even if it did not fully incorporate them into its social structure.[34]

Boucicault's physical presence also troubled the codes of manliness and discipline that dominated Edwardian England. According to Anne Wilson, Barrie's play voices the anxieties of the middle class in England at the turn of the century. Mr. Darling exemplifies these anxieties. Though he is the head of his household, he is not capable of leading it in an effective manner. It is Peter, not Mr. Darling, who can take action and help the children. Casting a woman as Peter in the 1904 production had the potential to challenge the notions concerning class and gender that helped to structure Edwardian society, but the play actually reinforces these distinctions. For instance, while Peter defeats the father figure, he cannot replace him. Barrie's play thus attempts to suppress or at the very least contain the changes that Peter symbolizes. As Wilson states, "*Peter Pan* offers a nostalgic view of the middle class, offering roles for men and women that were no longer available in an unstable society in order to manage the anxiety that comes with such rapid change."[35] In the play, Peter attacks the old order, but he does so without asserting his sexuality, and this may have been partly responsible for the audience's reaction to Boucicault's performance. Her Peter remained a lonely character who does not fit within the Darling family when they return to London.

Unfortunately, Boucicault could not take the physical and emotional strain that came with playing Peter for an extended run. May Martin, who had played Tootles and served as Boucicault's understudy, assumed the role shortly before the first run ended on April 1, 1905.[36] When reviewing subsequent revivals of the play at the Duke of York's Theatre, London's critics regretted Boucicault's absence and suggested "for her own sake and ours" that she go back to *Peter Pan* as soon as possible.[37] Cecilia Loftus and Pauline Chase followed Boucicault as Peter Pan, but neither actress was able to recreate the pathos that Nina had displayed in the original production, which was, as we have seen, a product of Boucicault's unique familial and societal origins.[38]

Of Boucicault's successors, Chase played the part the longest and offered the most interesting interpretation. Like Maude Adams, Chase was an American actress that Frohman had trained with his stock company. He brought her to London after she gained his attention as the Pink Pajama Girl in the Madison Square Theater's production of *The Liberty Belles*. Once Chase came to London, she played one of the twins in the 1904 production of *Peter Pan*. During the following year she was cast as Peter's understudy in a touring production. When the lead actress became ill, Chase was scheduled to play Peter in Liverpool. Frohman and Barrie attended the performance and later cast her as Peter for the 1906 revival in London.[39] As a result, a young and athletic American played Peter in London from 1906 to 1913.[40]

Pauline Chase, J. M. Barrie, and Charles Frohman became close friends, and Chase chose Barrie and Ellen Terry to be her godparents when she was confirmed. Her close relationships with Barrie and Frohman as well as her physical abilities gave Chase the freedom to make Peter a more feminine character. She wore pajamas in the underground scene and repeated the pajama dance that had made her a sensation in New York.[41] London reviewers were not initially receptive to Chase's interpretation, and the *Times* compared her playful Peter Pan to Nina Boucicault's defiant character: "Let us say at once that Miss Pauline Chase has not a tithe of the dramatic ability, nor of the boyishness, in a sense, which her first predecessor, at any rate, showed. Of common ordinary British boyishness she has none whatever. Spirit she has in plenty; but she shows no love of a good fight."[42] Londoners appear to have ignored this poor review and embraced the American dancer. The *New York Times* reported that audiences at the Duke of York's "bubbled over with enthusiasm" when they attended the latest production of Barrie's play, and in the following year a London critic wondered at the cultlike appeal of *Peter Pan*.[43] Frohman was so pleased with Chase's consistent performances that he brought the production to Paris in 1908 and 1909 at her request.[44]

Despite the adulation of London's fans and Frohman's satisfaction with her interpretation, other theater artists and critics believed that Chase had exploited her youthful looks and strong legs to make Peter an amusing fairy and never attempted to play him as a defiant boy.[45] As an American actress in London performing in the most popular play of its time, Pauline Chase also had the opportunity to capitalize on her colonial identity, much as the Irish Boucicault had, to reinforce her character's rebelliousness, but she preferred to display her dancing skills and portray Peter as a spirited girl.[46]

This is not an entirely objective or fair assessment of Pauline Chase's performance as Peter Pan. Chase did not have the same authority that Nina Boucicault enjoyed and had to deal with the play's strong performance traditions. After the initial run of *Peter Pan* at the Duke of York's in 1904, all other English productions mounted before Barrie's death were not original interpretations but revivals. Aside from the work of a small number of performers, these productions did little to reshape Barrie's characters established in that initial run. However, there were a few notable exceptions. Noel Coward played Tootles with Pauline Chase as Peter in 1913 and again in 1914 under the management of Dion Boucicault, Jr. Charles Laughton played Hook in 1936 after appearing in *The Bounty*. Barrie advised him not to be too sinister as the pirate.[47] Despite the inclusion of a few interesting actors, the managers in England did not want to risk financial ruin by staging a new interpretation of Barrie's play.[48] Dion Boucicault, Jr. continued to direct the revivals through the period that Pauline Chase played Peter. He knew every line of the play and could personally demonstrate each bit of stage business. According to Roger Lancelyn Green, Dion became "the human repository of the Peter Pan tradition."[49]

The commercial success of the initial production and the popularity of its revivals further strengthened the authority of the original play's form. The set, costumes, and stage business of the play's first production were also preserved, and they helped to maintain the play's form over time. Many of the play's traditions limited the contributions of individual actors in the English productions staged during Barrie's life. The London revivals used the scenery from the original production until 1941, when a German bombing raid destroyed the sets that had been stored under an arch of Waterloo Bridge. Some actors wore parts of the original costumes from until World War II.[50] Certain cast members also remained in the London production for many years, including: Hilda Trevelyan as Wendy, George Shelton as Smee, and William Luff as Cecco. Luff first played Cecco in a touring production of the play in 1906. He last performed in the same role in London in 1954.[51] Between 1906 and 1911, Barrie and Frohman maintained the camaraderie and cohesion of the cast with an annual golf outing and dinner party.[52] Finally, the audience demonstrated what actions were appropriate for the play. Avid fans established the Peter Pan Club in London, and the members of this organization would sit in the gallery and hiss if someone missed a line or misinterpreted their business.[53] As a consequence of these constraints, the casts of the English revivals had less agency than the players who first embodied Barrie's characters. The actresses and actors involved in the revivals had to faithfully perform the actions that others had invented with the playwright and director's input.

Lichfield Owen replaced Dion Boucicault, Jr. after Owen served as the stage manager for the 1904 production. Owen had recorded Boucicault's original stage directions, and he believed that his revivals should follow them to the letter. Some actors found participating in Owens's meticulous reproductions to be tedious, while others imagined themselves as guardians of a national treasure.[54] Even the touring company had a "stage manager's production." This special dress rehearsal used Boucicault's production script to test whether or not the cast of the tour conformed to the actions outlined in the play's original stage directions. Barrie attended many of these rehearsals to check the quality of each tour. In 1929, these constraints gained legal authority when Barrie offered the rights of his play to the Great Ormond Street Hospital for Sick Children. Between 1929 and 1939, the Daniel Mayer Company produced the London revivals and tours for the hospital, and the company promised Barrie that it would not experiment with his play.[55]

MAUDE ADAMS, EVA LE GALLIENNE, AND PETER IN AMERICA

Charles Frohman hoped to replicate the success of his London production in America and, after a brief workup at the National Theater in Washington,

D.C., *Peter Pan* opened at the Empire Theater in New York on November 6, 1905. It was an instant hit and set a record for the longest single engagement at the Empire. Frohman believed that his young star, Maude Adams, was an essential part of the production's popularity, and the show toured extensively with Adams as the indefatigable Peter Pan.[56] Green, who wrote the authoritative performance history of *Peter Pan* in England, believed that the success of the first American production did not depend upon Adams's acting, as Adams was not capable of creating an original interpretation of the avenging boy. According to Green, Adams was much like Pauline Chase. Both were products of Frohman's stock company in New York, and neither provided a Peter as powerfully haunting as the tragic character Boucicault created. Green argues that Adams relied on her delicate beauty and personal charm instead of her abilities as an actress to fill the Empire.[57]

Green's judgment privileges Boucicault's interpretation without taking into account what Adams achieved. She was the first and only actress to play Peter in America from 1905 to 1916.[58] She appeared in every revival that Frohman and his successors staged in New York during this period and took the production to cities and small towns across the country. Though it only accounts for the tour that followed the 1906 revival of *Peter Pan*, the following list provides an example of Adams's exhaustive schedule: Brooklyn, Philadelphia, Chicago, St. Louis, Cincinnati, Cleveland, Dayton, Columbus, Indianapolis, Louisville, Kansas City, Omaha, Denver, Salt Lake City, Pittsburgh, San Francisco, Oakland, and Los Angeles. Adams only had one break on this tour after she appeared in Chicago. Her endurance alone should have earned her a Tony![59] Adams did not display the range and depth of Ethyl Barrymore or Ellen Terry in more tragic roles, but through her determination, she made Barrie's character an American icon and became the most famous American actress of her generation and the wealthiest woman to appear on Broadway at the turn of the century.[60]

Adams was uniquely qualified to play Peter Pan in America. She was born in Salt Lake City in 1872. Her mother, Annie Adams, was a Mormon, and her family claimed that their ancestors included a passenger on the *Mayflower*. Her Puritan genealogy and an alleged connection to John Quincy Adams made Maude Adams a wholesome American heroine, and hoped to compensate for her Mormon past and independent lifestyle.[61] Enthusiastic audiences ignored the fact that Adams's maternal grandfather had been a polygamist and reframed her father's alcoholism and early death not as blights on her heritage, but as obstacles that the young actress had to overcome while growing up in the West.[62] Americans embraced Adams as Peter Pan. When she came down to the edge of the stage and asked the audience if they believed in fairies, it "registered a whole new and intimate relation

4.2 Maude Adams as Peter Pan in the 1905 New York production. Note feathered cap. Photography Collection, Miriam and Ira D. Wallach Division of Art, Prints, and Photographs, the New York Public Library, Astor, Lenox, and Tilden Foundations.

between the actress and the audience."[63] Birkin explains that it is difficult to communicate how important the 1905 production and subsequent tour was in America. Audiences across the country responded to Adams's Peter Pan "with a fervor that made the London production seem trivial."[64] In the American productions, Neverland became the New World, and Peter and his allies, both the island's natives and the children who fled the Old World, now fought against the tyranny of a fallen despot, rejecting the corruption of an older European world order. Instead of raising the Union Jack after defeating Hook, the American cast raised the Stars and Stripes.[65]

Adams was an accomplished actress who recognized the responsibilities of her fame. When creating a new character she always asked what her interpretation would mean to the people who would see it.[66] She argued that Peter Pan was "the idealization of everything that was wonderful and wistful in childhood."[67] With an almost spiritual fervor, she infused her Peter with a boyish optimism. According to the review of her performance in New York, her fans found Adams "delicately suited" to play the "half child, half fairy." Her performance helped them to momentarily live a second childhood, a fantasy of a lost purity that only Adams's "winsome, lonely little dreamer of dreams," could conjure for them.[68] Her Peter was not an athletically masculine dryad ready to exact vengeance on the enemies of vulnerable children. On the contrary, she was slight, girlish, and frail. She was five feet tall and weighed one hundred pounds. American audiences found her small size and pretty features to be endearing, and her interpretation of Peter did not threaten their patriarchal norms. Adams's characterization of Peter combined with carefully crafted reports of the actress's domestic life to portray her as "lovely, sweet, and wholesome."[69]

Despite her apparent frailty, Adams was stronger than she appeared, and her success created a seeming contradiction.[70] She was a small and shy woman, but she was also ambitious and independent. It required incredible stamina and discipline to reinvent her character over a long tour. These were qualities that Americans in general, and theatergoers especially, admired and enjoyed in Adams's portrayal of Peter Pan. Barrie's play gave her the freedom to display these characteristics in the persona of a boy, but she had adopted them from her mother and developed them with the support of Charles Frohman long before she played Peter Pan. Annie Adams had the greatest influence over her daughter's development, and the younger Adams inherited her mother's self-sufficiency. Without the support of her husband, Annie Adams raised her daughter while working in professional theaters from Salt Lake City to San Francisco. Eventually, Frohman noticed the mother and daughter team and invited them to join his stock company in New York.[71] With her mother's guidance and Frohman's assistance, Maude Adams soon became a leading actress. After Frohman prepared her for more serious roles, he cast her in his most important shows at the Empire.[72] These productions included two of Barrie's popular plays, *The Little Minister* (1897) and *Quality Street* (1901). Barrie and Adams met at Frohman's theater in New York in late 1896, and the playwright, actress, and producer quickly established a strong artistic team. They collaborated on the plays that Barrie wrote for Adams, including *Peter Pan*, and the actress believed that Barrie was her most important and unseen audience.

Adams's success in *The Little Minister* and *Quality Street* established her stardom, but the roles also typecast her as a whimsical and charming little woman. She did not want to be a character actress and pressed Frohman to select material that would challenge her artistically. Frohman admired her ambition and respected her talent. With his approval, Adams appeared at the Empire as Juliet in *Romeo and Juliet* and the son of Napoleon in Edmond Rostand's *L'Aiglon* before 1905. Rostand's play did not generate much profit or critical acclaim, but it was the first of a series of productions in which Adams portrayed a male character in a leading role.[73] Like the other important actresses of this period, Adams played male characters in serious dramas and cross-dressing females in comedies before and after she appeared as Peter Pan. Between 1908 and 1911, she starred as Viola in *Twelfth Night*, Rosalind in *As You Like It*, and St. Joan in *Joan of Arc*.[74]

Annie was a capable character actress, whom Brigham Young knew and supported, and she introduced Maude to the professional theater at an early age. When Maude decided to pursue acting as a career, she adopted her mother's maiden name for the stage, and only used her father's surname when she traveled incognito. Annie and Maude worked together in professional productions in Salt Lake City and small cities in California before they moved to San Francisco and eventually to New York.

Maude Adams was a household name in America before she played Peter Pan and remained popular long after the first production of Barrie's play in New York. Her first significant performance at the Empire was in the 1892 production of *The Masked Ball*, in which she played opposite John Drew, Frohman's leading actor.[75] After Frohman discovered Adams's talent, he relied upon her to star in shows at the Empire and to take them across the country. Frohman also agreed to stage plays that featured Adams as a male lead between revivals of *Peter Pan*. These plays included translations of Miguel Zamaceis's *The Jester* and Edmund Rostand's *Chantecler*.[76]

Adams considered herself a serious theater artist. She developed a rigorous and systematic approach to her rehearsals, and she prepared for each performance in a meticulous manner.[77] She employed the same methods when she created her Peter Pan. Barrie and Adams corresponded about the play and its lead character before she rehearsed for the role. After she received a copy of the latest script, she retreated to her cottage in New York's Catskill Mountains and used the summer to craft her interpretation in isolation.

She spent a month walking, riding, and studying Barrie's script in the wooded vales near Tannersville. When she had appeared as Napoleon's son in *L'Aiglon*, she failed to capture the complexities of the doomed boy, and the production revealed her limitations in playing tragic roles. Therefore, she did not attempt to mine the pathos inherent in Barrie's play. After her time away from the crowds and bustle of New York, Adams emerged from among the verdant mountains of upstate New York having created a winsome sprite full of boyish energy.[78]

As an artist, Adams helped make *Peter Pan* a national phenomenon, but her accomplishments took a toll on her body and impacted her personal relationships. While many theater critics lauded her work onstage, other reporters described her private life less sympathetically. In 1894, rumors in a gossip column reported that Adams had liaisons with other actresses, and the rumors resurfaced when reporters claimed that a young woman of Cuban descent had spent too much time backstage during a run of *Peter Pan* in New York.[79] Frohman attempted to suppress these reports and fabricated an account that Adams was engaged to a writer, Richard Harding Davis. But she had no serious personal or professional relationships with men other than Frohman and Barrie.[80] Besides the time that she spent with the producer and the playwright abroad, Adams traveled only with her closest female companions, and she worked hard to protect her privacy.[81] Only one actor attempted to court the actress, but she rebuffed him and asked Frohman to remove him from the play's cast.[82] In another instance, a stagehand at Frohman's theater made his unrequited love for Adams a public matter. Morris Gottlieb, one of the crew at the Empire responsible for operating a spotlight, also fell in love with Adams. Gottlieb had become entranced with Adams while she rehearsed her part and played it at the Empire, and he believed that she had responded in an encouraging manner to his love letters. She had not. Gottlieb's actions became erratic, and he was admitted into an asylum.[83]

Both positive and negative accounts of Adams's private life contributed to the ways in which American audiences understood the characters that she brought to life. Gottlieb's case offers one example of the complicated dialogue between actor, character, and audience. His sad story also provides the means of identifying an audience member's reception of Adams's Peter Pan that does not jibe with its official description in contemporary reviews. The first question is simple: did Gottlieb fall in love with Adams, with Peter Pan, or with Adams as Peter Pan? It is ironic that Gottlieb controlled the lights that represented Tinker Bell. In the play, Tinker Bell loves Peter and acts irrationally to protect him. Gottlieb claimed to have fallen in love with Adams, and a judge found his actions to be irrational as well. However, as a stagehand familiar with the machinations of the theater, he was not so delusional that he believed Adams *was* Peter Pan. He fell in love with the *actress* playing Peter Pan. Can this fact reveal anything about Adams's popularity as Peter Pan in America?

This second question is more complex, and frankly impossible to answer. Did other audience members find Adams attractive in her guise as Peter Pan? Once again, each audience member attending a theatrical performance participates in the production and reception of the meanings that constitute the event. Compared to the reviews in the papers, Gottlieb's actions demonstrate that no two audience members construct the same meanings or experience the same emotions while viewing a theatrical performance. When Adams appeared at the Empire, her costume, movements, and encounters with Wendy may have offered certain audience members the same excitement that aroused Gottlieb's affections, while for others her character may have represented uniquely American virtues. The reviews support the latter argument, which may explain her widespread popularity to broad audiences. The official accounts and Adams's biographical information do not identify how different audience members reacted to her Peter Pan. Yet critics claimed that most American audiences did not take such stories seriously. Reporters applauded her artistic achievements and domesticated her daily activities. Others glorified her independence and courage by recounting her travels to exotic sites in Europe, North Africa, and Palestine, but in almost every case, the popular press valorized Adams as an ideal American woman.[84]

Though Adams was a popular and talented actress, she did not make *Peter Pan* a national sensation without the help of powerful men. Much of the production's success in America belongs to Barrie's writing and Frohman's management. Frohman was to the American productions what Dion Boucicault, Jr. had been to their English counterparts. *Peter Pan* was his most cherished project, and he had the ultimate authority over the production's aesthetic. As a consequence, the play's long runs and even longer tours both supported and limited Adams's growth as an artist. Though he was a dear friend, still, Adams worked for Frohman. He made decisions concerning every aspect of the productions in which she appeared. Later in her career, he included her in this process, but she did not direct the shows or rehearsals for his productions in New York. It was not until Eva Le Gallienne established the Civic Repertory Theatre in New York that a woman both directed and starred in *Peter Pan*.

On December 1, 1933, Ethel Barrymore gave an impromptu address to the women's club in Philadelphia. She stated that the fine ladies gathered at the luncheon had no knowledge of difficulties that actresses faced, the sacrifices they made, and that they had no appreciation for their guest speaker. She was not speaking of herself or Maude Adams. She spoke out in support of Eva Le Gallienne. Le Gallienne was late for the meeting due to a schedule change, and the members of the club had complained. According to Barrymore's impassioned speech, her young protégé had "done more for the American theater than any one," and she deserved greater respect.[85] Le Gallienne was a dedicated artist from an important theater family. Two of her aunts and one of her uncles performed on the London stage. Her father, Richard Le Gallienne, was a famous poet and theater critic from England, and her mother was a journalist from Denmark. Le Gallienne was born in London on January 11, 1899, and after her parents divorced four years later, her mother raised her in Paris. In 1906, she attended one of her first and most memorable theatrical performances. Her mother took her to see Sarah Bernhardt play Prince Charming in *The Sleeping Beauty* at Bernhardt's theater in Paris.[86] Just as Bernhardt's achievements motivated Maude Adams to refine her craft, Bernhardt's performance as a young man inspired Le Gallienne to become an actress in the first place. Like Adams, Le Gallienne came from a single-parent family and relied on her mother for support and approval. Also like Adams, she began her professional career very young. Yet the two artists did not share the same education or training. While Adams had little formal schooling and learned her trade in the theaters of Canada's Western Territories, Le Gallienne had attended an arts school in Paris, moved to London, and was working in New York's theaters by the time she was sixteen.[87]

During the 1920s Le Gallienne received positive reviews for her strong performances in serious roles, but she differed from other successful actresses on Broadway. She was not satisfied to repeat the language and gestures of a single character in a long-run and tedious tour. Le Gallienne believed that commercial concerns dominated American theater and limited the form and content of mainstream productions. She wanted to produce, direct, translate, and write the latest and most challenging plays with a permanent company of similarly engaged and courageous artists. This company would stage classical plays and contemporary drama in repertory and keep admission prices at a minimum, much like the national theaters of Europe.[88] She opened the Civic Repertory Theater in 1926 with a combination of her savings and a subscription campaign. Most actresses in this period and in such a male-dominated profession worked for producers and managers. Le Gallienne, however, created her own company, controlled its play selection and production design, and held the lease for its theater. She did all of this without a government subsidy or the profits of a commercial hit.

The Civic Repertory Theater staged the plays of Shakespeare, Molière, Ibsen, and Chekhov at affordable prices to full houses in Lower Manhattan for six years. Unfortunately, the repertory theater never made its budget, and the Depression forced Le Gallienne to close it in 1933. Despite the loss of her theater, Le Gallienne's work gained national attention and helped promote the Off Broadway and Little Theater movements. Eleanor Roosevelt met Le Gallienne when she brought her company's production of *Alice in Wonderland* to Washington, D.C., in 1933. They discussed the possibility of establishing a national fund for professional theater, and President Franklin Roosevelt invited Le Gallienne to return to the capital and outline her plans to him and Harry Hopkins, FDR's righthand man. Roosevelt wanted her to run the theater program proposed in the Works Progress Administration, but she argued that his plan would promote mediocrity. Hopkins gave the post instead to Hallie Flanagan, who became the director of the Federal Theater Project. Eva's hopes for government support were never fully realized.[89]

A clear description of Le Gallienne's political activity helps explain why she decided to stage *Peter Pan* and how she interpreted its main character. When she produced Barrie's play, Le Gallienne became the third American actress to appear as Peter Pan in New York. Marilyn Miller had staged Barrie's play at the Knickerbocker Theater during the 1924–1925 season in what was a short and uneventful run.[90] Le Gallienne opened her production on November 26, 1928, at the Civic Repertory Theater. Compared to the work of Adams and Miller, Le Gallienne offered a new approach to *Peter Pan*. Though it was not a serious piece of dramatic literature like the works of Ibsen or Chekhov, Le Gallienne had many reasons to include *Peter Pan* in her repertoire. The *Wall Street Journal* described her as a dauntless advocate for freedom and moral courage, and her version of Barrie's play helped the Civic Repertory Theater bring in large numbers of paying audience members and provide benefit performances for orphans and poor children, and, in many ways, Barrie's play epitomized Le Gallienne's political beliefs.[91]

Le Gallienne gained Barrie's approval to stage *Peter Pan* through R. H. Philipson, an actor from London and an old friend of Barrie's. She also asked Maude Adams for permission to revive the play in New York. Le Gallienne found the older actress to be polite and rather dull.[92] Le Gallienne's Peter would not be as conventional as Adams's. She had decided to stage Barrie's play in repertory along with seven other works, including *The Cradle Song*, *The Master Builder*, *Twelfth Night*, and *The Three Sisters*. In the span of one week audience members could see Le Gallienne play a nun, an architect's wife, a girl pretending to be a boy, a Russian aristocrat longing for Moscow, and a boy who refused to grow up.[93] Le Gallienne directed most of the productions at her theater in New York, and she cast her permanent company members in *Peter Pan*'s most important roles. Egon Brecher played Hook, and a young Charles McCarthy was John Darling.

4.3 Like Maude Adams, Eva Le Gallienne played Napoleon's son in *L'Aiglon*, and this image illustrates the youthful defiance that she infused in her interpretation of Peter Pan. Photograph of Eva Le Gallienne in the 1934 production of *L'Aiglon* used with the kind permission of the Library of Congress.

Le Gallienne cast herself as Peter and selected Jo Hutchinson, her live-in partner of six years, to play Wendy.[94]

Like Adams, Le Gallienne prepared for her role away from the city, at a farm that she had bought in rural Connecticut, practicing her lines and developing her movements in its open fields. She created a new flying system for her production and was the first actress to soar above her audience. This was a courageous act that exposed her to possible injury. It also brought her body closer to the audience, a move that had made Adams more appealing to American audiences in 1905. The difference with Le Gallienne's interpretations was that she was even more willing to break barriers. Her costume consisted of a cap, a very short tunic, and bare legs. Swinging her exposed legs above the audience made Le Gallienne more vulnerable and her character more exciting. Yet Le Gallienne's Peter was not a feminized elf or an opportunity to exploit her body. She created a daring and reckless boy that did not ask for forgiveness.[95] One critic argued that though Le Gallienne lacked "the sweet, keen wistfulness" that Maude Adams gave to Peter, she made up for it with her élan and ability to convincingly portray a boy who would not be mothered.[96]

Le Gallienne and her company continued to stage *Peter Pan* as a part of their repertoire through 1932.[97] In 1928, she offered a free matinee in New York to orphans and settlement children. The tradition continued while the Civic Repertory Theater remained in business. Barrie supported the event, and Le Gallienne organized the parties, at which children received toys, balloons, oranges, and candy.[98] Such charity and advocacy was a hallmark of Le Gallienne's long career. She was committed to helping underprivileged children and advancing women's issues through her work in the theater and at various speaking engagements. Le Gallienne surrounded herself with talented women, lived with her closest companions, and was more open about her lesbian relationships. Her family, the members of her company, wealthy friends, and theater critics supported her choices, and they did not balk when Le Gallienne cast Jo Hutchinson as Wendy opposite her Peter Pan. The popular press did, however, often ask why she did not marry a man.[99]

After the Civic Repertory Theater closed, Le Gallienne did not play Peter Pan again. No other actress appeared as the elfin boy on Broadway until Jean Arthur starred in the 1950 production at the Imperial Theater.[100] Many Americans now imagine Mary Martin as the definitive Peter Pan, and electronic media has played an important part in establishing the dominance of her interpretation over the country's collective imagination. With the accessibility and apparent permanence of Martin's performance on video we lose the shadows of previous performances of Peter. These shadows bear the traces of an evolving tradition in which powerful actresses achieved greater autonomy by playing a boy while remaining women. In the time between Le Gallienne's last appearance as Peter in 1932 and the opening of the musical in 1954, the generation of actresses who had flown, crowed, and fought as Peter Pan had grown older, died, or were simply forgotten, a fate that Barrie's character will most likely never suffer.

Le Gallienne continued to perform in other roles, and these performances included strong male characters and cross-dressing women. In
this regard she extended the tradition of powerful actresses performing in
unconventional roles, a tradition that included her personal models, Ele-
onora Duse and Sarah Bernhardt. Though she had played Barrie's character
to great acclaim for six years, Le Gallienne did not meet the playwright
until after her repertory theater had closed. He was happy to finally make
her acquaintance and explained that he had wanted to return to America
and see her perform as Peter, but he had grown older and had not been
healthy enough to travel.[101] It is a shame that he did not see her in the role
that he had created. Le Gallienne had followed a difficult and lonely path to
become a gallant, earnest, and memorable Peter Pan.

Each actress identified in this essay reshaped Peter in her likeness.
Through her Irish heritage and her involvement in her father's productions,
Boucicault gave her Peter the ability to appropriate and subvert a form of
masculinity particular to Edwardian England. This was not a conscious
choice to politicize Barrie's play. The codes are embedded in Barrie's work,
and Boucicault's personal experiences and professional training enabled her
to bring out the tragic aspects of Peter's character. It appears that Adams's
childhood moved her to create an altogether different version of Peter Pan.
Growing up in the Western Territories, Adams was the daughter of an alcoholic, penniless father and a working actress mother. These difficult circumstances reinforced the importance of wealth and made elite society all
that more attractive. Adams was a hard worker and a skilled artist, and she
fashioned a Peter Pan that was safe and sexless. She did not attempt to question patriarchal norms, and instead created a character that exemplified the
best American virtues. This interpretation was quite popular, and its success
gave Adams artistic agency and personal freedom. If Boucicault provided
the darkest version of Peter, and Adams created the sweetest and most wistful sprite, then Le Gallienne embodied the most daring and defiant boy. She
was the one actress to play Peter that openly espoused political activism. Le
Gallienne took personal and professional risks to champion women's rights
and advocate for the protection of poor and sick children, and she invested
that passion into her productions of *Peter Pan.*

NOTES

1. Anthony Lane, "Lost Boys: Why J. M. Barrie created Peter Pan," *New Yorker,*
   November 22, 2004, 98. Please note that I have spelled the name of each theater
   as it appears in local papers from the period.
2. Stacey Wolf's article concerning Mary Martin's performance of Peter Pan in
   the 1960 film inspired my research and helped me limit its scope to the most
   significant productions between 1904 and 1933. Stacy Wolf, "'Never Gonna Be

a Man/Catch Me if You Can/I Won't Grow Up': a Lesbian Account of Mary Martin as Peter Pan," *Theatre Journal* 4 (1997): 497.

3. The phrase "Shadow of [a] girl," comes from the "Fairy Notes" that Barrie created while working on a draft of *Peter Pan* in October 1903. Note 210 reads, "Shadow of girl—P expected to find it cold—it's warm! Then she's not dead, &c." Peter Pan, "FAIRY NOTES," http://www.jmbarrie.co.uk.

4. Stephen Orgel, "Introduction: A View from the Stage," in *From Script to Stage in Early Modern England*, ed. Peter Holland and Stephen Orgel (New York: Palgrave Macmillan, 2004), 1–8.

5. Marvin Carlson, "Theater and Dialogism," in Janelle G. Reinelt and Joseph R. Roach, eds., *Critical Theory and Performance* (Ann Arbor: University of Michigan Press, 1992), 320.

6. Pam Morris, *The Bakhtin Reader* (London: Edward Arnold, 1994), 8–9.

7. Stephen Orgel, "Introduction: A View from the Stage," 1–3.

8. The performance occurred at Arena Stage in Washington, D.C., May 30, 2007. *Peter and Wendy: Program Book*, ed. Cathleen Tefft (Washington, D.C.: Arena Stage, 2007).

9. Mabou Mines, http://www.maboumines.org.

10. Ibid.

11. I dedicate this essay to Colm, Lauren, Katherine McClain, and Finn. I have read different versions of *Peter Pan* to them, and we have enjoyed staging scenes from the 1928 play. However, the Mabou Mines's production offered a new way to imagine Barrie's narrative, and I learned a great deal from Colm's enthusiastic response to the performance at Arena Stage.

12. "A CurtainUp Review of Peter and Wendy," CurtainUp: *The Internet Theater Magazine of Reviews, Features, Annotated Listings*, http://www.curtainup.com/peterandwendy.html.

13. Timothy Young, *My Heart in Company: The Work of J. M. Barrie and the Birth of Peter Pan* (New Haven, CT: Yale University: University Press of New England, 2005), 55.

14. Ibid., 231.

15. Andrew Birkin, *J. M. Barrie and the Lost Boys* (New Haven, CT: Yale University Press, 2003), 38–39. For more about the significance of Frohman's death, see the chapter by Linda Robertson in this volume.

16. Frohman had leased the theater for nineteen years in order to promote his American projects as well as look for emerging playwrights and actors. It was located "in the heart of London's theater district." Isaac Marcosson and Daniel Frohman, *Charles Frohman* (1916), 236.

17. Roger Lancelyn Green, *Fifty Years of Peter Pan* (London: Peter Davies, 1954), 91.

18. Armond Fields, *Maude Adams: Idol of American Theater, 1872–1953* (Jefferson, NC: McFarland, 2004), 186.

19. Green, *Fifty Years of Peter Pan*, 81.

20. Ibid., 135–136.

21. Ibid., 72–73; 105.

22. Ibid., 91–92.

23. Andrew Birkin details how the Llewelyn Davies boys inspired Barrie to write *Peter Pan*. Their mother, Sylvia Davies, was Gerald du Maurier's sister. Andrew Birkin, *J. M. Barrie*, Introduction to the Yale Edition; Green, *Fifty Years of Peter Pan*, 128.

24. "Duke of York's Theatre, 'Peter Pan,'" *The Times*, December 28, 1904.

25. Fields, *Maude Adams*, 186.

26. Marcosson and Frohman, *Charles Frohman*, 246.

27. "Duke of York's Theatre, 'Peter Pan,'" *The Times*, December 28, 1904.

28. Green, *Fifty Years of Peter Pan*, 90–91.

29. Lane, "Lost Boys."

30. "Duke of York's Theatre, 'Peter Pan,'" *The Times*, December 28, 1904; "Duke of York's Theatre, 'Peter Pan,'" *The Times*, December 19, 1906.

31. Green, *Fifty Years of Peter Pan*, 126.

32. "Peter Pan's New Adventure," *New York Times*, January 28, 1906.

33. These plays include: *The Octoroon, London Assurance*, and *The Colleen Bawn*. Phyllis Hartnoll, *The Oxford Companion*, 95–96.

34. Nina Boucicault was famous for appearing as Napoleon in the original production after Peter forces Hook from his ship. Barrie had the actors recreate William Orchardson's portrait of Napoleon aboard the *Bellerophon*. While Boucicault posed as Napoleon, the rest of the cast sang "Rule Britannia." Other actresses appeared in the same tableaux, but British history as well as Boucicault's Franco-Hibernian ancestry gave the image greater importance and subversive humor. Birkin's website has a clear picture of the tableaux. The action occurs in the first scene of act five in the 1928 edition of Barrie's play.

35. Ann Wilson, "Hauntings: Anxiety, Technology, and Gender in Peter Pan," in *Modern Drama: Defining the Field,* ed. Ric Knowles, Joanne Tompkins, and W. B. Worthen (Toronto: University of Toronto Press, 2003), 128–143.

36. Green, *Fifty Years of Peter Pan*, 100.

37. "Lyric Theatre 'The Sin of William Jackson,'" *The Times*, August 29, 1906.

38. Green, *Fifty Years of Peter Pan*, 123.

39. Marcosson and Frohman, *Charles Frohman*, 262.

40. Birkin, *J. M. Barrie*, 215.

41. *Fifty Years of Peter Pan*, 80.

42. "Duke of York's Theatre, 'Peter Pan, or the Boy Who Wouldn't Grow Up,'" *The Times*, December 19, 1906.

43. "'Peter Pan Back in London," *New York Times*, December 25, 1912; "The Cult of 'Peter Pan,' Another Revival at the Duke of York's," *The Times*, December 24, 1913.

44. Green, *Fifty Years of Peter Pan*, 147.

45. "Duke of York's Theatre, 'Peter Pan,'" *The Times*, December 17, 1907.

46. Green, *Fifty Years of Peter Pan*, 124.

47. Ibid., 132; 139.

48. Ibid., 23.

49. Ibid., 184.

50. Ibid., 155.

51. Ibid., 131.

52. Ibid., 146.

53. Ibid., 155.

54. Ibid., 136–137.

55. Ibid., 153–157.

56. Marcosson and Frohman, *Charles Frohman*, 171.

57. Green, *Fifty Years of Peter Pan*, 159.

58. IBDB: Internet Broadway Database. http://www.ibdb.com.

59. Fields, *Maude Adams*, 201; 206.

60. Barrymore was the niece of John Drew, the handsome leading man who played opposite Adams when she first appeared at the Empire. Barrymore and Adams were friends and developed their skills and fame during the same period. Marcosson and Frohman, *Charles Frohman*, 158–159.

61. Fields, *Maude Adams*, 3–5.
62. Maude Adams and Nina Boucicault both had Irish ancestry. Adams's father, James Kiskadden, left Ireland in order to make his fortune as a miner in the Western Territories. He drifted from one job to another and died a penniless alcoholic. As a consequence Annie Adams raised Maude in the Western theaters with little support. Fields, *Maude Adams*, 11–13.
63. Marcosson and Frohman, *Charles Frohman*, 170.
64. Birkin, *J. M. Barrie*, 126.
65. Ibid., 126–127.
66. Marcosson and Frohman, *Charles Frohman*, 162.
67. Ibid., 169–170.
68. "A Joyous Night with 'Peter Pan,'" *New York Times*, November 7, 1905
69. Ibid.
70. Fields, *Maude Adams*, 89–93.
71. Ibid., 5–6.
72. Maude Adams was a household name in America before she played Peter Pan and remained popular long after the first production of Barrie's play in New York. Her first significant performance at the Empire was in the 1892 production of *The Masked Ball*, in which she played opposite John Drew, Frohman's leading actor. Marcosson and Frohman, *Charles Frohman*, 140.
73. Adams's first experience at cross-dressing in a major production was a formative but difficult experience that nearly overwhelmed her. Despite this setback, Frohman agreed to stage plays that featured her as a male lead between revivals of *Peter Pan*. These plays included translations of Miguel Zamaceis's *The Jester* and Rostand's *Chantecler*. Marcosson and Frohman, *Charles Frohman*, 424–426; 172; 180–181; Fields, *Maude Adams*, 150.
74. Marcosson and Frohman, *Charles Frohman*, 173–179.
75. Marcosson and Frohman, *Charles Frohman*, 140.
76. Ibid., 172; 180–181.
77. To prepare for each performance, Adams delivered her lines in front of a mirror at home, arrived at the theater two hours before curtain, and wandered among the seats and backstage to better understand the special qualities of each playhouse before she went to her dressing room. Fields, *Maude Adams,* 127; 95.
78. Ibid., 189.
79. Ibid., 195.
80. Ibid., 107.
81. One of Adams's most memorable sojourns included a visit to Egypt, where she saw the Sphinx in the moonlight after a long ride on a mule. She also traveled to desert villages and was entertained by a sheik whose harem danced for her and her companions. Only her female secretary and a friend, Miss Ray Rockam, accompanied her on the trip. They had begun the journey in England, where they visited Barrie. After traveling to France and Egypt, they visited Jerusalem and returned to New York City in June 1903. In an interview after *Peter Pan* opened at the Empire, Adams recommended traveling from the East to the West to witness the march of civilization through the ages. Fields, *Maude Adams*, 169–171; J. D., "Over the Teacups with Maude Adams," *New York Times*, January 7, 1906.
82. Fields, *Maude Adams*, 129.
83. "Gone to Stay in Never-Land. Morris Gottlieb Crazy for Peter Pan, and He Can't Come Back," *New York Times,* April 10, 1906.
84. J.D., "Over the Teacups with Maude Adams"; Fields, *Maude Adams,* 172.

85. Helen Sheehy, *Eva Le Gallienne: a Biography* (New York: Alfred A. Knopf, 1996), 227.
86. Sheehy's text offers a detailed account of Eva's experience at the production of *The Sleeping Beauty.* Ibid., 5–6.
87. "The First Two Years, Miss Le Gallienne Tells Her Own Story and That of the Civic Repertory," *New York Times,* November 18, 1928.
88. "Eva Le Gallienne, Actress," *New York Times,* June 5, 1991.
89. Sheehy, *Eva Le Gallienne,* 225–226.
90. IBDB: Internet Broadway Database. http://www.ibdb.com.
91. "The Theatre," *Wall Street Journal,* March 12, 1927; "'Peter Pan' Given for 1,300 Children," *New York Times,* December 21, 1929.
92. Sheehy, *Eva Le Gallienne,* 184–185.
93. "To Give 7 Plays in Week," *New York Times,* April 16, 1927; "Eva Le Gallienne Back in Cast," *New York Times,* March 31, 1927.
94. "Eva Le Gallienne a Wistful Peter Pan," *New York Times,* November 27, 1928.
95. Sheehy, *Eva Le Gallienne,* 185–186.
96. "Eva Le Gallienne a Wistful Peter Pan," *New York Times,* November 27, 1928.
97. Sheehy, *Eva Le Gallienne,* 201.
98. "'Peter Pan' Given for 1,300 Children," *New York Times,* December 21, 1929.
99. Sheehy, *Eva Le Gallienne,* 167–170.
100. The production did not change Barrie's dialogue, but it replaced John Crook's score with new songs by Leonard Bernstein. The cast included Boris Karloff as a comic Hook. IBDB: Internet Broadway Database. http://www.ibdb.com.
101. "Liner Paris Delayed Six Hours by Storm," *New York Times,* August 29, 1934.

CHAPTER 5

Peter Pan and the Possibilities of Child Literature

Martha Stoddard Holmes

THE INTRODUCTION TO Donna R. White and C. Anita Tarr's groundbreaking anthology *Peter Pan In and Out of Time* closes with a wish that *Peter Pan* will "always . . . be read."[1] They do not say by whom, and it is an issue that bears discussion. In the first half of the twentieth century, J. M. Barrie's Peter Pan fictions were used as readers in British state schools; appear on a nurse's list of books for "entertaining convalescent children"; and were listed as recreational reading choices of children grades 4–6 in the "Z-section" (lowest 20 percent in terms of intelligence tests, sometimes termed "dullards"). These days, they are noticeably absent from K–12 reading lists issued by state departments of education; recommended reading lists provided by the American Library Association and the National Endowment for the Humanities; and other sources of recommended reading for children.[2] Further, an informal survey of teachers suggests that Barrie's actual texts may rarely, if ever, be assigned as part of the required or elective middle- or high-school curriculum.[3] While *Peter Pan*'s iconic status is regularly connected to its position as a classic work of "children's literature," it is unclear how many children actually read it. They are undoubtedly familiar with Peter Pan, but their knowledge comes mainly from films, both animated and live, from Disneyland and Disneyworld, and via pervasive cultural references, particularly advertising.[4]

This paradox illuminates a key issue in the scholarly study of *Peter Pan* and other "children's classics." If children no longer read a text apparently written with them as the imagined audience, is the text still "their" literature? In this distinctive situation of literary production, in which an author often writes for a reader (real or imagined) of a different age and with disparate life experiences, how important is it that a children's book be read by an actual child? Further, how important is it to classify a work as belonging to adults or children?

With their hybrid narrative voice; thematic emphasis on adult-child conflict, insecurity, pain, loss, and death; and mixed tone of sentiment and cynicism, the Peter Pan fictions have become an emblem of the problematic investment of adult writers (and readers) in writing "for" children that serves the adult's own need for an imagined concept of childhood, a situation suggested by Barrie's biography but potentially applicable to all adults. Psychoanalytic critic Jacqueline Rose's important study *The Case of Peter Pan; or, The Impossibility of Children's Fiction* was the primary catalyst for an ongoing critical engagement with *Peter Pan*'s misapprehension by adults as a narrative for and about children, and the narrative's particular utility in keeping alive for adults their desires about children and childhood. While some scholars have responded directly to this argument, others have taken Pan criticism in directions Rose addresses with lesser emphasis, such as the Peter Pan fictions' engagement with gender and nationalism/empire, their textual and genre history, their status (with childhood itself) as cultural artifacts and their relevance to queer theory, while focusing less intently on the problem of adult sexuality as the meaningful context for analyses of the texts' narrative and linguistic instability and suggesting an exciting diversification of literary criticism on *Peter Pan*, spurred on by the growth of the academic discipline of children's *literature*.

The unresolved controversies over its status *as* "children's literature," however, remain crucial to the important question of our investment in taxonomies of literary texts and in the adult-child binary that underpins the term. If few children read *Peter Pan*, some impassioned points about its appropriateness for children may have become moot; but the questions the novel raises about our ideologies of childhood and adulthood remain vital. *Peter Pan* as a classification problem is a powerful spur for the discipline of children's literature to reformulate its project in broader terms, defining a genre in which adults and children have different engagements throughout their lifetimes, but which they nonetheless share. Simultaneously, *Peter Pan* can continue to prod us to explore our larger cultural investment in ideologies of children, adults, and the boundary between them, beyond a narrow concern with sexuality and sexual transgression.

The term "children's literature" has been the site of conflict almost from its inception as a category. Historian F. J. Harvey Darton offered this definition in 1932: "printed works produced ostensibly to give children spontaneous pleasure, and not primarily to teach them, nor solely to make them good, nor to keep them profitably quiet."[5] Insightful as Darton's phrase is, with its wry awareness of some of the reasons why adults may give books to children, it seems increasingly unable to contain the genre. As Katharine Jones notes in a recent essay, "When children's books hit the headlines because of their popularity . . . the same questions always come up: are they really for children, are they good for children, how do we evaluate such books, why do adults read them, what is children's literature?"[6] The most basic questions have proved hard to answer. For example, should we categorize the genre by intended audience, actual audience, protagonist's age, and/or aspects of its content and purpose? Given children's reading differences, can we even define "child reader" in any productive way?[7] More complex issues wait in the wings: for example, if we define "children's literature" by a specialized audience of a particular psychological development, do we need to think differently about didacticism and other effects generally treated as aesthetic failures?[8] Further, the term "children's literature" now defines an academic subdiscipline produced and promoted through a host of undergraduate and graduate courses, a growing body of critical scholarship, and several lively professional organizations, creating important contexts that shape and complicate any shared definitions we might establish. While a meaningful conversation about the subgenre of children's literature would be especially welcome today, a lack of consensus makes discussion increasingly difficult.[9]

Jones's promising solution is the term "child literature . . . a literature written almost entirely by adults that assumes various conceptions of the child, childhood, and the childlike, with child readers usually being the target of the book."[10] I will return to this term, and to *Peter Pan*'s importance to a broader, more hybrid vision of the genre and its multiple stakeholders, after discussing some of the novel's early history as a provocateur within the critical study of children's literature.

PETER PAN UNDER THE SCHOLARS' LENS

One of Peter Pan's most significant identities in the past twenty-five years has been as a subject of scholarly critical analysis in the rapidly growing academic field of children's literature. In this context, Barrie's Peter Pan has catalyzed vigorous debate about the cultural construction of childhood, the role of the generic category of children's literature in such a construction, and the investment of adults in both.

Like the story of Peter Pan, its criticism has been a fascinatingly hybrid enterprise. J. B. Priestly argued in 1929 that "the nineteenth century knew Barrie as a novelist, whereas the twentieth century thinks of him as a dramatist, so that he has appeared to be suspended in the air between the two forms of the novel and the play."[11] While Priestly points out critical omissions that resulted from Barrie's doubleness, a more recent effect is that scholarship focused on the fiction often includes the play, and vice versa.

Further, as this volume demonstrates, single essays in Pan studies often engage both film and material culture; when Peter Pan is not just fiction(s), play, and films, but also a peanut butter, a syndrome, and (once) a collar, the criticism itself tends toward hybridity. With that proviso, I will emphasize critical studies of the fiction and particularly the emergence of important new trends in Pan criticism in the past decade.

The critical history of the Peter Pan fictions was until fairly recently marked by two linked threads, the biographical and the psychoanalytic. A number of studies of Peter Pan use Barrie's compelling and ambiguous biography (by this I mean both the life itself and the author's own life-narratives) as their foundation, locating the Pan fictions' origins in the traumas of Barrie's early life and his failure, as a grownup, to perform plausibly the gendered identity of adult male as defined by his social class in Edwardian Britain. A biographical emphasis in literary studies of Peter Pan persists despite an overall trend away from biography in scholarly practice. As Peter Hollindale notes, the fascination with biography is partly the product of Barrie himself, whose *The Little White Bird* is both "a fictionalised version of Barrie's relationship with the Davies family," whose five sons were in some sense Barrie's collaborators in creating Peter Pan, and also the work in which that first narrative of Peter Pan actually emerges into text.[12] The doubleness of *The Little White Bird* "anticipates the subsequent double history" of the story as fiction and a troubling biography involving Barrie's love for the five Davies boys, a history critics have been hard-pressed to avoid (201). Thus, earlier critical studies of Peter Pan like Humphrey Carpenter's chapter in *Secret Gardens: A Study of the Golden Age of Children's Literature* integrated biography into their critical analysis of the fiction, while (almost as a given) noting a wide range of additional thematic and textual devices.[13]

This biographical trend evolved into a psychological and sometimes psychoanalytic approach, both toward Barrie and the Pan narratives' status as modes of "remembering, repeating, and working through" his life traumas, and more broadly, toward "the Barrie in all of us" adults. Jacqueline Rose's *The Case of Peter Pan; or, The Impossibility of Children's Fiction* stands out as not only the most significant work with a psychoanalytic emphasis, but also the critical work on Barrie's Peter Pan fictions that has generated the most "buzz" to date, some of it of a negative nature. For Rose, Barrie's novel exemplifies the impossibility of the term "children's fiction" because it is neither "for" nor "about" children in any meaningful way. Rather, like most such works, it is about adults' desire for a fantasy of childhood: *Peter Pan* is a front—a cover not as concealer but as vehicle—for what is most unsettling and uncertain about the relationship between adult and child. It shows innocence not as a property of childhood but as a portion of adult desire.[14] Along with adults' libidinal investment in an ideology of childhood innocence, Peter Pan illuminates their need to "use the translucent clarity of childhood to deny the anxieties we have about our psychic, sexual and social being in the world."[15] While Barrie's story's generic, narrative, and linguistic instability (and resulting transgression of any well-defined concept of "children's literature") makes it a particularly visible example of Rose's argument, she argues that Peter Pan shares its "front" with the literary subgenre it both "belongs to" and implodes: through its overt challenges to a self-contained definition of "children's literature," *Peter Pan* illuminates that definition as a fantasy produced by and for adults.

Others have made related arguments, such as John Rowe Townsend's point that the child "hardly enters into the process by which quality children's books are assessed and distributed. . . . a children's book can go far on the road to success before a single child has seen it."[16] Rose's study, however, in pointing a finger at adults' libidinal engagement with ideas about children and children themselves, touched a major nerve within the field. Among other things, it generated a discussion of what might constitute a "genuine" or uncolonized children's literature that serves the interests of children themselves, as opposed to the "impossible" variety Rose theorizes.[17] While Rose's text takes critics of children's literature to task while referencing very few of them, later scholarship in the growing academic field of children's literature has undoubtedly been shaped in reaction to her provocative thesis. It has also been informed by her work on the textual history and cultural uses of *Peter Pan* as a representative text in children's literature, and children's literature as one of the institutions that divide childhood and adulthood.

The next work to generate a parallel cultural charge to Rose's was James R. Kincaid's *Child-Loving: The Erotic Child and Victorian Culture*, which argues that the child's position as an object of desire (solidified in various ways by Victorian texts, Barrie's among them) underpins our current cultural values in ways that we resolutely deny and "manage" through the scapegoat figure of the pedophile, whose explicit, extreme, and uncontrolled desire for children serves to keep other adults' desires in check. In that context, Kincaid affirms this "children's novel" as the vehicle for adults' desire for children—not necessarily for sex with them, but for the qualities, such as innocence, for which children have become cultural repositories. In contrast to Rose, whose readings of *Peter Pan* are arguably loaded with excitable language, Kincaid is more likely to remind us that it takes a culture to make a pedophile.[18] Despite their differences, Rose and Kincaid both highlight Barrie's book's complex position in relation to both "children's literature" and, more fundamentally, the adult/child binary.

Later psychologically and psychoanalytically oriented studies of the Pan fictions respond to Rose and Kincaid, extending and arguing with their provocative statements about Peter Pan's importance as a register of the desires of adults. Karen Coats, for example, in "Child-Hating: *Peter Pan* in the Context of Victorian Hatred," argues that the "fantasy spaces of childhood" like Neverland "almost always include beings that hate both the state of childhood and childhood itself" and that Barrie "sets up a deliberately antagonistic relationship between childhood and adulthood . . . grounded in an irrational hatred."[19] As its title makes clear, Coats's essay responds directly to Kincaid's *Child-Loving*, with whose argument about the cultural function of the pedophile as scapegoat she agrees, while brilliantly pointing out the ways in which the emphasis on "child-loving" both obscures the range of "child-hating" and particularly elides its presence in both Victorian culture (for Kincaid, the origin of child-loving) and *Peter Pan*. For example, when Hook discovers the sleeping Peter—a scene Kincaid anatomizes for the seductiveness of Peter's pose—Coats points out that, were he at liberty, "Hook surely would not have caressed the sleeping boy, but killed him." Coats extrapolates from her earlier chapter on Peter as embodiment of Lacanian *jouissance* to develop Peter's plenitude and "cockiness" as the source of Hook's obsessive animosity and offers, in place of Kincaid's pedophile, Hook as the misanthropic scapegoat that helps us manage our hatred of children.[20]

While critics continue to engage the *Peter Pan* fictions from a psychoanalytic perspective, queer and cultural studies analyses of gender and sexuality in *Peter Pan* have abounded in the last quarter-century. In addition to provocative work by Marjorie Garber and others on the cross-dressing and queerness that have defined most of the story's theater and film history, several essays have explored what Susan Kissel calls "the drama of gender" in *Peter Pan*, including a recent one by M. Joy Morse that unpacks the trope of thimbles and kisses as representative of late Victorian women's ambivalence about their social roles, arguing that Barrie's recognition of women's situation both echoes his compassionate identification with his mother's early life and makes him an iconoclast. Christine Roth provocatively contextualizes the Pan fictions in terms of an Edwardian cult of girlhood that was followed by an obsession with boyhood, situating *Peter Pan*, with its alternating emphasis on Wendy and Peter, in both camps.[21] Chris Routh's fascinating analysis of the history of Peter Pan illustrations and their continuing juxtaposition of Peter to Wendy (the latter as powerful needlewoman and storyteller, threatening to Peter because of her acceptance of growing up), offers a second productive analysis of *Peter and Wendy* as a bildungsroman à deux, albeit one in which only one child grows up.[22]

The dynamic of "race" and empire in Peter Pan is probably its most problematic element for contemporary readers (including teachers, as demonstrated by my survey), but has generated surprisingly few sustained analyses. Laura Donaldson's "Of 'Picaninnies' and Peter Pan: The Problem of Discourse in a Marxist Never-Never Land" articulates the ways in which Barrie's novel invokes the discourse of the "picanniny," used to "map the binary oppositions high/low, adult/child, culture/nature, light/dark, and superior/inferior onto European/'native' bodies, respectively," to recuperate Tiger Lily as a colonized subject despite "embu[ing] her with the possibility of challenging dominant interpretations of gender in fin-de-siècle imperial England."[23] Clay Kinchen Smith's "Problematizing Picaninnies, or How J. M. Barrie Uses Graphemes to Counter Racism in Peter Pan," argues rather that Barrie uses the Picaninnies in a way that provokes readers to notice the operation of racialized stereotypes. The connection between colonialist ideology and the politicization of nature in Peter Pan is another new emphasis, explored in M. Lynn Byrd's ecocritical essay "Somewhere Outside the Forest: Ecological Ambivalence in Neverland from The Little White Bird to Hook," in Dobrin and Kidd's anthology Wild Things: Children's Culture and Ecocriticism. Byrd argues that despite Barrie's reliance on nature as a representative of domesticity's Other, the narrative habitually moves toward domestication rather than wildness; "[n]ot only are nature and natural space [in the Pan fictions] constructed entities and confined spaces, but also the idea of nature is distorted onto domestic or fantasy spheres that ultimately elide nature itself."[24]

From its initial emphasis on biography and psychology, recent work on the Peter Pan fictions has undertaken a series of cultural studies analyses, including the larger context of pirate lore and the study of fairies and folklore in late Victorian culture. Genre has been a particularly productive thread, generating a number of essays placing Peter Pan in the context of the evolving genre of children's fantasy. Sarah Gilead's important essay "Magic Abjured: Closure in Children's Fantasy Fiction" draws on Barrie's novel (and the work of L. Frank Baum and C. S. Lewis) to articulate genre conventions involving multiple worlds and narrative closure. Amy Christine Billone and John Pennington extend this important idea, drawing comparisons between Barrie's fiction and the novels of J. K. Rowling and Philip Pullman.[25] Other intriguing comparative approaches have connected Barrie with Romantic ideologies of childhood (in Wordsworth, for example) and fin-de-siècle aestheticism.[26] As well as its textual relations with other works, Peter Pan has always presented a rich focus for a study of textual history, with its multiple audiences and versions. R.D.S. Jack's work on the Pan manuscripts remains the most extensive and definitive.[27] One of the biggest surprises is that with all the interest in embodiment in the narratives, from the uncanniness of Peter's baby teeth to Tinker Bell's bosom, there has been no disability studies analysis of the use of Hook's hook (much less P. J. Hogan's fascinating decision in the 1993 film to reveal his amputation).

Some of the most rewarding new work integrates an attention to cultural and historical contexts, including biography, with a broader attempt to identify these fictions' lasting allure. Such is the work of Coats and Hollindale, both of whom have worked in Pan studies in a sustained way; it also characterizes newer work by scholars such as Karen McGavock, whose essay "The Riddle of His Being: An Exploration of Peter Pan's Perpetually Altering State" resolutely argues for the lack of fixity in Barrie, the texts' genre identities, origins, audiences, and resonances, and Peter Pan's resulting "central yet tense position in the canon of children's fiction."[28] What marks new scholarship on Peter Pan is a "both/and" approach that acknowledges critics' desire to pin the works (and Barrie) down in various ways, but makes the texts' productive refusal of such fixity their object of study. While such studies identify many of the textual, thematic, and linguistic effects that are Rose's concern, they gain value by drawing conclusions that are less sweeping and less alarmist about the Pan fictions and their connections to children at risk of being violated by adults.

DEFINING ADULT: CHILD THROUGH PETER PAN

This is my focus as well. As I will illustrate, the novel creates an adult/child binary, but not simply to support adults' desire to maintain the desirable fiction of children and childhood (as Rose suggests), or keep alive "a monument to eternal enticement" in a boy forever on the verge of growing up, as Kincaid characterizes Peter Pan.[29] Rather, while the Peter Pan texts enshrine, with their many windows and gates, the boundary between childhood and adulthood and the binary it creates, they are also open in various ways to users on both sides of the binary. Like McGavock and Wasinger, I am interested in the irresolvable hybridity and malleability of the Pan texts that results from their play with socially constructed boundaries. As well as catalyzing debates relevant to children's literature in general, the Peter Pan fictions can transform the very terms of this critical conversation into those of a multiply-owned "child literature and culture."

Through dual or hybrid narrative address, a thematic emphasis on loss and death, the workings of its dual-world plot, and above all, its emotional landscapes, *Peter Pan* may mark itself as "for adults," but in the process it creates an imagined "adult" as much as it does a fictionalized "child." While most critics locate certain elements as the adult desires in the texts, and treat them as its "genuine" elements, *Peter Pan*'s disturbing and fascinating democracy of themes and affect, and its vertiginous linguistic border cross-ings, make this a shaky assumption in many instances. Unless we assume that Barrie, a clear adult, has complete control over his texts (and this sen-tence is already full of problematic conditions), then we must acknowledge that *Peter Pan* leaves the doors open to readers of all ages, making the real impossibility our limited model of adults and children, and the unworkable genre distinctions this binary engenders.[30]

Several of these characteristics gesture toward genre conventions but ultimately diverge from them in significant ways. One of the first things new readers of *Peter and Wendy* notice is that Barrie's narrator repeatedly gestures toward more than one type of reader, explicitly addressing readers with diverse levels of maturity.[31] A complex writing and reading dynamic in which the text is written "for" one audience, but is also accessible to another, is common in children's literature, for obvious reasons: texts below a certain age level are written with an awareness that they may have two audiences, the child reader/listener, and the parent who reads a book's denotative content to a child, but who can also "overhear" the connotative messages. Further, so the theory goes, the adult reader can act as a gate-keeper, gradually titrating the text for the child as s/he matures and is ready for its full content. The different levels of maturity implied by the narrative voice also connect *Peter and Wendy* to some conventions of children's fantasy literature in general. As U. C. Knoepflmacher observes,

> children's books, especially works of fantasy. . . . can be said to hover between the states of perception that William Blake had labeled inno-cence and experience. From the vantage point of experience, an adult imagination re-creates an earlier childhood self in order to steer it towards the reality principle. From the vantage point of innocence, however, that childhood agent may resist the imposition of adult values.[32]

In Barrie's texts, in contrast to these expectations, the dual-address nar-rative does not hover so much as dart strategically, even sadistically, between mature and naive modes. *Peter and Wendy's* narrator is by turns coy, desper-ate, tender, superior, and opaque. As Hollindale characterizes it,

> below the surface another narrative voice is speaking which is likely to be audible only to grown-ups [including] the putative adult reader-aloud. The adult reader is a helpless intermediary between Barrie and the child, caught in storytelling crossfire and receiving bullet wounds intended for him or her alone. Under the surface is a sharp and some-times ferocious dialectic, exploring the collision and relation of the child and adult worlds.[33]

An example of such a moment in *Peter and Wendy* is the scene in which Peter tells the Lost Boys why he dislikes mothers. The narrator adds a comment in free indirect discourse with any child reading or listening: "So this was the truth about mothers. The toads!"[34] As a narrative strategy, the comment potentially places the child reader/listener in an uneasy position (or one of power, since it may voice the child's very thoughts) in relation to a parent who may be holding the book—and the child—in his or her lap. Thus, it is not only the reading adult who may censor or titrate meanings, but also the listening child.

If for Hollindale this hybrid narrative produces conflict, for Rose it is a violation of "the barrier between adult and child . . . not experiment . . . but *molestation*. . . . the writer for children must keep his or her narrative hands clean and stay in his or her place."[35] While her metaphor is more disturbing than Barrie's narration, the dual address unsettles any impression of children's literature or fantasy conventions.

Thematic conflicts in the stories reinforce the tensions within the narrative voice. *Peter and Wendy* builds on a binarist construction of children as distinctly different from adults mainly to articulate the troubled relationships between the two groups, most often presenting the adult-child relationship as one of antagonism, longing, and frustration on both sides. The explorations are often nuanced: as Celia Wren observes, the Peter Pan narrative "seethes with psychosexual subtext and existential angst."[36] If Hook's threats of violence toward Peter are simple enough, given his role as the villain, his insecurity toward Peter Pan's "cockiness" and his worries about "good form" (and about the bad form of thinking of good form) are complex forays into adult neurosis.

Mr. Darling, Hook's alter ego and a poster child for Judith Butler's theories of the performance of gender, is another excellent example of Wren's point. He asserts his force over the household, loses his children as a result, and abjects himself in the kennel. When the children return, Lost Boys in tow, Mr. Darling is still insecure and emotional; when reproved by his wife for his concern for the cost of keeping additional children, he bursts into tears because "he thought they should have asked his consent as well as hers, instead of treating him as a cipher in his own house."[37] The drama of the father's failed authority and self-embarrassment through bullying is a classic adult narrative with which many adults are uncomfortably familiar. Unlike the concept of "good form" (a phrase delimited less by age than by class and nationality), however, this element is also uncomfortably familiar to many children; adults may simply not want to see that idea in a children's book.

Other features of *Peter Pan* can be more easily identified as "adult." For example, like many other works of fantasy literature, its plot is structured by two separate, individually coherent worlds whose relationships to each other can produce some of the text's most layered and interesting meanings. That Neverland is in some ways a parody of London can best be perceived and appreciated by experienced readers. In the meanings attached to transit between worlds, also significant to fantasy fiction, *Peter Pan* again seems to be speaking to an adult rather than a child. Sarah Gilead's important essay on three modes of closure in children's fantasy literature uses *Peter Pan* as her major example of "the tragic mode of return" to the primary world of the novel (in this case, London). In books like *Peter Pan*, she argues, the return is "dominated by a sense of loss unmitigated by a playful or softened tone."[38] For example,

> The children lose their powers of flight, their belief in the possibility of escape through fantasy, and also, perhaps, their belief in the inviolability of childhood itself. Peter, forgetting the past, is trapped in an eternal present without emotional or cognitive meaning. Those who have returned to reality are "grown up and done for." Mrs. Darling is "now dead and forgotten," as is Nana.[39]

To accept this message as central to a book that speaks to children rather than adults, we would need to imagine childhood as a time characterized by a sense of inescapable loss that pervades both of its worlds, As Gilead observes, "Like the author of children's literature, Peter kidnaps the child to escape the nursery, gravity, and other limitations and burdens of ordinary reality; but he takes us to a world infused with morbid reminders of that reality."[40]

If much of the affect that dominates the Peter Pan texts seems weighted toward an adult perspective, however, not all of it can be easily assigned to adults alone. Karen Coats has brilliantly argued that, while both Hook and Mr. Darling are vehicles for dislike of children, *Peter and Wendy* is also memorable for its representation of children's hatred of adults.[41] After the scene about mothers, for example, the narrator reminds the reader of "a saying in Neverland that every time you breathe, a grown-up dies" and says that "Peter was killing them off vindictively as fast as possible."[42]

Desire for adults—and adulthood—in the Peter Pan stories is hard to pin solely on Barrie's psychology and the needs of mature readers. Peter's wish to have Wendy be his mother is accompanied by Wendy's desire for her own mother, whose "sweet mocking mouth had one kiss on it that Wendy could never get, though there it was, perfectly conspicuous in the right-hand corner."[43] Further, Wendy desires the state of adulthood itself, so much so that she grew up "a day faster than the other girls."[44]

While *Peter and Wendy* may indeed be marked by adults' longing for an idea of children—and even by their hatred of children—it is also marked from start to finish by children's strong emotions toward adults. Even if these feelings, too, are part of an ideology of the child, they cannot be said to be the property of Barrie alone, or of the adults who read the texts, but available to all who read and hear them. They are not necessarily *not* about children.

It is not their suffusion with adult affect, but the availability of their strong feelings for ownership by both adults and children, that makes the Peter Pan books disturbing. A key example is the back story for Peter's hatred of mothers, which is only fully developed in *Peter Pan in Kensington Gardens*. Having played with the idea of returning home to his mother, but stopped short of commitment, Peter finally rushes back to the nursery window, assuming it will still be open:

> But the window was closed, and there were iron bars on it, and peering inside he saw his mother sleeping peacefully with her arm round another little boy. Peter called, "Mother! mother!" but she heard him not; in vain he beat his little limbs against the iron bars. . . . Ah, Peter, we who have made the great mistake, how differently we should all act at the second chance. But . . . there is no second chance, not for most of us. When we reach the window it is Lock-out Time. The iron bars are up for life.[45]

This may be the single most compelling passage of *Peter Pan in Kensington Gardens*, and a final example of the power of Barrie's ambiguity in relation to an imagined audience comprised of both adults and children. The tone is simple enough for children to understand. At the same time, the harshness of the message often shocks new readers of the text. It is impossible to specify to whom Barrie directs this message of lost opportunity, or who can receive it. Adults may feel they have been pointed at, their wasted chances and experiences of "Lock-out Time" made a bit too plain. At the same time, even the imagined, not to say real, presence of a child reader or listener may make the adult reader cringe, just as the child may have cringed at the insult to mothers. Finally, as much as we know that real children fear that they could be locked out of their mothers' hearts, and can apprehend much of the meaning in this scene, the narrator's plain statement of this hard truth seems almost an assault in a children's book.

In violating our sense of what realities may be broached in a children's book, the passage makes us acutely aware of our expectations for the genre. Like Wendy's desire for Mrs. Darling's kiss, Peter's longing and desperate shock may indeed be representative not only of adults' desires and fears, but also of the inner lives of children. One of the lines in the play, and the novel *Peter and Wendy*, which has been most subject to censorship and/or editing

is "To die will be an awfully big adventure." This, however, was not Barrie's creation but the comment of George Llewellyn Davies at age six during their collaborative creation of the Peter Pan stories.[46] Barrie's texts may
illuminate our investment in sorting the feelings of children and adults into
two distinct groups, our expectation that children's literature will help us
do that, and our dismay when it does not. For as much as the Peter Pan texts
are interested in the adult/child binary and the fraught border between
the two sides, they are equally committed to inventive boundary-crossings
and an overall hybridity: the Darwinian hybridity of *Peter Pan in Kensington Gardens*, in which babies are first birds and Peter becomes a "betwixt-
and-between"; the gender fluidity and even cross-dressing suggested by the
narrator's polymorphous identifications; and finally, at bottom, the hybrid
location—neither adult nor child literature, neither adult nor child audience, neither adult nor child writer—of the entire Peter Pan corpus.[47]

Peter Pan is, above all, a book that brings to the foreground and actively
troubles the adult/child binary, one of the foundational ideas of our cultural moment. The question of how adults and children are different is at
the heart of children's literature partly because it is so often at the heart
of contemporary culture in regard to relations of power and (even more)
desire. We might borrow from Eve Kosofsky Sedgwick's foundational essay
"Axiomatic" and reconsider as foundational a binary that has been seen as
marginal, of interest only in special cases or to special populations. Sedgwick asserts that "many of the major nodes of thought and knowledge in
twentieth-century Western culture as a whole are structured—indeed, frac-
tured—by a chronic, now endemic crisis of homo/heterosexual definition."
The adult/child binary has been similarly monumental in its impact on
culture since the "invention" of childhood as a special status distinct from
the adult.[48] As well as the relations of power and desire between and among
people of different age groups, this binary as metaphor and paradigm has
been used to structure a host of other social identities, including people
of atypical cognitive, neurological, or emotional function, people of color,
non-Europeans, women, and others at a disadvantage socially and politically, such as slaves.

The barrier between adults and children, so actively troubled by Barrie's work (and life), opens to us all many of the other issues that are provocative in the Peter Pan books, such as sexuality, gender differentiation,
family relations, colonialism, and racism.[49] Further, the child/adult binary
has always been central to the definition and study of this problematic entity
called "children's literature," the border of which is habitually patrolled by
different authorities and always alive with crossings. For the academic discipline that bears the name "children's literature," in the process of trying

to sort out whether or not it actually has a content area, how to define it, and what significance the actual reading (required or voluntary, guided or independent) of children has to it as a field of study, *Peter Pan* provides a continuing, invaluable source. This is especially true as we move toward Jones's model of child literature, which allows more potential modes of participation for all ages and includes those texts that may no longer frequently be read by children, but which are increasingly crucial to the genre.[50] The Peter Pan texts, which have from the start beckoned to many kinds of readers and listeners and whose readership continues to change, may allow us to create terms with enough consistency to allow us to have a conversation about child literature that can accommodate the hybrid and cross-over texts of the twenty-first century and beyond.[51]

At the very least, exploring both children's literature and twenty-first century culture from the perspective that the distinction between children and adults is the most significant binary of our time can move us to substantial insights not only regarding children's literature, but social relations more generally. *Peter Pan* may not open all of these doors simultaneously, but it is a powerful beginning.

APPENDIX. RESPONSES TO A QUESTIONNAIRE ON TEACHING PETER PAN; TWO VERSIONS OF THE QUESTIONNAIRE

Thirteen teachers completed the following survey questionnaire voluntarily over the months of June–August 2007. Nine teach at the community college/college/university level and four teach grades 7–12, with an emphasis on grades 11 and 12 (one is an 8th grade teacher). All are in the United States except one university teacher in the U.K. The four secondary school teachers were known to me and recruited; all but one of the college/university teachers were unknown to me, and none were recruited. All respondents were encouraged to reply even if they had never taught, or considered teaching, the Peter Pan texts. Three of the recruited secondary school teachers took a revised questionnaire (Questionnaire 2) that was simplified and asked for additional information (that is, had they heard of any other teachers teaching the Peter Pan texts; how many years had they been teaching).

All but one of the college/university teachers had taught one or more of the Peter Pan texts; a few had also taught film versions in the context of primarily literature courses. None of the secondary school teachers had ever taught any of them, or any of the films, nor had they heard of others teaching them at the secondary school level.

Of the five respondents (one college/university, four secondary level) who had never taught any of the Peter Pan texts, three expressed in their responses to the questionnaire a plan to think about teaching them. College and university teachers reiterated the importance of Peter Pan as a cultural icon: the exact phrase "cultural icon" came up at least twice, as did "cultural touchstone." The novel apparently comes up in literature classes in which it is not taught, and most American students see to have some awareness of Peter Pan; "many students believe [it] is a classic." As one teacher who doesn't particularly like the novel argues, "I especially think we need to consider why it has now become one of our most commonly retold stories."

While the majority of teachers include *Peter Pan* in some form of children's literature courses, some teach it in specialty courses on fantasy literature or popular British fiction. One teaches it in general survey courses and argues for its significance in "surveys of non-children's texts of the early twentieth century, both the play and the novel." Other suggestions about the place of Peter Pan in the college/university curriculum focus on the cultural study of childhood, adulthood, and adolescence. One thought it could be productively included in lower-division courses asking students to "reconsider the texts of their childhood and various retellings of those texts." Another respondent agreed that *Peter Pan* is "one of those phenomenal texts (like *Little Women, Tom Sawyer,* and *Secret Garden*) that takes up so many key issues related to children and the experience of childhood" and focuses on teaching *Peter Pan* as "an agent of socialization into cultural expectations of behaviour" (specifically, gender development/representation); as an engagement with "the classic tension that children feel between the need to reject the world of adult responsibility and care . . . and the simultaneous desire to be a part of that world"; as "a social document that reflects critically upon the middle class nuclear family unit," especially in connection with paternal authority and capitalism; and finally, as an example of cultural imperialism, "both in regards to the racism of the text and the representation of animals and wilderness vs. humans and civilization."

One of the most interesting aspects of the responses was the fact that college and university teachers, many of whom used *Peter Pan* as a focus for discussing gender ideologies, imperialism, and racism, thought that these issues might make secondary school teachers reluctant to assign it. A few of the respondents taught Barrie's texts in courses filled mainly with future secondary school teachers, and had discussed with them the challenges of "classic" children's literature texts in this regard.

The secondary school teachers, on the other hand, offered curricular restrictions as the major reason they had not considered teaching the Barrie texts.

NOTES

1. Donna R. White and C. Anita Tarr, *J. M. Barrie's Peter Pan In and Out of Time: A Children's Classic at 100* (Lanham, MD: Scarecrow, 2006), xxiv.
2. See Jacqueline Rose, *The Case of Peter Pan; or, the Impossibility of Children's Literature* (Philadelphia: University of Pennsylvania Press, 1993), 115–136; Lena Dixon Dietz, "Entertaining Convalescent Children," *American Journal of Nursing* 32, no. 12 (1932): 1255–1256; John A. Hockett, "Reading Interests of Z-Section Pupils," *Elementary School Journal* 3, no. 1 (1935): 26–34; "Summertime Favorites," http://www.neh.gov/projects/summertimefavorites.html; and California Department of Education, "Recommended Literature (K-12): Collection of Outstanding Literature for Children and Adolescents in Grades Kindergarten through Grade Twelve," http://www.cde.ca.gov/ci/rl/11/, accessed July 22, 2007. While "classic children's literature" texts such as *The Secret Garden* or *The Wizard of Oz* appear here, on the American Libraries Association lists, or on Oprah's booklists for children, Barrie's books do not. See http://www.ala.org/ala/alsc/alscresources/summerreading/recsummerreading/recommendedreading.htm and http://www.oprah.com/obc/kids/age13/obc_kids_13_a.jhtml, both accessed August 16, 2007.
3. Martha Stoddard Holmes, unpublished survey of fourteen high school, college, and university teachers on teaching *Peter Pan*, June-August 2007.
4. I use Barrie, *Peter Pan in Kensington Gardens and Peter and Wendy*, ed. Peter Hollindale (Oxford: Oxford University Press, 1991). I will refer individually to *Peter Pan in Kensington Gardens* and *Peter and Wendy*, but also call the combined narrative *Peter Pan* or the Peter Pan fictions.
5. F. J. Harvey Darton, *Children's Books in England: Five Centuries of Social Life* (Cambridge: Cambridge University Press, 1932), 1.
6. Katharine Jones, "Getting Rid of Children's Literature," *Lion and the Unicorn* 30 (2006): 287–315.
7. Farah Mendelsohn pursues this question in a book-in-progress. I am grateful for her permission to read this unpublished manuscript.
8. These are only samples of longstanding debates inside and outside the academy; Jones provides a useful summary of the more heated ones. See also Jack Zipes, "Why Children's Literature Does Not Exist," in *Sticks and Stones: The Troublesome Success of Children's Literature from Slovenly Peter to Harry Potter* (New York: Routledge, 2001), 39–60; Karin Lesnik-Oberstein, "Essentials: What Is Children's Literature? What Is Childhood?" in *Understanding Children's Literature*, ed. Peter Hunt (New York: Routledge, 1999), 15–29; Maria Nikolajeva, "Exit Children's Literature?" *Lion and the Unicorn* 22, no. 2 (1998): 221–223; Felicity Hughes, "Children's Literature: Theory and Practice," *ELH* 45 (1978): 542–561; and C. S. Lewis, "On Three Ways of Writing for Children," in *Of Other Worlds: Essays and Stories* (New York: Harcourt, 1966, 1982), 31–43. Barrie, to my knowledge, never explicitly joined this conversation to which his works have been central.
9. The growth of the field of children's literature criticism has begun to remove the stigma from the scholarly study of the genre produced by the dismissal of children's literature as not "serious" literature that began in the 1800s. See Felicity Hughes, "Children's Literature: Theory and Practice," *ELH* 45 (1978): 542–561; and Beverly Lyon Clark, *Kiddie Lit: The Cultural Construction of Children's Literature in America* (Baltimore: Johns Hopkins University Press, 2003). For a useful history of the discipline, see Suman Gupta, "Sociological Speculations on the Professions of Children's Literature," *Lion and the Unicorn* 29, no. 3 (2005): 299–323.

10. Jones, "Getting Rid of Children's Literature," 305. She also suggests the term "generational literature" to indicate a reader's possibly multiple stances toward a text over a lifetime.

11. J. B. Priestly, "Sir James Barrie," *English Journal* 18, no. 2 (1929): 106–119: 106.

12. Peter Hollindale, "A Hundred Years of Peter Pan," *Children's Literature in Education* 36, no. 3 (2005): 197–215; 201–202.

13. Carpenter, for example, includes a hypothesis of Pan and Hook as Christ and (Milton's) Satan, and a discussion of Barrie's reworking of the Romantics' Pan and other uses of Romantic notions of childhood.

14. Rose, *The Case of Peter Pan,* xii.

15. Ibid., xii, xvii.

16. John Rowe Townsend, "Didacticism in Modern Dress," 1967. Reprinted in *Crosscurrents in Children's Literature*, ed. J. D. Stahl, Tina L. Hanlon, and Elizabeth Lennon Keyser (Oxford: Oxford University Press, 1967), 16–19: 17. Gupta extends the conversation, arguing that "children's literature is a playing field that has little to do with children as reading subjects, but a great deal to do with 'children' as a politically efficacious category in the adult world." See Gupta, "Sociological Speculations," 299.

17. See, for example, Mary Galbraith, "Hear My Cry: A Manifesto for an Emancipatory Childhood Studies Approach to Children's Literature," *Lion and the Unicorn* 25, no. 2 (2001): 187–205.

18. See James Kincaid, *Child-Loving: The Erotic Child and Victorian Culture* (New York: Routledge, 1992) and *Erotic Innocence: The Culture of Child Molesting* (Durham, NC: Duke University Press, 1998).

19. Karen Coats, "Child-Hating: *Peter Pan* in the Context of Victorian Hatred," in Donna R. White and C. Anita Tarr, *J. M. Barrie's Peter Pan In and Out of Time* (Lanham, MD: Scarecrow Press, 2006), 3–22; 3, 4.

20. Coats, "Child-Hating," 7. Where Coats argues that Peter is joy itself, David Rudd in "The Blot of Peter Pan" in White and Tarr, *Peter Pan In and Out of Time*, draws on Lacan to argue that Peter persists in a pre-Symbolic stage of development in which he "persists in trying to be all for the mother" (269).

21. See Christine Roth, "Babes in Boyland: J. M. Barrie and the Edwardian Girl," in White and Tarr, *Peter Pan In and Out of Time*, 47–67.

22. See Garber, *Vested Interests: Cross-Dressing and Cultural Anxiety* (New York: Routledge, 1992); Susan Kissel, "'But When at Last She Really Came, I Shot Her': *Peter Pan* and the Drama of Gender," *Children's Literature in Education* 19, no. 1 (1988): 32–41; M. Joy Morse, "The Kiss: Female Sexuality and Power in J. M. Barrie's *Peter Pan*," in White and Tarr, *Peter Pan In and Out of Time*, 281–302; Roth, "Babes in Boyland," in White and Tarr, *Peter Pan In and Out of Time*, 47–67; and Chris Routh, "'Man for the Sword and for the Needle She': Illustrations of Wendy's Role in J. M. Barrie's *Peter and Wendy*," *Children's Literature in Education* 32, no. 1 (2001): 57–75.

23. See Laura E. Donaldson, *Decolonizing Feminisms: Race, Gender, and Empire Building* (Chapel Hill: University of North Carolina Press, 1992), 86, 77.

24. Sidney I. Dobrin and Kenneth Byron Kidd, *Wild Things: Children's Culture and Ecocriticism* (Detroit: Wayne State University Press, 2004), 48–70; 49.

25. See Amy Christine Billone, "The Boy Who Lived: From Carroll's Alice and Barrie's Peter Pan to Rowling's Harry Potter," *Children's Literature* 32 (2004): 178–202; and John Pennington, "Peter Pan, Pullman, and Potter: Anxieties of Growing Up" in White and Tarr, *Peter Pan In and Out of Time*, 237–262.

26. See Glenda A. Hudson, "Two is the Beginning of the End: *Peter Pan* and the Doctrine of Reminiscence," *Children's Literature in Education* 37, no. 4 (2006):

313–324, which develops a point Carpenter also notes in his chapter on Peter Pan; Jean Perrot, "Pan and Puer Aeternus: Aestheticism and the Spirit of the Age," *Poetics Today* 13, no. 1 (1992): 155–167; and Paul Fox, "The Time of His Life: Peter Pan and the Decadent Nineties" in White and Tarr, *Peter Pan In and Out of Time*, 23–45.

27. See R.D.S. Jack, "The Manuscript of *Peter Pan*," *Children's Literature* 18 (1990): 101–113.

28. See Karen McGavock, "The Riddle of His Being: An Exploration of Peter Pan's Perpetually Altering State" in White and Tarr, *Peter Pan In and Out of Time*, 195–215.

29. Kincaid, *Erotic Innocence*, 144.

30. As Glenda A. Hudson notes, Barrie satirizes the Romantic child (as created by Rousseau and particularly by Wordsworth in his "Ode: Intimations of Immortality") and presents him not as "trailing clouds of glory" but as a creature steeped in primal urges. See Hudson, "Two is the Beginning of the End." Other connections she does not make might include Barrie's "iron bars" as an allusion to Wordsworth's "shades of the prison house," another key line from the "Ode."

31. In arguing that *Peter Pan* reads and reveals our desire for an adult/child binary, and works continually with such a division without delivering it in conclusive ways, I find the terms "adult" and "child" inescapable for describing the texts' variegated and amorphous textual landscapes. I do not repeat the scare quotes, but my suggestions that some parts of the text are earmarked for "adults" and others for "children" should be taken to mean *imagined* identities rather than actual or essential ones.

32. U. C. Knoepflmacher, "The Balancing of Child and Adult: An Approach to Victorian Fantasies for Children," *Nineteenth-Century Fiction* 37, no. 4 (1983): 497–530; 497.

33. Peter Hollindale, "Introduction," *Peter Pan in Kensington Gardens and Peter and Wendy* (Oxford: Oxford University Press, 1991), xxi. Hollindale comments that the inclusion of a domestic/intimate voice that makes readers feel they are intruding was one of the things Barrie imported from the chapter in *The Little White Bird*, a 1902 novel for adults, when he transformed his ideas into *Peter Pan in Kensington Gardens* (1906). When he finally published *Peter and Wendy* (1911), the only version of the original story explicitly written for children, Barrie incorporated the same narrative layering as part of his method, with effects ranging from confusing to potentially disturbing. Like Hollindale, Jack affirms that Barrie's first Peter Pan manuscript was clearly intended for adults; Jack also argues that the revisions to the manuscript argue for Barrie's intention to make the text hybrid and layered: "From the outset I believe he hoped to attract both sections of his audience but in different ways and on rather different levels. This is, after all, only a development of Boccaccio's vision of art as presenting a series of veils for the reader or listener to remove according to his capacity for understanding." See Jack, "The Manuscript of *Peter Pan*," 101–113; 111–112.

34. Barrie, *Peter and Wendy*, 167.

35. Rose, *The Case of Peter Pan*, 70.

36. Celia Wren, "Fear of Flying," *American Theatre* (February 2003): 44–48, 44.

37. Barrie, *Peter and Wendy*, 216.

38. See Sarah Gilead, "Magic Abjured: Closure in Children's Fantasy Fiction," *PMLA* 106, no. 2 (1999): 277–293; 285.

39. Ibid., 287.

40. Ibid., 286. As the previous points remind us, if much of the affect that dominates *Peter and Wendy* is weighted toward an adult perspective, little of it seems

obviously pleasurable. While there seems to be critical consensus about the novel's attractions as a fulfillment of "Romantic and Surrealist yearnings to live through the imagination, with unfettered, unrepressed fantasy" that "presupposes that the child has access to a form of desirable wisdom, of potent innocence which cannot tell pretend from real, and sex from sexlessness," it's important to note that the Peter Pan fictions enact the fulfillment of such desires in the most painful ways possible. It is not only "a morbid book, rich in themes of guilt, revenge, obsession, and murder," but also a book about discomfort. See Marina Warner, "Little Angels, Little Monsters: Keeping Childhood Innocent" in Stahl, Hanlon, and Keyes, ed., *Crosscurrents of Children's Literature*, 133–140, 137; Gilead, "Magic Abjured," 286.

41. See Coats, "Child-Hating."
42. Barrie, *Peter and Wendy*, 168.
43. Ibid., 69.
44. Ibid.
45. Barrie, *Peter Pan in Kensington Gardens*, 40.
46. Hollindale, "A Hundred Years," 206.
47. See Carrie Wasinger, "Hybridity, Androgyny, and Terror in *Peter Pan*," in White and Tarr, *Peter Pan In and Out of Time*, 217–236.
48. See Eve Kosofsky Sedgwick, *Epistemology of the Closet* (Berkeley: University California Press, 1991), 1.
49. While Wasinger, for example, focuses on gender indeterminacy as the key of many troubled binaries in *Peter Pan*, I would argue that child-adult indeterminacy is the more central catalyst.
50. Jones, "Getting Rid of Children's Literature," 307.
51. Examples include the Harry Potter books and, even moreso, Philip Pullman's *His Dark Materials* trilogy, as Billone and Pennington argue. For useful discussions of these series' connections to Peter Pan, see Amy Christine Billone, "The Boy Who Lived: From Carroll's Alice and Barrie's Peter Pan to Rowling's Harry Potter," *Children's Literature* 32 (2004): 178–202; and John Pennington, "Peter Pan, Pullman, and Potter: Anxieties of Growing Up," in White and Tarr, *Peter Pan In and Out of Time*, 237–262.

CHAPTER 6

Disney's *Peter Pan*

GENDER, FANTASY, AND INDUSTRIAL PRODUCTION

Susan Ohmer

WHAT WE THINK OF as the narrative of "Peter Pan"—the exploits of Peter, Wendy, and her brothers in Neverland, among Captain Hook, the pirates, Tinker Bell, and the Lost Boys—is composed of a collection of texts whose construction spanned thirty years. J. M. Barrie's drive to represent the evanescent fantasies of childhood, along with his modernist awareness of the process of representation, led him to explore the medium of film. In 1920 he wrote a scenario developed from both the play and the novel intended to show "that the film can do things for *Peter Pan* which the ordinary stage cannot do."[1] Yet when Paramount Studios produced the first and only silent film version of the tale, he was disappointed at its lack of creativity and felt that it was only repeating what had been done on the stage.[2]

Given Barrie's interest in exploring cinema as a medium of representation, and his belief that film has a capacity to "strike a note of wonder . . . and whet the appetite for marvels," it is interesting to consider the first animated film based on *Peter Pan*, the 1953 Walt Disney feature.[3] Walt Disney himself felt that animation was the best medium for realizing Barrie's vision. "I don't believe that what James M. Barrie actually intended ever came out on the stage," he said in an interview. "If you read the play carefully, following the author's suggestion on interpretation and staging, I think you'll agree. It's almost a perfect vehicle for cartooning. In fact, one might think that Barrie wrote the play with cartoons in mind. I don't think he was ever happy with the stage version. Live actors are limited, but with cartoons we can give free rein to the imagination."[4] Cartoons provide opportunities to escape the constraints of the material world, and they also evoke childhood pleasures. As Kristin Thompson has pointed out, this linkage of animation and childhood has made it difficult for both the industry and critics to take cartoons seriously. The pleasure cartoons give us is so natural that there seems to be no need to analyze them; in fact, Thompson argues, viewers may resist the idea of examining cartoons, fearing that to do so could reduce their enjoyment.[5]

Disney animation poses additional challenges. More than any other cartoon producer, the Disney studio is enshrouded in myth. As Donald Crafton has noted, the studio's work is repeatedly described as "timeless" and as having a "universal" appeal.[6] Advertisements for the studio's new theatrical films and video releases refer to the "magic" of Disney and its tradition of "classic" works. Documentaries about the studio's past and behind-the-scenes glimpses of current productions portray the Disney audience as encompassing viewers of all ages and backgrounds, underlining the universal appeal of its product. The company's continuing ability to attract the public is often attributed to the wisdom of its founder, known within the organization simply as "Walt." Studio mythology often presents Walt Disney as a benevolent patriarch whose intuitive understanding of his audience guided the company to worldwide success.

Seen from an ideological perspective, the image Disney constructs for itself, of being able to make audiences happy everywhere and at all times, implies that the pleasure these films give is natural and automatic, while glossing over historical and cultural differences that influence audience reactions. Disney animation appears to float free of the very down-to-earth material conditions that enmesh other kinds of films and filmmakers. Similarly, the studio's own accounts of its history portray its films as the product of internal discussions and the creative insights of its founder; they do not take into account the effects of social, cultural, and economic forces.

Yet as recent criticism has taught us, viewing pleasure is not innocent and universal, but the result of specific industrial practices and social and cultural formations. Richard deCordova, Eric Smoodin, and Mark Langer have provided crucial models for analyzing the production, exhibition, and marketing of Disney films. This essay seeks to break through the myths surrounding Disney cartoons in order to understand how the studio's construction of *Peter Pan* responded to shifting ideologies of fantasy, gender, childhood, and sexuality in postwar American culture. My goal is not to "read off" images as simple reflections of social issues, but to analyze how production processes, and the studio's sense of itself and its films, reflected changing conditions within the company and within the industrial and social environments in which it operated.

Peter Pan in Disney's Production

The production of Disney's *Peter Pan* encompassed the Depression, when the studio stood at the apex of animation; World War II, when the studio expanded beyond cartoons; and the postwar period of crisis, uncertainty, and relative prosperity. During the most intense period of production on the film, from 1948 to 1952, the company began producing live action films, moved into television, launched international coproductions, and laid the groundwork for what became Disneyland. The very meaning of "Disney" shifted rapidly in this period. Within the broader framework of U.S. culture, this period marked an era when gender roles, the nature of fantasy, and the meaning of childhood also fluctuated. Disney's *Peter Pan* bears the marks of these industrial, economic, and social changes.

Disney's cartoon incorporated many familiar characters and dramatic elements from the earlier texts, but the studio also reframed the story to create new iconic moments and character types aimed at contemporary audiences (it had now been half a century since the first Peter Pan theater productions). Disney commissioned market research on the project before launching production, and these early studies of public attitudes formed the basis for many later decisions. Transcripts of production conferences that took place between 1948 and 1952 allow us to track decisions made at the storyboard stage and during the early animation or "rough reels." At one point executives divided these remarks by gender, making it possible, perhaps for the first time in Hollywood history, to study the influence of gender on filmmaking while a project was still in production. Decisions about *Peter Pan*'s characters, narrative, and visual style involved a process of negotiation and compromise that reflected changing social norms and shifting expectations for what "Disney" should be. These transcripts reveal that the uncertain masculinity of the film's central character posed a challenge for Disney animators that shaped their approach to elements involving sexuality and gendered behavior.

Another means of understanding the impact of Disney's *Peter Pan* is by analyzing its critical and audience reception. The film's reception illustrates how viewers, and not only Disney personnel, were working through shifting ideologies of gender, childhood, and sexuality in the postwar period and the extent to which Disney films could, or should, represent them. This criticism demonstrates how the pleasure evoked by animation is not universal but is embedded within a particular place and culture, and that films have the power to stretch the category of pleasure to include nodes of cultural anxiety that can either evolve into a source of pure pleasure, revert into pure anxiety, or remain—like Peter Pan—between these two categories.

Disney's *Peter Pan* did not live only on the screen. The film's release launched the most massive merchandising campaign to date, by a studio already known for its promotional skill. Hundreds of product tie-ins and widespread coverage in various media reveal a company keenly aware of the possibilities of synergy decades before it became a buzzword. *Peter Pan* not only marks a pivotal moment in Disney animation, but also a crucial turning point in the studio's growing multimedia empire. The Disney studio continues to update *Peter Pan* with new electronic formats, computer games that recast the film for new technologies, and spin-offs that focus on characters who were not as visible in the 1950s. The new multimedia packages and the studio's continual recasting of its history demonstrate Disney's success at renewing *Peter Pan* again and again for generations, just as it renewed the story for the first time in the 1950s.

"PETER PAN" AS INTERTEXT

Walt Disney and the animators who worked on *Peter Pan* read and studied several versions of Barrie's tale, and Disney even annotated the studio copy of Barrie's 1911 novel *Peter and Wendy*.[7] Visual sources, however, were not so popular among the Disney crowd: Walt Disney avoided attending the play that was criss-crossing the country in 1950 while his animators were hard at work on the cartoon.[8] A brief survey of the major themes that occur across all of these versions of the story will highlight issues central to the Peter Pan narrative and enable us to understand how the Disney film reworks them. These issues include the viability of fantasy as a form of experience; how creative ideas can be represented in textual form; childhood as a point of privileged access to the imagination; the special position of mothers as the adult figures who bridge the worlds of fantasy and daily life; and the complications introduced into fantasies by gender and sexuality. Disney's film incorporates these thematic elements of the Peter Pan intertext but filters them through its own studio culture and perceptions of postwar U.S. culture.

The conjunction of fantasy, nature, and childhood is central to the narrative of Peter Pan, and it appeared first in the stories Barrie exchanged with the Llewelyn Davies boys starting in the summer of 1897. Barrie incorporated some of these tales into *The Little White Bird; or, Adventures in Kensington Gardens* (1902), and it is in the last six chapters of this book that Peter Pan first appears in print. The stress on fairies and babies in these stories was meant to reflect the boys' ages and interests. As they matured, however, new dramatic elements were incorporated into the ongoing tale, including adventures with shipwrecks, pirates, desert islands, and "redskins" prompted by the rental of a lake cottage in Surrey in 1901.[9]

As they had in London, the Llewelyn Davies boys often acted out these scenarios, and to commemorate their dramas, Barrie took a series of photos that he collected in an album called "The Boy Castaways," the first visual representation of the Peter Pan narrative. The book contains many of the pirate adventures seen later in stage and film versions of the tale: Hook makes his first appearance as Captain Swarthy, and Tinker Bell was born from the glow of the lantern lights the boys used in the woods.[10] Barrie continued to rework the tales and in 1904 completed a three-act play, "Peter Pan; or, The Boy Who Wouldn't Grow Up," which included the addition of Wendy, a character modeled after the daughter of another friend. Barrie continued to revise the play during its first year and in subsequent seasons, incorporating the ideas and experiences of the younger Davies boys.[11]

As this brief history demonstrates, "Peter Pan" is not a unitary narrative but one that is dispersed across various textual sites. The disparate texts that constitute "Peter Pan" illustrate the process by which fantasies can be constructed and reworked. That Barrie altered characters and actions to reflect the Davies boys' changing perceptions and experiences foregrounds the process of narrative construction. The texts themselves also reflexively explore the language through which fantasies are represented. As literary historian Leonee Ormond notes, the Darling children employ the syntax and vocabulary of twentieth-century London, but Hook speaks in eighteenth-century phraseology, and the Indians communicate in what would today be seen as a crude parody of pidgin English.[12] Barrie's interventionist narrative voice is also heard in the extensive stage directions, witty asides, and detailed background information that add another level of commentary and humor to the play. Within the film scenario, Barrie uses parenthetical remarks to articulate differences he perceives between the stage and cinema. Thus texts that embody the narrative of Peter Pan highlight the mutability of language and the difficulty of representing fantasy.

Though its history and language dramatize the difficulties adults have in producing fantasies, "Peter Pan" also celebrates children's ability to believe in them. A central trope of "Peter Pan" in all its forms is that childhood represents a moment of privileged access to the imagination. Adults' inability to comprehend Peter and the fantasies he embodies is represented literally as a failure of vision. In the play, adults can't see him; when he knocks their hats off their heads, they think it's a gust of wind. Yet between this world of children who imagine, and adults who cannot see, there are transitional spaces they can share. Mothers, in Barrie's narratives, occupy a unique position. As in the theories of the French psychoanalyst Jacques Lacan, mothers have special access to the world of the imaginary. In contrast to Disney films such as *Snow White* and *Pinocchio*, where mothers are absent, the multiple narratives of "Peter Pan" valorize maternal figures. In the play, both the pirates and the Lost Boys talk about the importance of having mothers. When Hook's pirates make the Lost Boys walk the plank, Wendy calms them by saying that their mothers would want them to die like English gentlemen. And in the end, Peter decides to allow Wendy and her brothers to fly home when he sees the distress their absence is causing their mother.

Though mothers serve as positive models in many ways, gender marks a site of conflict in most of the "Peter Pan" narratives. Neverland is at first defined as the place where "boys" have adventures; girls don't join them until Barrie begins to write the play and adds the character of Wendy. Casting changes during early performances of the play also complicated the gender issue. In the first London production in 1904, actresses played most of the Lost Boys as well as the role of the youngest brother, Michael. One year after the play's debut, however, an actor took over the role of Michael, though the Lost Boys continued to be performed by actresses, with one exception: Slightly was usually played by a male (at one point by Noel Coward). In touring companies outside London, however, the role of Michael sometimes reverted to an actress. It was not until around 1928 that boys began to play the Lost Boys. Peter Pan, of course, was most famously played by actresses, and Nana the dog was usually played by a man.[13]

It is not surprising that a play that exhibits such instability regarding gender should exhibit an equal instability in the realm of sexuality. The actress who originated Peter Pan, Nina Boucicault, was praised for her ability to transcend these thorny issues, and admired because she "obtruded neither sex nor sexlessness."[14] Both the play and the novel portray Peter as existing outside the circuit of sexual desire, oblivious to feelings that even Tinker Bell understands. Jacqueline Rose has argued that the ambiguity surrounding Peter Pan is symbolic of the difficulty adults have in dealing with children's sexuality. Andrew Birkin suggests that the character was for Barrie a way of evading the demands of heterosexuality that may have made him uncomfortable. Descriptions of a middle-aged man showing an interest in young boys and taking them on island adventures may remind today's readers of recent scandals involving pedophilia, and rumors of this kind have also swirled around Barrie. Two of the Davies boys have denied that there were any such problems in their relationship with Barrie, yet the continuing questions about that relationship and others between adult men and young boys demonstrate the sensitivity of this subject.

As this brief survey of the Barrie texts shows, questions about the nature and viability of fantasy, gender roles, and sexual identity are fundamental to the Peter Pan narrative. Barrie's text formed a complex social and cultural matrix even before the Disney studio began its work on the project. Records of various stages of the film's production illustrate how these issues became part of Disney's animated feature and how Disney deployed its particular brand of fantasy to deal with them.

UPDATING A CLASSIC

The Disney studio bought the rights to make an animated version of *Peter Pan* in the late 1930s, but its feature film of the story did not appear until 1953, and the long journey to the screen occurred during a time of economic and aesthetic crisis at Disney. The construction of a new studio in 1940 and the shift to a more efficient, factory-like mode of production reshaped the animators' day-to-day work environment. A bitter 1941 strike led some senior animators to leave the studio and left many who remained suspicious about their employer's motives. Walt and Roy Disney's decision in 1940 to raise funds by issuing public stock brought more outside scrutiny and required more attention to the bottom line. World War II drew the studio away from animation when markets for its cartoons declined. And when Warner Bros. and MGM began winning more animation Oscars than Disney did, the company's doubts about its work increased.[15]

Disney negotiated the purchase of the film rights to *Peter Pan* with both Paramount Studies, which bought them when it produced Brenon's live-action film in 1924, and the estate of James Barrie, who died in September 1937. Barrie had bequeathed the copyright for the play to the Hospital for Sick Children in Great Ormond Street, London; accordingly, Disney thanks the hospital in the opening credits of the film. Disney paid $20,000 in October 1938 for the rights to make an animated version of the tale and announced plans to produce it while the studio was developing *Bambi* and *Pinocchio*.[16] Despite this initial enthusiasm, the studio shuffled the project around on its schedule for several years. In February 1940 Disney announced that *Peter Pan* would follow *Bambi* and *Fantasia*,[17] but by September Disney's attention had turned to *Dumbo* and *The Reluctant Dragon,* and *Peter Pan* had moved to the back burner.[18] When Disney applied to the Securities and Exchange Commission for its stock offering, the studio listed *Peter Pan* as one of the films for which it wanted to raise money, and in November 1941 the company announced that it had stopped work on every other production to concentrate on that film so it would reach the screen in late 1942 or early 1943.[19]

The attack on Pearl Harbor and the United States' declaration of war forced Disney, like other Hollywood studios, to change its plans. The rapidly shifting economic and political circumstances affected the studio's attitude toward animation in several ways. When the United States declared war on the Axis powers, theaters in most of Europe could no longer screen Hollywood films. *Pinocchio* lost money as a result, and *Fantasia* did not recoup its costs on its first run. The studio's 1940 deficit of $120,000 ballooned to $1.2 million by 1942.[20] Though its feature-length cartoons lost money, Disney kept afloat by producing training films and educational shorts, many of which combined animation with live action. Projects for the Navy, Nelson Rockefeller's Office of Inter-American Affairs, the Treasury Department, and the Canadian government absorbed Disney's time and resources.[21] The success of these new ventures, and the loss of money on its animated features, spurred Walt Disney to reevaluate the company's commitment to the latter. Walt Disney had experimented with mixing live-action figures and cartoon characters in his *Alice* series of the 1920s, and continued this work in his films of the immediate postwar period, such as *So Dear to My Heart* and *Song of the South*. During the production of *Peter Pan* the studio was also working on live-action versions of *Treasure Island* and *Robin Hood*. As late as 1950 there was open discussion as to whether *Peter Pan* would be filmed in live-action or as an animated feature.[22]

In September 1943 the Disney studio commissioned a poll from the Audience Research Institute (ARI) to help determine whether it should proceed with *Peter Pan*. Launched by George Gallup in 1937, ARI applied techniques used in political polling to motion picture research. Walt Disney met Gallup while Disney was making films for the Treasury Department and through his distributor RKO, which hired ARI to test public reactions to *Fantasia*.[23] Disney's initial request to ARI on September 10, 1943, reveals that the studio was debating not only whether the film should be animated or live-action, but whether Disney should make it at all, and the fact that Walt Disney asked for outside opinions about one of his films underlines the pressure he was under. The Disney studio asked ARI to study four questions. What kind of interest was there in *Peter Pan* as a Disney film in particular? Would viewers rather see it as an animated film or a live-action feature? And how did public interest in the project compare with interest in "A" pictures from other Hollywood studios? The company also wanted to know which demographic groups liked and disliked live-action and animated films.[24] The survey reflects the increased use of live action in Disney's films and the doubts about the place of animation in its future.

The results of the survey were not encouraging. ARI found that *Peter Pan*'s appeal as a cartoon fell below the average for that of live-action Hollywood films. One-quarter of those surveyed said that they didn't like feature-length cartoons at all. Viewers between the ages of eighteen and thirty expressed the least interest and labeled the story "silly" and "childish." In earlier studies ARI had determined that those between eighteen and thirty accounted for two-thirds of the box office for an average film, so this lack of interest meant that Disney probably would not recoup its costs. ARI's research indicated that there was little enthusiasm for a Disney feature-length cartoon about the story.

As part of its services to clients, ARI offered suggestions for enhancing a film's popularity. One idea it proposed was to modernize the film by using a popular bandleader or composer. Disney asked ARI to study reactions to the music of Irving Berlin, Cole Porter, and Jerome Kern, and ARI added swing bandleader Harry James to the list. Two surveys in November 1943 found that the addition of Harry James boosted interest among women and viewers between the ages of eighteen to thirty by 20 percent, but Cole Porter and Irving Berlin, songwriters associated with the 1920 and 1930s, failed to rouse any enthusiasm.[25] In addition, ARI suggested that Disney hire a screenwriter that adults would recognize, such James Hilton, author of *Goodbye, Mr. Chips* and *Lost Horizon*; the New York satirist Dorothy Parker; or Sally Benson, author of the stories that became *Meet Me in St. Louis*. Though the idea of a Dorothy Parker *Peter Pan* is provocative, ARI's survey found that only Hilton had much name recognition with the public. Only a swing version of *Peter Pan*, then, seemed to draw any interest from the public.

Despite the lack of interest indicated by these surveys, the studio decided to go ahead with production on *Peter Pan* and use ARI's research as an early-warning system about areas that needed attention. A 1943 production file for the film contains a large sheet with two columns listing "negative factors" and "positive factors" drawn from ARI's findings. Under "negatives," the chart notes that only one out of ten people surveyed wanted to see *Peter Pan* as a Disney feature and most said they would prefer a live-action film. Viewers between the ages of twelve and thirty did not like the theme of eternal youth and wanted a more adult romance. Under a much smaller list of "positives," the studio noted that 40 percent of respondents said they liked Disney films in general. So even though there was little evidence that the public wanted to see this particular story as a Disney film, there was still interest in "Disney," and this seems to have been enough for the studio to continue. Drawing from ARI's findings, the studio decided it could offset the story's association with childhood by using popular actors and music and by stressing the comic possibilities of puppy love between Wendy and Peter. More importantly, the studio decided to answer the general doubts about animation head-on, by playing up the greater possibilities for fantasy that cartoons offered compared to the stage.[26] Romance, music, popular actors, and creative animation: these were the elements the studio decided would make a winning combination.

"PLENTY OF ACTION, AND JUST ENOUGH ROMANCE"

The response to ARI's findings reveals that some at least within the studio believed that a Disney *Peter Pan* could still succeed. Yet the issues revealed in the survey reflect production conferences about *Peter Pan* that took place between 1948 and 1952. Records of these meetings reveal how Disney animators and employees at various levels struggled to respond to changing social norms and attitudes toward animation while affirming the value of the Disney style.

One of the enduring traditions of the Disney studio during the 1930s was the production conferences, in which writers, animators, and Walt Disney himself hammered out ideas for the company's short and feature films. These meetings figure prominently in the memoirs of several animators who worked at the studio in that period. Frank Thomas and Ollie Johnston describe conferences as fairly harmonious gatherings where talented professionals formulated the dramatic structures, character types, and visual design that came to characterize Disney animation.[27] Shamus Culhane recalls that Walt Disney dominated these meetings and strove to impart (or impose) his vision of animation.[28] For Leo Salkin and Jack Kinney, production meetings provoked panic, anxiety, and even terror, as colleagues tore apart each other's work.[29] The differences in these accounts reflect each man's position within the studio and the extent to which he shared Walt Disney's goals. Culhane, Kinney, and Salkin eventually left the company, whereas Thomas and Johnston were later canonized as part of the exemplary "Nine Old Men."

Production conferences held in the late 1940s differed from earlier ones in several respects. In the 1930s they were usually informal affairs that included whoever was handy and functioned as a way for Walt Disney and senior animators to train new members of the staff. Beginning in the late 1940s, however, the studio began to organize production conferences more systematically. Using a format ARI developed, participants in these meetings filled out detailed questionnaires, sometimes as long as six or seven pages, giving their opinions of characters, dramatic situations, and individual sequences of the film. In the 1930s, stenographers typed the discussions as they occurred and often found it difficult to capture off-the-cuff remarks. The questionnaires used in the late 1940s enabled the studio to ask very specific questions and keep records of the responses. Walt Disney received typed summaries of the comments so that he could stay informed about the progress on a film during a period when he was often away from the studio and engaged on other projects.

In addition to collecting the reactions of what was called the "critical" group of senior animators, the Disney studio also organized meetings for what it called a "noncritical" group that consisted of junior members of the animation staff—assistants, in-betweeners, and the women from ink and paint—and other studio employees who did not work directly in animation, such as janitors, gardeners, secretaries, and switchboard operators. These noncritical groups helped the studio to get a broader range of reactions to a film. The decision to seek reactions outside of the senior animation staff again reflects ARI's influence. The Institute had begun to organize previews for other studios, selecting audiences who mirrored the demographic composition of the majority of American filmgoers in terms of age, gender, education, income, and place of residence. Disney, however, took a shortcut and decided to invite comments from its own employees, rather than go outside the studio. Executives felt that including both senior and junior staff members would incorporate differences in age and income, and that inviting the ink and paint department, which was all female, would account for gender diversity in the general public.

Disney's twist on ARI's methods makes these conference records valuable for several reasons. First, these documents enable us to track changing views at different levels of the company, and to contrast the senior animators who had been at the studio for a long time and the newer, junior staff members who were not as immersed in the Disney tradition. The meetings also allowed employees who were not normally involved in these early stages of production to participate in a film's development. Second, for the first time in Disney's history, these conferences offered women a chance to express their views on a film while it was in progress. Files on these meetings include memos and scrap paper indicating that the research department worked hard to include an equal number of males and females in the noncritical group. Gender differences thus became inscribed within the process of production itself. Finally, near the end of *Peter Pan*'s production, the studio began to separate the production comments by gender. Thus it becomes possible to study gender differences in reactions to specific characters, dramatic moments, and songs in the film. These records, then, mark one of the few instances when one can study gender differences in responses to a film, in a historical period during which ideas about gender were very much in flux.

The first storyboard conferences on *Peter Pan* began on December 9, 1948, with two meetings, one for a "noncritical" group at 1:30 P.M. and another for a "critical" group at 3:15. Participants were asked to respond to a series of storyboard drawings about the film on a questionnaire that consisted of four open-ended questions: 1. "Please tell us fully and frankly what you thought of the Peter Pan story material." 2. "Do you think that Peter Pan could be made into a good Disney all-cartoon feature? ( ) Yes, ( ) No. Please explain." 3. "Was there anything about the story material that you didn't like?" 4. "Please feel free to make any other remarks that you feel are appropriate at this time."[30] Thirty-seven people filled out forms in the noncritical group, and the list of those attending, though not the comments themselves, was divided by gender.

Judging from the comments, these early storyboards mixed fantasy and live-action elements. Remarks refer to the Barrie book itself being part of the story and discuss the human characteristics of Peter and Tinker Bell. On the whole, the noncritical group didn't like this mixture of live-action and fantasy and felt the film should embrace animation. Like the general public surveyed by ARI, they questioned whether the film would appeal to adults. Many felt that its young protagonists and its roots in a children's book would make adults lose interest. Unlike the general public, however, respondents within the studio felt that *Peter Pan* could be a great animated film because of the possibilities it afforded for humor and fantasy. To illustrate how the project might develop, the noncritical audience referred several times to *Snow White*. They felt that *Peter Pan*'s pirates, fairies, and animals, like the seven dwarves, were "exploitable from every angle." The characters and situations presented at the meeting more than measured up to the Disney standard, they agreed, thus affirming the company's traditions. Records indicate that Roy Disney, Walt's brother, and Gunther Lessing, the studio's attorney, were in the audience for this meeting, which may have influenced these responses.[31]

Though both the noncritical and critical groups felt the project would make a great Disney feature, the animators offered more concrete ideas about how to modernize and update the classic tale. Their suggestions mirror ARI's advice and the 1943 memo about creating a sense of "puppy love" between Wendy and Peter. The critical group recommended that the story crew build up the role of Captain Hook as a way to inject "more guts and fun" into the narrative. One respondent worried that viewers attuned to action cartoons such as the Fleischers' *Superman* series would need more action and adventure. The senior animators also wanted to create a "love and jealousy" angle between Tinker Bell and Wendy to make the film more "modern" and attract adult audiences. The all-male group worried that "Peter can't be a sissy." The female-involved noncritical group, by contrast, felt that Peter's character was becoming too sexual. One member of the noncritical group wrote: "I had a little dislike of the idea of Wendy being emotional about a 'Clark Gable' type. Seems to me that injects a little disturbance of thought in [the] story line. Couldn't she just like Pan as a playmate or as someone who needed care?" This concern was echoed by the senior animators at later meetings, when the critical group expressed that they had gone too far in making the jealousy between Wendy and Tinker Bell too adult, and Tinker Bell too "voluptuous."[32]

Though responses are not divided by gender at this point, the critical group consisted solely of men, and the noncritical group of men and women. It was the latter group that expressed concern about the sexualized nature of the project, while the critical group of male animators worried about Peter's lack of masculinity and the need for "guts" in the narrative. Thus the animators' sense of how to appeal to changing audience tastes came into conflict with the noncritical group's sense of what was appropriate for children and of what constituted a "Disney" film. While the animators wanted to modernize the characters and update the kinds of adventures they had, many in the noncritical group wanted to preserve the "youthful innocence" of the tale they loved.

The next set of comments from the critical and noncritical groups comes three years later, from storyboard meetings held on January 8, 1951. Again, the noncritical group met separately before the critical group and included seventeen women from ink and paint. At this meeting, both groups completed a six-page questionnaire that consisted of twelve questions. In addition to asking their overall feelings and impressions, and what they liked best and least about the story and characters, the questionnaire requested specific comments on seventeen individual sequences from the film and asked respondents to rank particular characters such as the crocodile and the mermaids as excellent, good, fair, or poor. The forms also asked attendees to compare the *Peter Pan* project with the studio's work on *Alice in Wonderland* and *Cinderella* and to offer ideas for gags and voice casting.[33]

During the 1951 storyboard meetings there were points of agreement between the critical and noncritical groups. The majority of both critical and noncritical viewers gave the storyboards a rating of "excellent" and felt the project would appeal to children and adults. "This is just right for Disney," wrote one member of the noncritical group. "Charming, appealing, and excellent," said others. "Plenty of action, and just enough romance," another summed up. But differences between the two groups did emerge. The noncritical group singled out for praise the scenes depicting the flight to Neverland, the comedy between Hook and Smee, and Peter Pan at Skull Rock, though they were divided on the merits of the scenes involving the mermaids, Indians, and Lost Boys. The critical group, on the other hand, was much more negative toward these sequences. Ninety percent of the noncritical group liked the flying scene compared with 68 percent of the critical group, and 75 percent of the noncritical group liked Wendy's arrival in Neverland and the introduction of the Lost Boys compared with only 47 percent of the critical group.

The senior animators often criticized each other's work—an attitude that was encouraged in the studio's quest for quality films—so it is not surprising that they expressed more reservations than the noncritical group toward the storyboards. What roused their enthusiasm, however, were the scenes involving the pirates and Captain Hook. The noncritical group also enjoyed the pirate fights and scenes of the Indians capturing the boys, but their enthusiasm paled by comparison to that of the critical group. Ninety percent of the senior animation staff gave these sequences the highest rating, compared with 70 percent of the noncritical group, and 88 percent of the critical group liked scenes of the Lost Boys being captured by Indians and fighting with the pirates versus 73 percent of the noncritical group. The animators were almost unanimous in their praise of Captain Hook. A follow-up screening for the critical group alone took place five months later, on June 6, 1951, at which the animators looked at both storyboards and "rough reels" showing sequences in animated, black and white film. The critical group responded very positively, with 95 percent rating the material they saw as "excellent." In particular the animators praised three scenes involving Captain Hook: the humorous shaving sequence with Smee, his duel with Peter at Skull Rock, and his tricking Tinker Bell into revealing the location of Peter's hideout.[34]

The next meetings of both the critical and noncritical groups took place nearly one year later, on April 16, 1952, and presented rough cuts of the first twelve sequences of the film. Both groups still felt very positive about what they saw, with 93 percent of the noncritical group and 85 percent of the critical group rating the material "excellent." The critical group was still not satisfied with the flying sequence, the arrival in Neverland, and the treatment of the mermaids, compared with the noncritical group. Both groups equally liked Hook and Smee, and 88 percent of each group gave Hook and the crocodile the highest rating. The two groups also differed in their reactions to some of the characters. The noncritical group gave Wendy the lowest number of "excellent" votes, while the critical group ranked Peter lowest. Only 30 percent of the critical group ranked the treatment of Peter as excellent compared with 72 percent of the noncritical group.[35]

It is interesting to note that the senior animators in the critical group continued to be displeased with the scenes that involved flying, material that the 1943 memo said could define the film as "Disney." The animators also devoted a great deal of time to the mermaid sequence, which was expanded from the brief scene in the book, and the studio shot live-action footage of three women in bathing suits to help the animators capture the movements better. Their continuing dissatisfaction with these scenes reflects their professionalism and desire to craft an imaginative sequence. Card Walker, the marketing executive who organized these screenings, noticed that the junior animators who formed part of the noncritical group also tended to be more negative toward work by their senior colleagues. The men in the junior group often came from clean-up and in-between, he noted, and had strong ideas about the type of cartoons the studio should make. The women in the noncritical group, on the other hand, tended to be more critical toward storyboard material than the critical group, perhaps, Walker thought, because they had a harder time imagining what the drawings would look like when they were animated. When it came to the rough reels, though, the women tended to like everything about the animation, in contrast to their more critical counterparts.[36]

Walker explained the differences he saw in terms of the different professional experiences of each group. To take into account these recurring patterns and maximize the value of these conferences, Walker decided to divide the remarks of the noncritical group by gender, separating the male junior animators (and other male employees) from the women in ink and paint (and other female employees). Though Walker decided to do this to uncover the differences in the professional opinions of each group, he inadvertently makes it possible to analyze the reactions of these employees by gender. It becomes possible to compare each group's remarks to the senior animators' assumptions about gender preferences and to prevailing gender norms of the time, to see whether this audience of employees reinforced or departed from gender stereotypes.

On June 17, 1952, the studio held another screening of eighteen sequences of rough animation for the noncritical group and divided their comments by gender. The remarks of this group do not line up along traditional gender lines. The women criticized scenes of the pirates fighting, but so did the men. Both groups enjoyed the song "Your Mother and Mine," but the men mentioned it more often in their comments. The greatest disparities in the comments seemed to be, as Walker noted, a result of the differences in their professional roles. As in previous screenings, the males in the noncritical group gave low marks to work relating to their senior colleagues while the women were more enthusiastic. The scenes involving flying, for example, earned highest marks from nearly all of the women but only two-thirds of the men. Both groups disliked the treatment of the Indian characters, though 57 percent of the women praised them compared with only 17 percent of the men. Captain Hook, however, won nearly unanimous praise from both groups. In general, the men in the noncritical group were much more negative toward their senior colleagues in every area compared with the women, but this reflects their place in the studio hierarchy more than their gender.

A shift away from conventional gendered responses continues through the final meeting of the noncritical group on September 9, 1952. Forty-six men and women assessed eighteen sequences presented on rough reels and in some color footage; their comments were again divided by gender in the typed summary. Though the women are still more positive overall about the material than are their male colleagues, the men show much more enthusiasm for the work of their senior colleagues than they did in June. Twice as many males in the second survey enjoyed the scenes of Wendy going home and the song "Your Mother and Mine." Interestingly, Wendy at this screening fell out of favor with the women, who criticized the quality of the drawing, but gained noticeably with the men: 84 percent gave her character a rating of excellent this time, compared with 62 percent in June. Women still rated the character of the Indian Chief more highly than the men did (81% vs. 47%), but liked the pirate crew less than did the men (48% vs. 74%). This was the first screening where the women were not as enthusiastic as their male colleagues about Captain Hook: 79 percent of the men gave him the highest rating versus 63 percent of the women. In general the men were more positive about the action and adventure elements than were the women, but the women still liked many of them, and while the women tended to prefer scenes emphasizing children and home, the men enjoyed them as well.[37]

What we see broadly is men and women moving closer together in their preferences. The process of adaptation at Disney thus emerges as one of negotiation, in which each group comes at least to acknowledge the interests of the other. A "successful" film, by this system, is one that permits multiple points of identification, in which viewers can cross traditional gender boundaries in their enjoyment of the film. Though *Peter Pan's* narrative presents characters that conform to gender stereotypes, the men and women in the audience do not accept these easy divisions. The film is considered successful when it retains the elements that elicited positive reactions from women and adds more that the men liked. In this case, both groups liked elements of the pirates and Indian characters, and the men began to like Wendy and the themes of mother and home as well. The ideal film in this scenario is one in which both genders find elements to enjoy.

One of the distinguishing features of the noncritical group is that it included women. A large contingent of this group was from the ink and paint department, who the senior animation staff sometimes described as "pure and clean." From the beginning, the noncritical audiences enjoyed the framing scenes in the film—the images of family life at Mr. and Mrs. Darling's home that surround and contain the fantasy sequences in Neverland. In later versions of the storyboards, the ideal of the nuclear family begins to permeate the fantasy scenes as well. Wendy, no longer a temptress, becomes a nurturing maternal figure. Scenes of her reading a bedtime story to the Lost Boys, and the addition of the song "Your Mother and Mine," reinforce her association with a sexless domesticity. Despite their adventures, the Lost Boys acknowledge that they are missing something, something Wendy labels "home." The fact that the noncritical group liked the family sequences from the beginning suggests these elements may have been expanded to accommodate the desires of these women.

One might argue, then, that the action scenes were created to please the male animators in the critical group, and the scenes of the family and the depiction of Wendy as a maternal figure were meant to soothe the women in the noncritical audience. Walt Disney himself probably shared these stereotypes. In a 1956 interview with his biographer, Pete Martin, he described his views of audience preferences. "The males don't go for sentimental things . . . they go more for vigorous action or excitement or big belly laughs or scientific things or mechanics. The females always go for the personalities, the little sentimental things, for the beauty in it and it never fails. All the women love this—the man is bored with it."[38] Yet when we examine the last two conferences, this is not the case. While it is true that the women in the noncritical group responded strongly to the elements involving mothers and children, so did the men, and the women also liked the pirates and Indian characters. Rather than break down along rigid gender lines, the remarks in these production transcripts show that both groups came to share common interests.

TICK TOCK

ARI's surveys and the studio's own in-house studies reveal an anxiety about whether Disney animation would continue to appeal to postwar audiences and a new generation of filmgoers. The studio's initial strategy for "updating" Barrie's play involved adding suggestions of a romance between Peter and Wendy and making Tinker Bell's feminine attributes more explicit. The animators also decided to enhance the elements of adventure and comedy in the pirate scenes and to exploit the possibilities of animation wherever possible. Though Disney's *Peter Pan* does not feature a musical score by Cole Porter or instrumentation by Harry James, it does include original songs by contemporary composers that extend emotional moments in the text. As a postwar creation by a major media company, the film clearly reaffirms traditional values of home and family, while creating a space in which fantasies of adventure can be entertained.

The first few minutes of the animated *Peter Pan* anchor the film firmly within the Disney tradition. The opening image of a night sky and twinkling star recall the beginning of *Pinocchio* and that film's theme of making dreams come true. The members of the Darling family also resemble other

Disney characters. Mrs. Darling appears first, and her voice, face, hairstyle, and movements immediately recall Disney's Cinderella, as if the star of Disney's earlier feature had grown up to become Wendy's mother. Wendy looks like a younger version of Cinderella, and Nana the dog becomes entangled in the children's toys in ways that recall the antics of Pluto.

In contrast to Barrie's characters, Disney's live comfortably. The play introduces the Darlings in an almost offhand way, placing their house in "a rather depressed street in Bloomsbury," but adding "you may dump it down anywhere you like."[39] The male voiceover that introduces the Disney film, however, speaks with assurance. "All this has happened before. And it will all happen again. But this time it happened in London. It happened on a quiet street in Bloomsbury. That corner house over there is the home of the Darling family." Though Barrie describes the color of the Darling house as looking as if "it had been sprayed on by a hose," the house in the Disney film is part of a well-maintained upper-middle-class neighborhood. Barrie also emphasizes the shabbiness of the children's nursery and how hard Mrs. Darling worked to fix it up, "with nails in her mouth and a paste-pot in her hand." Having the dog Nana as the children's nursemaid serves as further proof of their limited means in the play. "The Darlings could not afford to have a nurse, they could not afford indeed to have children; and now you are beginning to understand how they did it."[40] The family in the film, however, experiences no such financial difficulties. Disney's Darlings live securely in their world.

In contrast to the Barrie texts, Disney's film creates firmer boundaries between the world of the imagination and the world of everyday life. Barrie's play includes a sequence of role reversals, in which the boys play at being their parents and present each other as babies; but in Disney's film the parents remain resolutely adult and do not cross over into childish fantasies. The children in the film play at being pirates, anticipating the scenes to come, but their antics are clearly framed as childish behavior, while the grown-ups go about their business. In the play Mrs. Darling herself sees Peter Pan come into the nursery and leave his shadow behind, and she rolls it up and puts it in the drawer; in the film it is Wendy who does this, and when she tells her mother about it, Mrs. Darling treats her murmurings as the dreams of someone half asleep. The animated Mrs. Darling believes in Peter Pan, but not as much as her children do, and Mr. Darling rejects the whole notion of a boy who can fly. In Disney's film the father of the family is grumpy and bumbling, but Barrie portrays him more sympathetically, saying that "he is really a good man as breadwinners go."[41] His decision to banish Nana outside, which makes it possible for Peter Pan to return, Barrie portrays as a vain attempt to reassert control when he thinks the children love the dog more than him. In the film Mr. Darling is also portrayed comically, as a man with a treasure chest drawn on his waistcoat, but he is determined to make his children grow up. Disney's father reprimands Wendy for "stuffing the boys' heads with silly stories" and declares Peter Pan to be "absolute poppycock." He tells Wendy that this is her "last night in the nursery" and puts Nana outside so that she, too, will learn that, "The children aren't puppies, they're people. And sooner or later, Nana, people have to grow up." The father in the play descends to the children's level when he tries to avoid taking his medicine, but Disney's father is resolutely grown up, and wants everyone else to grow up, too.

The film's introduction of Peter Pan exemplifies Walt Disney's belief that animation could illuminate the possibilities of Barrie's texts. We first see the nursery from outside a window where the window shade is pulled down part way and the family is shown in half-shadow. This theme of seeing and invisibility recurs when Peter first becomes visible standing on the rooftop, silhouetted against the moonlit sky, then again when he chases his shadow across the nursery, cavorting in ways that are not possible on stage. It is when the children fly, however, that the possibilities of animation are most fully realized. This sequence was one of the main reasons Barrie wanted to film the story. In his scenario Barrie indicated that he wanted the screen version of the tale to open with a scene of Peter flying through the woods, and that "the flying must be far better and more elaborate than in the acted play."[42] In the play the children practice flying in the room, bumping into the ceiling and each other, before the stage directions say that they fly "out of the window over the trees of the square and over the house-tops." In the film, their flight forms an extended sequence that is heightened by a song and by choral music on the soundtrack. On Peter's advice, the children "think of a wonderful thought" and then he sprinkles them with pixie dust: "All it takes is faith and trust, and something I forgot . . . just a little bit of pixie dust." As they launch out the window and into the sky, the soundtrack swells with "you can fly you can fly, you can fly." We see them circle the chimney and zoom in and out of the window in a celebration of being unfettered. Even Nana joins in when Michael sprinkles pixie dust on her and she rises as high as her leash allows. The children take off over London, landing on the hour hand of Big Ben and then soaring over St. Paul's and London Bridge.

The flight to Neverland lasts five minutes in the film—7 percent of its 75-minute running time—compared with a one-and-a-half page description in the play, or just under two percent of that text. The time and care devoted to this sequence underscores the crucial role it plays in celebrating the possibilities of animation and the opportunities cartoons offer to celebrate the freedom and joy of childhood. Disney also creates a new

6.1 The Darling children led by Peter Pan soar past Big Ben on their way to Neverland. Courtesy of Jerry Ohlinger's Movie Material Store.

iconography for *Peter Pan* in the moment when he and the children line up along the minute hand of Big Ben. This image does not appear in any of Barrie's texts, of course, but Disney made it famous by using it in studio publicity and photos that accompanied many newspaper reviews.[43] The shot of Big Ben is one that many viewers think is emblematic of the story, and Disney invented it. This image and the ones that follow it of Saint Paul's and London Bridge also create a view of London that is more specific that Barrie's description, a tourist's sense of what matters in the city.

The film continues to play with perspective in the scenes that take place in Neverland. We first see the island that Peter and the Lost Boys inhabit in an aerial perspective that would not be possible on stage, and as Wendy hurtles toward the ground the perspective shifts rapidly in ways that are only possible on film. As in the play, Tinker Bell tells the Lost Boys that Peter wants them to shoot "the terrible Wendy bird," but instead her fall offers an opportunity for Peter to catch Wendy and hold her momentarily, in a pose that was used in publicity stills. Tinker Bell turns red with jealousy and sets a leaf on fire with her anger, in a scene employing color and close-up only possible in film. Instead of building Wendy a house, as they do in the play, the Lost Boys set off with Wendy's brothers "to capture some Indians," marching through the jungle vegetation like the seven dwarfs going off to the mine. Their foray offers additional opportunities for gags; they slip on the rocks and use each other as planks to ford the river. When the Indians instead capture them and march the boys back to their camp, the music that accompanied the boys at the beginning of their trek is reprised in a squeaky style that mocks their supposed bravery.

The scenes with the Indians around the campfire are uncomfortable to watch today, as the Indian characters speak in broken English and claim that they are "red" because of the first Indian prince who blushed when he kissed a maiden. The scene was clearly intended to appeal to children caught up in the television craze for Westerns, and depicts Michael, John, and even Wendy garbed in headbands and feathers. In this sequence the Disney studio presents its own take on the kinds of adventures children enjoyed in other media and expands them with the music and color that are possible on film.

In the play the Lost Boys and the pirates are distinguished as individuals; they have names, ages, and family histories. Barrie's descriptions of the boys refer to the Davies children and were meant to evoke their shared experiences.[44] In Disney's film, however, the boys and the pirates are part of a crowd, and most of the attention focuses on Captain Hook. Disney elides the scenes where the boys discuss their families and life with Peter and concentrates instead on a long sequence in which Smee, a pirate who resembles several of the seven dwarves, shaves what he thinks is Hook's face but is really a seabird. Nothing resembling this sequence appears in any of the Barrie texts, but it is classic Disney, with the nearsighted Smee shaving the bird's behind until it squawks and flies off, and then, fearing that he has cut off Hook's head, dragging Hook around the ship until he realizes his mistake. In the play Hook talks with Smee about his fear of the crocodile, and the voracious animal is introduced simply. "It is a tick, tick as of a clock, whose significance Hook is, naturally, the first to recognize. 'The crocodile!' he cries, and totters from the scene. Smee follows. A huge crocodile, of one thought compact, passes across, ticking, and oozes after them."[45] Disney elaborates their encounter, with the full resources of animation. As Smee and Hook discuss the crocodile and the clock, the music begins to play in synchronization with the movements of what we gradually realize is the subject of their discussion. The crocodile's eyes rise above the level of the water as the tick-tock creates the kind of mickey-mousing effect that Disney invented in the 1930s. Captain Hook becomes undone when he hears the ticking and jumps on Smee's back, completely undercutting the dashing image he has tried so hard to project.

6.2 Captain Hook and Smee confront the hungry crocodile. Courtesy of Jerry Ohlinger's Movie Material Store.

The animators also expand the later encounters between Hook and the twin threats, Peter and the crocodile. When Peter frees Tiger Lily from Skull Rock he teases and taunts Hook, turning somersaults in the air that seem to defy the law of gravity. When Hook falls into the water, there is another comic sequence in which he jumps out of the animal's gaping jaws over and over again as the crocodile chases him into the sunset. The speed and agility of the characters, the humorous repetition of the movements,

and the tight synchronization of image and sound all vividly illustrate animation's possibilities. Similarly, the confrontation at the end of the film
between Peter and Hook on the ship is a tour-de-force of cinematic techniques: rapid editing, multiple and constantly shifting perspectives of the
ship, the ropes, and the deck; characters leaping and flying; and the music
synchronized with each of them. In the play much of the action takes place
inside a cabin, an offstage space, and the dramatic climax of the fight is
achieved largely through sound effects. Here again the animators celebrate
the possibility of their craft.

One of the elements that distinguishes Disney's *Peter Pan* is the extent
to which Hook is repositioned as the center of the narrative, displacing, or
at least competing with, Peter as the locus of interest. Initially the favorite
of the senior animators, he came to be beloved by the rest of the studio
employees and continues to draw attention today. In Thomas and Johnston's
Disney Animation: The Illusion of Life, the "bible" of Disney animation, there
are thirteen references to the film in the index and seven to Hook. Like
Peter, Hook's sexuality is ambiguous. While he is male, he is characterized
as an eighteenth-century fop, with long curly hair and a long waistcoat,
qualities that make him seem effeminate. His wooden arm signifies physical limitation, even emasculation, and his crude efforts to bully the boys
and torment Tinker Bell mark him as someone who does not know how to
wield power effectively. In some versions of the play, the actor who played
Hook also played the children's father, Mr. Darling, and this casting choice
was seen to deliberately undermine the idea of the patriarch. In the play
Barrie describes him as "sinister and grim," but he is neither of these things
in the film.[46] Thus, the character of Captain Hook mocks masculinity, but
in a comic and exaggerated way. At the same time, Hook is a pirate, a figure with historical referents who has nevertheless graduated to the status of
legend. The pirate life of adventure on the high seas underscores the possibilities of the imagination. Like Peter, Hook illustrates the power of fantasy,
and it took animation to bring him fully to life. In creating him, Disney
affirmed the viability of its own traditions.

WOMAN TROUBLE

The character of Peter Pan occupies an unstable position in a binary
system of gender. This difficulty is also displayed during the production of
Disney's film, in which Peter becomes a "problem" in narrative construction and character development. For the animators, the "problem" with
Peter was his sexual ambiguity, and the nature of his relationships with
Wendy and Tinker Bell. Crafton notes that this issue arose very early in
the film's production. In a November 1938 memo discussing James Barrie's

novel, story analyst Dorothy Blank urged that, "'we remove forever any doubts about sex, and make our hero all boy—fun, fierce, brave and a little tough."[47] In 1946 Walt Disney told Hedda Hopper that he found the character of Peter "too sugary" for modern tastes and planned on "toughening him up a bit, making him a real boy."[48] Several years later, he went further, saying that "it's been traditional for a girl to play the part of Peter on stage, but we're making him a real boy, using Bobby Driscoll to supply the voice and bringing the dialog more down to earth."[49] In the comments at the production conferences this issue surfaces again and again. From the first storyboard meetings, the senior animators expressed concern that Peter not be "a sissy." Later they congratulate one another for making him "less effeminate." In most of their responses he is usually referred to as "Pan." In the first rough animation screenings the critical group of senior animators rates his character lower than any other character in the film.[50] A lost boy who is described as having a "tough voice" scores higher.

The film presents Peter as a nonchalant young teenager who seems oblivious to any possibility of romance between himself and the female characters of Wendy and Tinker Bell. In contrast to Barrie's Peter, who seems too childish and naïve to know the difference between a thimble and a kiss, Disney's Peter would rather move on to the next adventure than dwell on such things. Barrie describes Peter as being made of "autumn leaves and cobwebs,"[51] but Disney's character is a young teenage boy with red hair and a voice showing the effects of puberty. Bobby Driscoll, who supplies Peter's voice in the film, was fifteen when he recorded the dialogue, and was known to Disney fans through his appearance as Jim Hawkins in Disney's live-action *Treasure Island* (1950) and starring roles in the animation/live-action combinations of *So Dear to My Heart* (1948) and *Song of the South* (1946). Driscoll was nine years old when he performed the role of the young boy in *Song of the South*, eleven when he played the child in *So Dear*, and thirteen in *Treasure Island*, so audiences watched him grown up on screen before he took the role of Peter. This Peter is not a boy but a young man; he introduces himself to Wendy but skips the play's detailed biography of growing up with the fairies. Rather than beginning a romance, this Peter seems indifferent to girls in general and just wants her to come to Neverland to entertain him. In the play Peter flatters Wendy and makes her feel needed; in the film he seems merely to think it would be amusing to have her around.

These efforts to enhance Peter's manhood also affected the initial construction of the characters of Wendy and Tinker Bell. Though Crafton suggests that Wendy's sexuality is the central issue in the film, transcripts from these production conferences reveal that decisions about how to handle her

6.3 A sexualized Tinker Bell checks her image in the mirror. Courtesy of Jerry Ohlinger's Movie Material Store.

character were part of the spillover from Peter's development. To shore up Peter's "lack," the animators/critical group decided to add suggestions of a romance between Peter and Wendy. In addition, the character of Tinker Bell was made more explicitly sexual. From the first moment we see her, she is exaggeratedly feminine: she checks herself in a mirror, pats her blond updo and fusses over the size of her hips. Critics praised Disney's characterization: *Newsweek* described her as "a particularly endearing little vixen compounded of blond hair, feminine curves, and a pout" who was "just a little too bosomy to squeeze through an oversize keyhole,"[52] while *Time* found her to be "a little vamp . . . who flits about enchantingly with a silvery tinkle of bells in a sprinkle of golden pixie dust."[53] Critics compared Tinker Bell to Betty Boop, Zsa Zsa Gabor, and Carol Channing. *Variety* argued that the Disney film was the first to bring Tinker Bell to a more complete visual form.[54] Herbert Brenon, the director of the 1924 Paramount film, praised Disney's portrayal as well, saying that, "That was something we had to do with just a light on the end of a wire. Cartoon is the ideal medium for portraying the role."[55]

The jealousy Tinker Bell feels for Wendy motivates Hook's scheme to destroy Peter. "A jealous female can be tricked to do anything," he says. After persuading Smee to kidnap her and bring her to the ship, Hook manipulates Tinker Bell into revealing Peter's whereabouts by playing on her sympathies. He accuses Peter of "taking the best years of her life. Casting her aside. Like an old glove" as he twirls his mustache in a parody of silent film melodramas. The scene is followed by one in which Wendy persuades the boys to return home by reminding them of their mother's love, in the song "Your Mother and Mine." Even Smee, who is waiting to kidnap the boys, begins to cry and reveals a tattoo of "Mother" on his belly. After the pirates capture the boys, Hook lowers a bomb into Peter's hideaway. Later, on the ship, Hook narrates the tale and we see Peter reading the inscription on the box containing the bomb and then the bomb inside the box, through a dissolve. Tinker Bell saves him, not from desire, but from a sense of loyalty and affection that Wendy recalled for the boys. What began as an effort to shore up Peter's sexuality ends as an affirmation of friendship and family.

TAILORED FOR THE MODERN GENERATION

The animators who produced *Peter Pan* recognized that the late 1940s and early 1950s marked a time of transition in public tastes. Their approach to characters such as Peter, Tinker Bell, and Captain Hook and the film's emphasis on scenes of humor and adventure represent a conscious effort to update the Disney style to appeal to a new generation of children and to adults adjusting to postwar culture. The film's depiction of gender and sexuality also reflects contemporary popular attitudes. Like the animators, critics responded to *Peter Pan* within the context of a changing era. Some applauded the film's efforts to update Barrie's classic tale and thought it represented a fresh, modern approach, while others mourned what they felt was a loss of innocence. Looking at the critical and popular reception of the film reveals viewers' shifting attitudes toward the Disney style, animation in general, children's entertainment, and Walt Disney himself.

Peter Pan was a huge success at the box office, and the studio credited the film with increasing its revenue more than 10 percent over the previous year.[56] At 8 A.M. on opening day at the Roxy theater in New York, the ticket line extended down the street, and 17,500 people saw the film by late afternoon.[57] In Washington, D.C., the film played for nine weeks at the Keith, two weeks longer than *Cinderella*, and a record for that theater.[58] *Peter Pan* was one of the U.S. entries at the 1953 Cannes Film Festival, along with *Call Me Madam* and Alfred Hitchcock's *I Confess*, and it played alongside Henri-Georges Clouzet's *Le Salaire de la Peur* (*The Wages of Fear*) and Jacques Tati's *Les Vacances de Monsieur Hulot* (*Mr. Hulot's Holiday*). The festival jury celebrated Walt Disney's involvement by awarding him a special prize "for the prestige he once more brings to the festival."[59]

Placing *Peter Pan* in the context of other films of the period helps us to understand its cultural significance and interpret critics' reactions. For many, Disney's film reaffirmed traditional values in film and in life. *Peter Pan* was released and reviewed at the same time as *The Bad and the Beautiful* (dir: Vincente Minnelli) and *Moulin Rouge* (dir: John Huston) and screened in major cities during the same period as Chaplin's *Limelight*, Jerry Lewis and Dean Martin's *The Stooge*, and John Ford's *The Quiet Man*, and *High Noon*. Newspaper columnist and TV host Ed Sullivan praised the Disney film as a wholesome contrast to more adult works because it featured "wit as opposed to smut."[60] For others, *Peter Pan* served as a reminder of the value of established filmmaking styles at a time when widescreen technologies such as Cinerama and Cinemascope had begun to appear. In New York, *Peter Pan* played at the same time as and within a few blocks of *Bwana Devil*, the first feature-length stereoscopic film.[61] Some critics weren't convinced that these new technologies would last and praised *Peter Pan* as an example of the "good old flatties" whose appeal would endure.[62] Seen in the context of other releases of the period, Disney's film served to reinforce traditional values and ways of representing imagined worlds on film.

Peter Pan also appeared on U.S. screens during a moment when babies and children were at the forefront of the news: press screenings took place during the week that Lucille Ball gave birth to her first child on *I Love Lucy*.[63] Several films released at the same time as *Peter Pan* explored the change from childhood to adolescence in more somber ways. Carson McCuller's *The Member of the Wedding*, with Julie Harris and Ethel Waters, and George Stevens's *Shane* portrayed older children who were beginning to see and understand the complexity of adulthood. *Theatre Arts* reviewed *Peter Pan* along with Rene Clement's *Forbidden Games*, which used a documentary style to tell the story of a little girl who saw both her parents die during the Nazi invasion of Paris. Disney's film suffered in the comparison, with Peter Pan seeming like a "brawny, if very cavalier, boy scout in mufti" when put next to the life-and-death situations of Clement's film.[64]

Most critics, however, praised Disney's efforts to update Barrie. They felt that the world had grown up and that it was time Peter Pan did, too. *Newsweek* argued that "the time has come, in the opinion of many people who have gotten around to growing up, when Barrie's determinedly elfin whimsies could benefit from a healthy dose of Disney's broad comedy."[65] *Commonweal* quoted the film's own words: "Whilst this Peter Pan goes out of its way to make it clear that sooner or later everyone has to grow up, it also makes clear that this fantasy really happened and will no doubt happen again."[66] Several writers noted that the film aimed at a more "modern" audience and praised the decision to tell the story with "a minimum of sentiment and a maximum of lively action."[67] *Variety* praised "the constant buzz of action and comedy" and *Time* the feeling of "pell-mell adventure."[68] Critics also admired Disney's updating of the character of Peter. "For once," said *Newsweek*, "Peter Pan is played by a boy . . . rather than by such fraudulent, if beguiling, facsimiles as Miss Adams, Betty Bronson, etc."[69] *Variety* applauded Peter's enhanced masculinity: "Gone are feminine curves that have predominated in previous interpretations of Peter Pan, and it is a change for the better."[70] Manny Farber complained that Wendy's brothers should have been more manly, too. Michael and John were "sissified," he felt, and gave the feeling that "someone has pinned the sign 'Kick Me' on the back of each one."[71] And most liked Disney's visualization of Tinker Bell as well, comparing her with Carol Channing and Marilyn Monroe.[72]

While many praised the general modernization of Barrie, critics were divided about the effect of filming the story in animated form. *Library Journal* complained that "the delicious tomfoolery of the book's dialogue has lost color or has omitted it entirely in favor of the broad familiar comedy of animation."[73] Disney's caricature of Captain Hook met with mixed reactions. *Films in Review* praised Disney's depiction of the crocodile and the studio's addition of the scenes involving the Indians, but said the film made Captain Hook more of a buffoon than a comic character with elements of pathos. "Disney seems to eschew the subtler points of human frailty. It has to be slapstick, bump-your-head, fall down, see stars."[74] Bosley Crowther, the influential critic for the *New York Times*, felt that Disney did not trust its audience to appreciate the subtleties of Barrie's story. He criticized the film for eliminating the famous scene in which Peter Pan asks the audience to clap if they believe in fairies. "Perhaps these eliminations were prompted by a belief that present-day adults and children are more literal than they were in Barrie's time. Perhaps they were due to some anxiety that the mention of pixiness in the modern American movie theatre might provoke some embarrassment. And it may also be that Mr. Disney and his artists, for all their craft and skill, are still a wee bit unresponsive where the delicacies of whimsy are concerned."[75]

Others, however, felt that Barrie's creative genius had finally been realized. "Thanks to the wizardry of the animated cartoon, Peter no longer needs to be a fragile girl hoisted around a stage on wires. The crocodile who ticked, Captain Hook, and Nana the nurse with the big ears and soulful eyes, need not be awkwardly contrived. They can and do perform any feat demanded by the author's imagination with the greatest of ease."[76] Nearly everyone applauded the flying sequence and recognized, as Barrie had in his

1920 film scenario, that it proved the creative possibilities of cinema. The *Monthly Film Bulletin* said that "because in this story so many of the characters fly, as we fly in dreams; and since the movement in cartoons must be so much faster than in life, this flying satisfies us far more than the usual whizzing earthbound chases of beasts and humans" and *Newsweek* added that "Disney's fantasy, unhampered by the limitations of an earthbound stage or screen, is truly airborne and magical."[77]

Critics easily recognized the qualities that marked *Peter Pan* as a Disney production but were divided as to whether that improved or marred the tale. Crowther enumerated the similarities between Michael and Smee and the seven dwarfs, and the *Washington Post* listed specific gags repeated from the Silly Symphonies: "the open bureau drawer, the objects falling on people's heads."[78] Several writers analyzed the changes in Disney's visual style and drew contrasts with earlier films. Farber noted that "the film intermittently tries out a new drawing style and a more hectic type of animation and timing" that he identified as one of caricature. "In place of the ovular features and symmetrical rhythms that make Peter and friends so insipid, Disney draws his pirates and crocodiles with an angular, hacking, cutlass stroke, and he puts the frenzy of a Widmark gangster into the personalities."[79] For Parker Tyler, the combination of visual styles in the film didn't work. Wendy and her mother resembled paper dolls, he felt, while her brothers and the Lost Boys were drawn like comic strip characters. "Though just as ingenious in terms of movement," he wrote, the Disney style "is now less beautiful than ever because so inconsistent."[80] In London, *Peter Pan* debuted at the same time as the Mr. Magoo cartoon *The Dog Snatcher,* and *Sight and Sound* found that Disney suffered greatly in the comparison. "As expected, Disney brings to Barrie's fairy tale his comic strip mind and sentimental vulgarity. The result is Superman—or Super-Pan. The mistiness, the rather dowdy fantasy, are lost; a not very convincing romp with Indians, pirates, etc. remains. . . . Disney has done this sort of thing so often before, and with more style."[81]

During production on the film, Walt Disney was engaged with many other projects, including several live-action features set in England and a new series of nature films. But studio publicity for *Peter Pan* portrayed him as being just as involved with this production as he had been with earlier films. *Peter Pan*'s release gave rise to a new wave of manufactured histories that positioned Walt as still being the center of the studio and linked his personal story not only with those of his characters but with American culture as a whole. During the month of *Pan*'s release *McCall's* magazine published an essay under the name of Lillian Disney, Walt's wife, titled "I Live with a Genius," that portrayed Walt as being like Peter Pan in his enduring youthfulness and vivid imagination.[82] The year of *Peter Pan*'s release also marked the twenty-fifth anniversary of Mickey Mouse's first screen appearance in *Steamboat Willie*. Studio publicity often spoke of Mickey and Walt as "maturing" together, and this was also the theme of the February 8, 1953, episode of Ed Sullivan's *Toast of the Town* television show, which surveyed Disney's career since Mickey's debut. As Sullivan described it, the story of Walt Disney was the story of both animation history and the American dream. "The Disney story is a classic of courage and imagination, of character and amazing craftsmanship. Luck and privilege are in it nowhere at all."[83] Not only did Walt Disney's life and work exemplify enduring American values, his popularity went beyond national borders. A Chicago critic gushed that while he watched the Sullivan show he "could not help but think that [Disney] appeals to all races, all nations, all colors. Possibly Walt Disney is THE Hollywood name that may outlast all others. Last night his work looked as if it would appeal to all ages and perhaps thruout all time."[84] We can see in the publicity surrounding *Peter Pan* the active process by which Disney became "timeless" and universal": not just because of qualities inherent in his films, but because of a publicity machine that created this image of him and his work.

HAIRCUTS AND TREASURE HUNTS

Merchandising has been a crucial part of the Disney empire since the 1920s, but with *Peter Pan* it took a quantum leap forward. The general sales manager of RKO, Disney's distributor, told the *Hollywood Reporter* that "in all his years in the industry he had never seen anything that even approached in scope the *Peter Pan* campaign."[85] As the film went into release, there were 661 manufacturers in twenty-three countries licensed to sell products with Disney characters, including ninety in the United States. *Business Week* pegged Disney's annual gross on licensed merchandise at $100 million in the United States and Canada alone.[86] The campaign for *Peter Pan* represented a big chunk of this activity. Fifty-two manufacturers signed licensing deals as part of a $25 million merchandising and tie-in campaign.[87] The merchandise included everything from matching aprons for girls and their dolls; a wooden Peter Pan toy on which children could push a button and watch him duel, bend, and twist; a Tinker Bell pinafore with real bells; hand puppets of Hook and Peter; and of course, peanut butter.[88] Looking at some of these items more closely reveals how the Disney studio helped create and also benefited from the baby boom of this period. The links its merchandise created between youth and a culture of consumption remain a cornerstone of the company's strategies today.

In the postwar era, the toy industry was one of the fastest-growing parts of the American economy. Before World War II Americans spent about $200 million on toys in a banner year, but in 1953, they spent four times that amount. *Nation's Business* argued that this was not just due to inflation, because even when the birth rate rose by 20 percent, toy sales surged by 200 percent. The magazine pointed to three factors to explain this change: Americans were more willing to indulge their children; toys could be bought year-round, and not just in toy stores; and kids wanted the merchandise featuring their favorite TV and film characters. Disney, the magazine argued, led the field because all of its merchandise got free advertising every time children saw one of its cartoons.[89] *Business Week* concurred, describing Disney and *Peter Pan* as the "juggernaut" of 1953.[90] Its analysis pointed to another reason for Disney's popularity with toy manufacturers, one that Richard deCordova has noted in his work on Mickey Mouse. Most toy companies produced toys for the Christmas season only, but Disney merchandise promised year-round sales. "He offers them smash one-shot promotions, like *Peter Pan*, then keeps them going between features with the steady, persistent Donald Duck group."[91] Disney merchandise even helped smooth out the ups and downs of industrial production.

In 1953, as today, the Disney studio maximized the synergistic possibilities of its films. The release of each new animated feature was accompanied by book and record tie-ins aimed at both children and their parents. For *Peter Pan*, the studio released a "Story Book" featuring characters from the film that reached number 12 on the *New York Times* bestseller list of children's books.[92] A "Little Nipper" Story Book album appeared even before *Peter Pan*'s release, in time for Christmas 1952. As proof of both the popularity and quality of Disney merchandise, the 45 and 78 rpm record of the film's songs cost three times as much as other children's albums from RCA, including those with Captain Video and Kukla, Fran and Ollie. Other tie-ins helped support Disney's fledgling ventures into television. One toy featured a wind-up television set with pictures from *Peter Pan* on its pretend screen.[93] The Admiral Corporation, which manufactured TV and radio sets, promoted the film with coloring books and play sets. Children who brought their parents into the store for a demonstration of Admiral products received a toy television studio in return.[94] The animated feature, then, also served to promote Disney's newest ventures beyond the cinema and prepared children to be eager viewers of the *Disneyland* TV show.

The Admiral Corporation's strategy of linking their adult product with Disney's film turned children into young consumers who would in turn spur their parents to consume. Other Disney strategies turned entire childhood events into promotional opportunities. A June 1952 market analysis prepared for the Disney studio by the Chester LaRoche agency recommended that Disney work with parents' and women's magazines to promote *Peter Pan.*[95] The March 1953 issues of *Women's Home Companion* featured an article telling mothers how to "Give Them a Peter Pan Treasure-Hunt Party." The how-to list of pointers suggested asking guests to dress up as a character from the film; sending maps of the host's house and neighborhood in the form of a pirate map; and dividing the children into teams of Crocodiles and Indians to search for the treasure. Suggested refreshments included "Mermaid Nectar" (orange juice or a fruit cup), Wendy's homemade sandwiches, Treasure Chest cake, or Hidden Treasure Meatloaf. The party favors would be Peter Pan toys and gifts—which were richly illustrated in the magazine.[96] Even children's birthdays could be seen as a site for consumption.

Children weren't the only group targeted by Disney, however. Adults, too, could experience the sensation of eternal youth by adopting Peter Pan haircuts. Macy's advertised the new style in language that promised grown women a younger feeling. "Isn't it fun! Isn't it enchanting! It has a never-grow-old look, a windy, flyaway look and all the guile of a Peter Pan collar. Everybody who wears it—looks prettier! And all it ever needs is a brushing! Peter Pan himself gave us the idea. See Walt Disney's Peter Pan movie soon!"[97] Even Walt Disney himself seemed to gain energy from being linked to his merchandise. One extraordinary ad for Willoughby's Camera Store in New York connected the man, the cartoon, and modern technology in one inventive swoop.

> Creative efforts are demanded of WALT DISNEY which are required of no other motion picture producer. Imaginative creations of style and quality associated with his name only. Fresh surprises of animation with each of his pictures. Sensational developments. That's because he understands his medium and has the extraordinary skills to carry out his imaginative entertainment processes. And nowhere have these processes been better exemplified than in the new Walt Disney Technicolor motion picture, "PETER PAN." . . . and here's a 35mm camera that's something extraordinary, too! [emphasis in the original][98]

But perhaps the most astonishing linkage of the film to trends even beyond this world came from a New Jersey man who placed figures from *Peter Pan* in the Christmas crèche he displayed in his front yard each year. Peter, Cinderella, and Br'er Rabbit stood shoulder to shoulder with a chorus of angels and Mary and Joseph. The man was forced to remove them after the mayor of Glen Rock complained that what had begun as a celebration of Christmas "had degenerated into commercial advertising."[99]

RETURN TO NEVERLAND

The Disney studio has, of course, continued its onslaught of commercial advertising since the first release of *Peter Pan* in 1953. As each new technology for home viewing becomes available, the studio reissues its classic films, often in restored versions. The 2007 release of *Peter Pan* is a two-disc DVD set that includes the film on one disc and an extensive array of extras on the other. The additional songs, trailers for future films, and games illustrate how Disney continues to update its older works for new generations by taking advantage of new technologies and new forms of leisure entertainment. New formats such as DVD not only modernize the film once more but create new iconic moments from a familiar text.

The DVD release of a "classic" film offers the opportunity to go into the studio vault and bring out previously hidden material. The two-disc set of *Peter Pan* contains several documentaries that fashion a history of the studio for audiences who may not know about the company. DVD releases today almost always include multiple examples of the music from a film. In many cases the DVDs present contemporary groups singing classic songs in an updated arrangement; for example, the *Peter Pan* DVD contains a music video of a multicultural group called T-Squad who perform a hip-hop version of "The Second Star to the Right" that includes clips from the film. The credits let audiences know that the music is available from Walt Disney Records. The 2007 release includes a song that was deleted from the film but that was finished for the DVD by Richard Sherman. "Neverland" creates a feeling of nostalgia and longing that is not found in the film: "there never was another land like never, never land," a feeling enhanced by the performance by Paige O'Hara, the voice of Belle in *Beauty and the Beast*. The 1950s film is thus connected to contemporary audiences through association with one of Disney's more recent releases.

Like Admiral's promotion of *Peter Pan* and television sets, Disney DVDs use new technology to awaken interest in older films. Most of its current DVD editions feature games designed to appeal to a generation raised on computer and video games. The *Peter Pan* DVD includes a puzzle game that enables children to "train to be a lost boy." By finishing the puzzle they can become one of Peter's forest companions. The pirate Smee offers "Smee's Sudoku Challenge" with three levels of difficulty. The viewer can free the Lost Boys from the pirate's lair by hitting targets in the right place. Finally, there is "Peter Pan's virtual flight," which presents a computer simulation of flying over London with voiceover narration by a young teen. Young players zoom over Neverland and see Hook's ship, the Lost Boys' hideout, and Mermaid Lagoon. The computer game allows them to dive in and out of space in a modern-day equivalent of the flying depicted in the film.

Like Peter Pan's Flight ride at Disneyworld, the game updates this iconic moment for new markets and new generations.

Other innovations spin off new narratives for the film's familiar characters. The DVD contains a trailer for a soon-to-be-released film called *Tinker Bell* that borrows elements from *The Lord of the Rings*. Tinker Bell and her friends Iridesca, Silver Mist, and Queen Clarion form a sort of sorority-in-the-shire called Pixie Hollow that resembles the home of Bilbo Baggins. A female voiceover who sounds like Cate Blanchett explains that the fairies are supposed to spread magic to the children of the world through pixie dust . . . but one day, the magic stops working. Only Tinker Bell can save the world of fairies. Like *Peter Pan*, the film has been supported before its release with book and video tie-ins that introduce girls to the characters and invite them to share the fairies' lives by drawing pictures and keeping a journal.

What some call two-dimensional animation has reached a critical moment again. The success of 3-D animated films such as *Shrek* and the increasing pervasiveness of computer graphics have called into question the financial viability, though perhaps not the popularity, of animated films that rely, at least in part, on drawings on paper. At such a key turning point in the history of animation, it is useful to look back to another historical period in which the viability of drawn animation was called into question in Hollywood. The production and reception of Disney's *Peter Pan* demonstrates how a studio can reinvent itself in response to shifting economic, cultural, and social conditions by changing its approach to design and narrative while still affirming its traditions. Its continual updating for new generations illustrates the careful planning and strategic decision that the company continues today.

NOTES

1. James Barrie, "Scenario for a Proposed Film of *Peter Pan*" [1920]. In Roger Lancelyn Green, *Fifty Years of Peter Pan* (London: Peter Davies, 1954), 172.
2. Green, *Fifty Years of Peter Pan*, 169.
3. Barrie, "Scenario," 172.
4. Edda Hooper, "Drama and the Arts," *Los Angeles Times*, May 11, 1952, E1
5. Kristen Thompson, "Implications of Cel Animation Technique," in *The Cinematic Apparatus*, ed. Stephen Heath and Teresa de Laruentis (London: Macmillan, 1980), 111.
6. Donald Crafton, "The Last Night in the Nursery: Walt Disney's *Peter Pan*," *The Velvet Light Trap* 24 (Fall 1989): 35.
7. *Once Upon a Time: Walt Disney*, Exhibition Catalog, Montreal Museum of Fine Arts (Munich: Prestel, 2007), 178.
8. Edda Hopper, "Complete Two-Thirds of the Animation," *Chicago Daily Tribune*, May 22, 1950, B13.
9. Janet Dunbar, *J. M. Barrie: The Man Behind the Image* (Boston: Houghton Mifflin, 1970); Green, *Fifty Years of Peter Pan*, 13–26.

10. Andrew Birkin, *J. M. Barrie and the Lost Boys* (New York: Clarkson N. Potter, 1979), 88–91.

11. Harry Geduld, *Sir James Barrie* (New York: Twayne, 1971), 53–54.

12. Leonee Ormond, *J. M. Barrie* (Edinburgh: Scottish Academic Press, 1987), 105.

13. Green, *Fifty Years of Peter Pan,* 97, 219–238.

14. Birkin, *J. M. Barrie and the Lost Boys,* 117.

15. Susan Ohmer, *George Gallup in Hollywood* (New York: Columbia University Press, 2006), 206.

16. Edwin Schallert, "*Peter Pan* Cartoon Rights," *Los Angeles Times,* October 19, 1938, 10.

17. Edwin Schallert, "*Peter Pan* to Follow *Bambi* at Disney's," *Los Angeles Times,* February 22, 1940, 13.

18. "Walt Disney's Cartoon Factory," *Washington Post,* September 1, 1940, A4.

19. "Shares in Disney," *Time,* March 25, 1940, 72; Schallert, "*Peter Pan* to Follow," 13; "Screen News Here," *New York Times,* November 25, 1941, 33; Louella O. Parsons, "The Kernel of a Splendid Idea," *Washington Post,* November 29, 1941, 8.

20. Annual Report, 1942, The Walt Disney Studio, Walt Disney Studio Archives, Burbank, California.

21. Thomas F. Brady, "Donald Doesn't Duck the Issue," *New York Times,* June 21, 1942, X3.

22. Philip K. Scheuer, "Disney May Have Found Peter Pan," *Los Angeles Times,* September 7, 1950, B11.

23. Ohmer, *George Gallup Goes to Hollywood,* 202–203.

24. "Audience Reaction to Peter Pan," September 10, 1943, "Peter Pan" file, Box 14 in Audience Research Institute files, Walt Disney Studio Archives, Burbank, California.

25. "Peter Pan with Henry James," November 9, 1943, "Peter Pan" file, Box 14; "Peter Pan with Irving Berlin," November 24, 1943. "Peter Pan" file, Box 14.

26. "Analysis of Peter Pan," September 20 1943, "Peter Pan" file, Box 14.

27. Frank Thomas and Ollie A. Johnston, *Disney Animation: The Illusion of Life* (Los Angeles: Disney, 1995).

28. Shanus Culhane, *Talking Animals and Other People* (New York: St. Martin's, 1986).

29. Jack Kinney, *Walt Disney and Assorted Other Characters* (New York: Random House, 1988); Leo Salkin, "Pigs is Pigs," in *Storytelling in Animation,* ed. John Canemaker (Los Angeles: American Film Institute, 1990).

30. "Peter Pan Storyboard," December 9, 1948, "Peter Pan" file, Box 7.

31. Ibid.

32. Ibid.

33. Ibid.

34. "Story Board and Rough Reels," June 6, 1951, "Peter Pan" file, Box 7.

35. "Rough Animation," June 17, 1952, "Peter Pan" file, Box 7.

36. Card Walker, memo to Walt Disney, October 1951. "Peter Pan" file, Box 7.

37. "Color and Rough Animation," September 9, 1952, "Peter Pan" file, Box 7.

38. Pete Martin, interview with Walt Disney, 1956, Walt Disney Studio Archive, Burbank, California.

39. Barrie, *Peter Pan,* 87.

40. Barrie, *Peter Pan,* 89.

41. Barrie, *Peter Pan,* 90.

42. Barrie, "Scenario," 171–172.

43. *Peter Pan,* Advertisement, *New York Times,* February 8, 1953, X15.

44. Barrie, *Peter Pan*, 103.
45. Barrie, *Peter Pan*, 110.
46. Barrie, *Peter Pan*, 108.
47. Crafton, "The Last Night in the Nursery," 37.
48. Hedda Hopper, "Looking at Hollywood," *Chicago Daily Tribune*, June 30, 1946, G3.
49. Hedda Hopper, "Drama and the Arts," *Los Angeles Times*, May 11, 1952, E1.
50. "Rough Animation," April 16, 1952, "Peter Pan" file, Box 7.
51. Barrie, *Peter Pan*, 97.
52. "*Peter Pan*; Real Disney Magic," *Newsweek*, February 16, 1953, 96.
53. "New Pictures," *Time*, February 2, 1952, 78.
54. "*Peter Pan*," Review, *Variety*, January 13, 1953, 6.
55. Gladwin Hill, "*Peter Pan* of Brenon's Fond Memory," *New York Times*, April 12, 1953, X5.
56. "Disney Fiscal Year Earnings Push Higher," *Los Angeles Times*, January 9, 1954, 12.
57. "Of Local Origin," *New York Times*, February 24, 1953, 21.
58. Richard L. Coe, "One on the Aisle," *Washington Post*, April 7, 1953, 24.
59. Robert F. Hawkins, "Postscript to the Cannes Festival," *New York Times*, May 10, 1953, X5.
60. "This Is Ed Sullivan Speaking," *Chicago Daily Tribune*, February 7, 1953, 15.
61. "Of Local Origin," *New York Times*, February 24, 1953, 21.
62. Coe, "3-D's Just Triple Bust," *Washington Post*, May 10, 1953, L1.
63. Hopper, "Looking at Hollywood," *Chicago Tribune*, January 19, 1953, B4.
64. Parker Tyler, "All That's Goldwyn," *Theatre Arts* (February 1953): 84.
65. "*Peter Pan*," *Newsweek*, , 96.
66. Philip T. Hartung, "The Screen: The Wild Blue Yonder," *Commonweal* (February 20, 1953): 499.
67. Films," *National Parent-Teacher* (March 1953): 26.
68. *Peter Pan* Review, *Variety*, 6; "Cinema: The Big Grossers," *Time*, February 2, 1953: 78; "New Pictures," *Time*, 78.
69. "*Peter Pan*" *Newsweek*, 96.
70. "Peter Pan Review," *Variety*, 6.
71. Manny Farber, "Films," *New Republic*, November 6, 1952, 535–536.
72. Hartung, "The Screen," 498.
73. Kathryn Hitte, "New Films from Books," *Library Journal*, February 1, 1953, 211.
74. Elspeth Chapin, "*Peter Pan*," *Films in Review* 4 (1953): 94.
75. Bosley Crowther, "The Screen: Disney's *Peter Pan* Bows," *New York Times*, February 12, 1953, 23.
76. Mae Tinée, "Disney's *Peter Pan* Tailored for the Modern Generation," *Chicago Daily Tribune*, February 5, 1953, A2.
77. "*Peter Pan*," *Monthly Film Bulletin*, 20: 228/239 (1953): 70; "*Peter Pan*," *Newsweek*, 96.
78. Coe, "One on the Aisle," *Washington Post*, 24; Crowther, "The Screen," *New York Times*, 23.
79. Farber, "Films," *The New Republic*, 536.
80. Tyler, "All That's Goldwyn," *Theatre Arts*, 84.
81. David Fisher, "Disney and U.P.A.," *Sight and Sound* 23, 1 (July/Sept. 1953): 40.
82. Lillian Disney, "I Live with a Genius," *McCalls* (February 1953): 40–41, 108.
83. "Walt Disney Tribute on *Toast of the Town*," Advertisement, *Chicago Daily Tribune*, February 8, 1953, S6.

84. Larry Wolters, "Television News and Views," *Chicago Daily Tribune,* February 8, 1953, B9. Emphasis is in the original.

85. "$25,000,000 Tie-in Campaign," *Hollywood Reporter,* February 2, 1953, 5.

86. "He'll Double as a Top-Notch Salesman," *Business Week,* March 21, 1953, 43.

87. "$25,000,000 Tie-in Campaign," *Hollywood Reporter,* 5.

88. "Housekeeping Today," *New York Times,* February 14, 1953, 14.

89. Albert Morehead, "There's Fun and Millions in Toys," *Nation's Business* (December 1953): 30.

90. "He'll Double as a Top-Notch Salesman," *Business Week,* 43.

91. Ibid.

92. "Best Seller List: Children's Books," *New York Times,* November 15, 1953.

93. Elinor Hillyer, "Give Them a Peter Pan Treasure-Hunt Party," *Woman's Home Companion* (March 1953): 78.

94. "Advertising & Marketing," *New York Times,* January 27, 1953, 41.

95. "Market Analysis of *Peter Pan,*" June 1952, "Peter Pan" file, Box 7.

96. Hillyer, "Give Them a Peter Pan Treasure-Hunt Party," *Woman's Home Companion,* 78–79.

97. "Peter Pan Haircut," Advertisement, *New York Times,* January 18, 1953.

98. "Willoughby's Cameras," Advertisement, *New York Times,* February 8, 1953, X15.

99. "Christmas Display in Jersey," *New York Times,* December 25, 1953, 1.

CHAPTER 7

Hooked on Pan

BARRIE'S IMMORTAL PIRATE IN FICTION AND FILM

Lester D. Friedman

"You people here have made Childhood your profession."[1]
—Ravello (aka Jas Hook)

OF HEROES AND VILLAINS

ALL HEROES, EXCEPT ONE, need a villain—and that one exception is Peter Pan. J. M. Barrie's original concept of a youth who would never grow up first appeared in an adult novel, *The Little White Bird* (1902), in which a London gentleman tells a young child stories about an ageless boy who inhabits Kensington Gardens at night. Following the spectacular success of *Peter Pan* on the London stage two years later, Barrie excerpted the chapters dealing specifically with his fanciful creation and reprinted them as *Peter Pan in Kensington Gardens* (1906), a slim volume with pictures by the famous illustrator Arthur Rackham. These two books provide the backstory of Peter Pan, explaining his extraordinary life before he journeyed to Neverland. While they contain ill-intentioned fairies, curmudgeonly birds, and a mother who locks out her first-born child, the most consistent villain is also the narrative's hero: Peter Pan's childish joys merge with a darker side that includes burying children lost in the park when they may still be alive.

Most surprising for those weaned on the versions of Walt Disney, Steven Spielberg, and Cathy Rigby, there are no pirates in these prose tales. According to Andrew Birkin, the foremost biographer of J. M. Barrie, Captain Hook was an afterthought in the original theatrical production, a required piece of stagecraft:

from his latest revision notes it's clear that he completed his first draft without any mention of Hook at all. He didn't need a villain for the simple reason that he already had one: Peter Pan. Hook's inclusion only came about as a result of a technical necessity. The stagehands needed a front cloth scene to give them time to change the scenery.[2]

Such are the lucky accidents of literary history.

As surely as the crowing boy has emerged as an almost universal symbol of youthful joy, so the miserable man with an iron hook has evolved into an enduring icon of malevolent adulthood: he "exemplifies all that is bad and grown up or all that is bad because grown up."[3] Misconstruing both figures as uncomplicated, these types of Manichean readings lock Pan and Hook into a crude series of one-dimensional dichotomies: good versus evil, old versus adolescent, purity versus corruption, virtue versus vice, eternal versus temporal, guileless versus scheming. In particular, they ignore the complexity of the man by interpreting him simply as the childish embodiment of evil, a bedtime nightmare that vanishes with the dawn or a motiveless malignancy bent on destruction for the flimsiest of reasons. To the contrary, a close reading of the relevant literary and cinematic texts reveals a far more sophisticated creation than generally acknowledged by critics and readers alike. The following analysis conceptualizes Captain James Hook not as an absurd cardboard villain, but rather as an obsessed man psychologically tortured by competing systems of moral and immoral behavior and emotionally constricted by interlocking codes of honor and masculinity. As such, he rightfully claims a place in the pantheon of literary—and ultimately cinematic—villainy that stretches far beyond the borders of childhood Neverland.

Peter Pan in the Fantasy Film Tradition

In his classic book *The Fantastic: A Structural Approach to a Literary Genre*, Tsvetan Todorov asserts that three narrative structures constitute fantasy fictions: the marvelous (events that involve the supernatural or spiritual); the fantastic (events that question common reality); and the uncanny (events produced by the unconscious). Building on Todorov, Wade Jennings argues that the only "indispensable element in a fantasy is a central situation that defies rational or even pseudo-scientific explanation . . . the situation cannot be explained; it must simply be accepted."[4] Classic fantasy films as diverse as *Lost Horizon* (1937), *The Wizard of Oz* (1939), *Mary Poppins* (1964), and the *Lord of the Rings* trilogy (2001/2002/2003), rarely explain beyond the simplest of histories how their strange worlds and exotic characters were created; instead, they provide the complex pleasure of allowing us to "believe without really believing."[5] We watch these movies knowing they defy the laws of common reality but, at the same time, give ourselves up to the delight of accepting them at face value.

In Coleridgian terms, our willingness to suspend our disbelief allows us to enter these magical worlds but, once there, the consistency of the norms within the environment must be as rigorously obeyed as in any conventionally realistic novel or film; in other words, we accept the author's fantastic creations as long as the internal logic of even the most outlandish narrative conforms to its own established rules and boundaries. This narrative constancy allows for the insertion of fantastical elements into everyday surroundings, encouraging readers/viewers to contemplate disruptive personal and communal questions made less volatile by the mediating forces of exotic or remote locations and encounters with supernatural beings. Because the basic narrative designs of fantasy works usually revolve around perilous physical quests that necessitate equally precarious internal journeys of personal understanding and self-realization, heroic protagonists must reassess their values in order to successfully complete their ordeals. In the process, they discover (or sometimes rediscover) joy and happiness, as well as a comprehension that rational knowledge alone remains insufficient for one to survive the dangerous obstacles that must be overcome and the death-defying tests that must be passed. More than merely being physically tested, therefore, they must tunnel deeply into their psyches to unearth the emotional strength and moral courage to defeat their malevolent enemies.

Most commonly, fantasy worlds are populated by three general character types: (1) the superman with powers beyond ordinary beings; (2) the child hero who battles evil armed with "natural innocence and goodness"; and (3) the supernaturally wise mentor to the human hero.[6] To do battle with seemingly invincible foes, the central figures find elements within themselves that, until revealed in a crisis, remain buried. Initially transported from their own worlds into these fantasy realms, these displaced protagonists ultimately have to choose either to stay within the new environment or return to their own worlds. In this manner, the fantastical situations that challenge them physically simultaneously force them to analyze their values and their place in the world they knew before the adventure. This same reevaluation is required of readers and viewers, who must either identify with or reject the protagonist's choice to remain in a new world or return to the routine and loved ones waiting on the other side of the wardrobe, at railway platform nine and three quarters, or in the nursery. This stark choice between remaining in the realm of adventure or returning to the original environment inevitably forces readers/viewers to consider the essential concept of "what constitutes home?"—a complex question that lies at the center of most fantasy films.[7]

This notion of "what constitutes home?" is a significant concern in all the Peter Pan narratives. Most critics characterize the choice as one between the joyful seductiveness of imaginative childhood found in Neverland and the inevitable responsibilities of conventional adulthood firmly entrenched in England. Though the Darling children experience exciting adventures with Peter—culminating with battling Captain Hook's pirate crew—they (along with the Lost Boys) freely choose to abandon Peter and return to the domesticity of London, a decision tinged with the dark knowledge of growing older and eventually dying. On the one hand, this choice perfectly matches the narrative arc of most fantasy films: the villain is vanquished, the social order is restored, and the main characters resume residence in their vacated domestic settings, be that a farm in Kansas or a comfortable home in the Shire. For the Darlings, rejoining the family offers the one pleasure unavailable in Neverland and that counterbalances the gloomy necessities of mortality: the love of a family, particularly a mother.

Wendy does such an admirable job of mothering the Lost Boys that her announced departure for London triggers a painful recognition: to remain on the island without a maternal figure now seems unbearable to them. Because her role-playing so powerfully evokes the compassionate warmth of family life forgotten during their coarse and exhilarating years with Peter, the Lost Boys willingly trade an endless round of exciting adventures for the tender affections of a mother, abandoning their leader with few regrets and barely a backward glance. Wendy, the only child without a mother while in Neverland, is the first who chooses to return home. Her determination to regain the secure comfort of being Mrs. Darling's daughter, as well as the anticipation of assuming the responsibilities of real motherhood herself, motivates her resolution to leave Neverland. Wendy's decision to go back to the nursery, and ultimately to her domestic life—and, eventually, death—drives the action for the rest of the story: it results in the showdown with Hook, the return of the Lost Boys to London (and the Darling family), and Peter Pan's isolation in a Neverland without a mother, a wife, a loyal band of brothers, or even a worthy enemy.

As with the figures of Pan and Hook mentioned earlier, the differences between the two main environments that constitute "home" in the Peter Pan narratives are not as clear and disconnected as they initially seem. In fact, a closer examination reveals some narrative anomalies not usually mentioned by commentators drawing the stark dichotomy between imaginative Neverland and dreary London. Neither setting fits into a rigid pattern that directly opposes the other. In London, for example, a Newfoundland dog, the loveable Nana, tends to Wendy, John, and Michael. While Barrie's narrator blithely asserts that the Darlings were "poor, owing to the amount of milk the children drank," the couple dresses quite well, employs a housekeeper (Liza), and attends fancy parties—facts more evident in the film adaptations than in the original novel.[8] On the surface, therefore, they appear able to afford childcare wages more costly than kibbles and bits. Even it they can only hire one servant, why not a human to do childcare instead of housekeeping? Which is more important? More to the point, if the money is unavailable, why doesn't the idealized Mrs. Darling take over the rearing of her brood? Surely the sight of a mother raising her own children would lift fewer eyebrows than using a dog as a nursemaid.

That is precisely the point: the London world of the Darlings is, at times, not particularly far from Neverland's fantastical elements and supernatural creatures. No one bats an eye when a dog that "belonged to no one in particular" knows most everything about caring for children and performs her duties admirably in the midst of a slightly satiric but otherwise quite naturalistic urban setting.[9] Barrie's narrator confidently declares, "no nursery could possibly have been conducted more correctly"[10] and, though Mr. Darling "had a passion for being exactly like his neighbours," he is far more troubled that Nana might "not admire him"[11] than that the neighbors might think him a joke because of his domestic arrangements. In fact, Nana's role strikes no one in the story as particularly strange or even incongruous—except the other nurses, who didn't like her because she revealed their derelictions of duty. In this sense, the seemingly rational London world that Barrie constructs to mirror our own sense of reality contains at least canine scraps of fantasy that would not be out of place in Peter's Neverland of mermaids, fairies, and pirates.

Understanding that an element of fantasy remains barely noticed in stolid London provides both a fuller understanding of Barrie's complex imagination and a warning about placing narrative and character elements in limited, or even predictable, categories. One scene that appears in *Peter and Wendy* and nearly all of the films, though in various iterations, describes the deliberate collision between fantasy and London reality. This scene makes readers and viewers accept that Neverland has come much closer to the world than it has before in previous works of art, and that pieces of the real world can also exist in Neverland. Upon teaching the children to fly, Peter slowly convinces them to leave the nursery with him—at the prospect of pirates, John grabs his "Sunday hat" and is ready to depart for high adventure. The hat will play an important role in Neverland, serving first to carry Tinker Bell and shield her light from the watching pirates, and second as a new nest for the Neverbird after she gives her's up to save Peter on the rock.

The incongruity of a top hat floating for eternity on the Neverland lagoon clearly demonstrates the incursion of the real into the fantasy world, just as Peter's entrance into the Darling household provides an equally incongruous flutter of fantasy into that bland environment. The film *Peter Pan* directed by P. J. Hogan (2003) features both worlds trespassing into each other through the hat. In this version, the children fly out of the nursery and soar over the house where their parents are attending a party held by Mr. Darling's boss. They swoop down over the adults leaving the festivities and John seizes the hat from his father's boss's pate, thanking him politely before zooming back into the sky and away to Neverland, where the hat plays the above-mentioned important role. Similarly, Hook, Pan, Wendy, and her brothers, the Lost Boys, Mrs. Darling, even Mr. Darling also have a foot (or at least a toe) dipping into Neverland's fantasy elements. This extreme collision of worlds is important, since the cultural exchange between Neverland and London makes any one-dimensional reading of any of the characters seem, at best, simplistic.

THE GENESIS OF CAPTAIN HOOK

Barrie, who always assumed the role of Hook in pirate games with the Llewelyn Davies boys, blended snatches of pirate life—from fictional sources, iconic representations, and newspaper accounts—to fashion one of the most memorable scalawags in literary history.[12] Though the writer never revealed his actual sources, he could easily have drawn upon a slew of seafaring adventure stories, the most famous being the work of his countryman, Robert Louis Stevenson. Hook clearly harkens back to the devious Long John Silver, that lethal peg-legged pirate who captures young Jim Hawkins in Stevenson's immensely popular *Treasure Island* (1883). Barrie refers specifically to Silver by his nickname, "the Sea Cook," in *Peter Pan*, his narrator telling readers that Hook "was the only man that the Sea Cook feared."[13] Given Barrie and Stevenson's lively, ongoing correspondence starting in February of 1892, Jill May claims that "Barrie's interest in Stevenson, as a fellow Scot who wrote about shipwrecked men, was genuine and it affected his creation of Hook and all the pirates."[14]

An equally important element in Hook's creation might have been the enduring reputation of Christopher Newport (1560–1617) in the Great Britain of Barrie's day. A swashbuckling Elizabethan mariner who lost his right arm off the coast of Cuba in a battle with Spaniards, Newport replaced it with a metal device resembling a hook. History books label him as a privateer, but the line between privateer and pirate was constantly under negotiation in the sixteenth century, since the only difference between the two was a contract from your monarch saying that you were robbing in his/her name and were willing to share your spoils. An unwillingness to do the latter was what frequently turned privateers into pirates and had them dragged into court. Whatever his official designation, Newport raided Spanish and Portuguese merchant vessels successfully for twenty years in the Caribbean, sharing his booty with the various London merchants who funded his voyages and at times serving in the employ of Queen Elizabeth I. One of his most famous deeds was to bring two baby crocodiles back to King James I in 1605, a feat that may have inspired the incorporation of Hook's reptilian nemesis. The daring Newport is best known in American history for a more legitimate role: as captain of the *Susan Constant*, the main ship among a trio that carried English settlers to Jamestown in 1607.

Other individuals often nominated as playing a part in Barrie's lush imagination include Captain James Cook, the eighteenth-century explorer famous for his maps of Australia and New Zealand, and Herman Melville's monomaniacal Captain Ahab, with his ivory leg and obsessive quest to destroy the white whale. Whatever combination of elements in the cultural ether coalesced to generate the sinister captain of the *Jolly Roger*, he has managed to take his place among the most celebrated villains of all time. His glowing red eyes (blue until he was about to kill someone), threatening expression, and above all the eviscerating hook make him a frightening spectacle of vicious cruelty. In fact, when originally played on the London stage by Gerald du Maurier (the brother of Sylvia Llewelyn-Davies and father of novelist Daphne du Maurier), children were often carried crying from the theater. Despite the campy portrayal given by Cyril Ritchard in the Mary Martin stage/television production (1960) and the pusillanimous clown voiced by Hans Conried in the Disney cartoon (1953), Captain Hook has remained a menacing presence within and beyond the Pan narrative, sending shivers down the spines of children for generations—and perhaps causing a shudder or two in their parents as well.

CAPTAIN HOOK IN THE POPULAR IMAGINATION

As Peter Pan graces countless jars of peanut butter and Tinker Bell flits around the Walt Disney empire, so Captain Hook has sliced his way into our cultural consciousness, often as a naughty rather than a truly wicked icon. A quick Google search reveals an expected listing of resorts, boat names, marinas, seaside restaurants, dinner cruises, bait and tackle shops, and fishing charters from Lake Erie to Tahiti all bearing his name. Yet unanticipated associations also appear, including a variety of nicknames such as Nine Ball champion Mike "Captain Hook" Sigel, baseball manger Sparky "Captain Hook" Anderson (known to yank his pitchers at the first sign of trouble), and malpractice lawyer Captain Hook Silver. Online, you can order the Trango Captain Hook ($159.95), a mountain climbing tool, or the Captain Hook trailer winch or the Captain Hook Dumpster. You might even view the Captain Hook Cluster at the Institute of Computer Engineering, a hi-tech device used in the field of medical image processing and parallel simulation of biological processes, or peruse the Captain Hook Awards for biopiracy (given to those who monopolize genetic resources). Elementary school teachers utilize the "Finding Captain Hook's Treasure" game to engage students in geography lessons, and their students can order Captain Hook party supplies (including costumes, cakes, and balloons) from a wide group of vendors. If you walk up behind a man and kick him squarely in the privates, you have performed a Captain Hook, according to the *Urban Dictionary*, an online source that also informs readers that a man whose penis is bent noticeably to the right or the left is called a Captain Hook. Finally, Shel Silverstein reminds Real Player listeners "There are lots of folks I'm glad I'm not, but mostly Captain. Hook" as he sings his poem "Captain Hook" (from *Where the Sidewalk Ends*) online. Much to the pirate's credit, a recent BigBadRead poll organized by the publisher Bloomsbury in London drew more than 16,000 votes from British schoolchildren and put Hook fifteenth among the greatest literary villains of all time, just a notch below Conan Doyle's Professor Moriarty (September 4, 2006).

But the vision of Hook offered by most commentators—that "Hook is to be taken seriously as the representative of the adult world"—needs some refining.[15] It seems strangely perverse to characterize Hook as the personification of responsibility in any sense of the word, even in juxtaposition to the perpetually childlike Pan. The captain surely is a grownup, but he is a pirate, hardly an appropriate embodiment of typical adulthood. By their very natures, pirates epitomize precisely the opposite of maturity as it is traditionally configured in our culture: with their flamboyant clothing and murderous actions, they incarnate a reckless disregard for conventional responsibility and traditional morality. Has anyone ever seriously cited Blackbeard or Captain Kidd as models for adulthood? Pirates are boy-men who spend their lives playing games, dressing up in costumes, and living by their own rules. In this sense, they most closely resemble older Peter Pans. Quite the opposite of responsible adults, pirates loom in our collective imaginations as romantic icons precisely because they attack the very values Hook has so often been interpreted to personify and, in so doing, become perpetual outsiders mocking middle-class values. Forsaking the dependable, mundane world for a life on the seas filled with adventure, plunder, and brutality, pirates seek their fortunes at the expense of other, less colorful men, jettisoning in their wake the middle-class values of marriage, child-rearing, and legal employment.

SPIELBERG'S CLOSE ENCOUNTER WITH CAPTAIN HOOK

Menacing and cruel though Captain Hook may be, one sound clips him "at the joint" and reduces him to "a little heap":[16] the approach of the ticking crocodile embodies the most negative aspect of growing older; the beast becomes a physical manifestation of time's passage and the fear of death. The most cinematic example of the former emerges in director Steven Spielberg's lavish production *Hook*. The film totally reverses Barrie's tale about children without parents, making it a story about a father who must leave his children to regain his childhood and thereby save his family. In this scenario, Peter Pan has chosen to live with the Darlings rather than to remain in Neverland. As the grownup Peter Banning (Robin Williams), his myopic preoccupation with his work makes him a feeble husband and, even worse, a negligent father. To visually underscore the importance of lost time, Spielberg fills the mise-en-scène with an almost numbing variety of time pieces, from postcard-perfect shots of Big Ben, to the intimate pocket watch Peter gives his son Jack (Charlie Korsmo), to Hook's (Dustin Hoffman) emblematic museum of broken clocks.

Throughout *Hook*, Spielberg emphasizes the fleeting fragility of time. Banning mishandles time by ignoring his children, even yelling at them "to shut up and leave me alone." Not visiting his adoptive mother Wendy (Maggie Smith) even once in the last ten years, he concentrates his attention on mergers and acquisitions. He "blows any resistance out of the water," an excited Jack tells his grandmother, who wryly notes that Peter has himself become a pirate. (Later, the Lost Boys tell Peter, "Grownups are pirates," perhaps because they steal time away from children.) Endlessly talking on his cell phone through his daughter Maggie's (Amber Scott) school play, he further compounds the transgression by sending an office flunky to videotape his son Jack's baseball game. "My word is my bond," he tells his son after missing the contest he promised to attend. "Yeah, a junk bond," responds the hurt and angry boy. Later in the film, when Captain Hook captures the children, he seduces away their affections by spending time and playing games with them. Seeing precious drops of time dripping away, Banning's wife, Moira (Caroline Goodall), reminds him that:

> Your children love you. They want to play with you. How long do you think that lasts? Soon Jack may not even want you to come to his games. We have a few special years with our children when they're the ones who want us around. After that, you're going to be running after them for a bit of attention. So fast, Peter. It's a few years, then it's over. You are not being careful. And you are missing it.

By foregrounding the relentless passage of time, *Hook* forces viewers to consider and take responsibility for how they allot their particular, and quite limited, portion in their own daily lives. In this case, it is the children who are the ticking clocks reminding viewers of the limits of mortal life, and it is Peter—the immortal child—not Hook who loathes them.

Only late in the film does Peter Banning remember that he accepted the responsibilities of the temporal world—and gave up being the eternally youthful Peter Pan—for a reason: "I wanted to be a father." That decision to put others before himself kills the invulnerable child-hero and replaces him with the fallible man. Far from being about remaining a boy forever, as most critics interpret it, *Hook* demonstrates the necessity to grow up, to choose external obligations over personal pleasures. To vanquish Hook and regain his children, Banning must learn how to balance his powerful childhood memories with his adult responsibilities, how to keep one from ever overwhelming the other. Peter "can't stay and play" in Neverland after he rescues his children; indeed, the happy thoughts that finally allow him to fly are not about his adventures with the prepubescent Lost Boys, games with the free-spirited Tinker Bell (Julia Roberts), or battles against Hook's nefarious pirates, but about his children and, by extension, his parental role to love, nurture, and protect them.

Hook, intuitively understanding that his permanence depends on the existence of Peter Pan, seeks to generate a timeless frieze: the perpetual boy endlessly fighting his unchanging adult adversary. After all, great heroes and villains need each other to guarantee their immortality. "What would the world be like without Captain Hook?" asks the pirate. The answer, as every parent knows, is that Hook's flamboyant wickedness pales in comparison with the genuine dangers, potential disasters, and real evils that threaten the safety and happiness of the children we love. Kidnappings, molestations, tortures, rapes, and murders clearly trump walking the plank. Beyond the childhood borders of Neverland, Hook is irrelevant, except perhaps as a stand-in for the darker dangers that threaten the innocence of children.

In the end, Peter Pan must return to being Peter Banning, though he will carry the memory of being "the Pan" with him forever. As another artist fascinated by childhood, the poet William Wordsworth, so poignantly observes in his "Ode: Intimations of Immortality": "nothing can bring back the hour/Of splendour in the grass, of glory in the flower" (11. 177–178).[17] Instead of the carelessly thrilling and exuberantly selfish pleasures of youth, Wordsworth's lost "visionary gleam" (1.56), Peter finds a deeper pleasure in fulfilling his familial responsibilities. The lessons he learns from his return—and final—voyage to Neverland are basic truths: that time can never be halted and that it moves far too fast. We each carry with us precious memories from our childhoods—those times, as Wordsworth says, of "trailing clouds of glory" (1. 64) behind us; but we cannot reproduce them as adults because we travel "daily farther from the east" (1.71) and drift into "the light of common day" (1.76). The play of an adult self-consciously assuming various disguises and parts remains accessible to Spielberg—after all, filmmaking is but an exaggerated and expensive form of fun and games—but it can never duplicate the natural, spontaneous and impulsive joys of childhood. In this sense, then, *Hook* is an elegy for, rather than a celebration of, impulsive childhood and youthful innocence, as well as an embrace of adult responsibilities. "All children, except one, grow up" in *Peter Pan*. "And even he must do so," concludes Steven Spielberg in *Hook*.

In stressing these ideas, Spielberg creates a startling deviation from Barrie's original work. The scene begins as a rejuvenated Peter flips open the ornate face of the grandfather clock that houses Tinker Bell, its hands frozen at X and XII and its cobwebbed face glowing in the silent darkness. Literally encircled by time as his face replaces the clock dial, Peter Pan finds a melancholy Tinker Bell sitting amid relics from Peter Banning's former life: driver's license, gold Master Card, box of Certs, and BMW keyholder—symbols of the daily obligations he has forsaken. When Peter tells Tink that he returned to Neverland "to always be a little boy and have fun," she reminds him that this is not true, that he came back to save the children he now barely remembers. Shattering the arrested time tower she inhabits, Tinker Bell transforms herself into a full-sized woman, dressed in a soft blue, off-the-shoulder evening gown, who gives Peter a "real" kiss and tells him that she loves him. "Moira. I love Moira. Jack and Maggie," he says haltingly, breaking the momentary spell and devising a plan for their rescue.

Tink realizes the painful truth embedded in this tenderly ambivalent moment. "When it's all over you'll leave and never come back again." In rejecting this stylized adolescent romance bathed in shimmering blue light for the mature though often frustrating marriage with Moria and his duties as a father, Peter accepts the joys and sorrows of emotional adulthood and, in the only version of the story to do this, makes the same choice that Wendy made—without the mockery of an eternal boy who flits to the window when he remembers to borrow her, her daughter, then her granddaughter, and down through the line to be his mother in adventure.

This acceptance of time's passage brings with it the sobering acceptance of death. Ironically for a film ostensibly concerned with eternal childhood, and directed by a man most critics attack as a perpetual adolescent, Spielberg stuffs *Hook* with pervasive dialogue about dying; it even contains the visualized death of a child, Rufio (Dante Basco), a rare moment in Spielberg's work that actualizes the director's worst fears. Both main characters discuss death at crucial moments in the movie. Peter reveals to Tinker Bell that he ran away from home to avoid getting older "because everyone who grows up has to die someday." A depressed Hook attempts suicide, albeit comically, telling his first mate Smee (Bob Hoskins): "I want to die. There's no great adventure here. Death is the only great adventure I have left," borrowing a line from Peter Pan who, in *Peter and Wendy*, chooses to die by drowning on the lagoon rather than trying to save himself because, "To die will be an awfully big adventure." Before their duel commences, Hook warns Peter to "prepare to die." "To die would be a great adventure," responds Pan, borrowing back the line from Hook and claiming a sentiment that was absent in the Disney cartoon version and most subsequent iterations of Barrie's far darker story.

For the second time, Hook answers that "death is the only adventure." Yet for all his bravado, Hook fears death more than any other character in the movie. His museum of broken clocks, each one having "ticked its last tock," testifies to his dread of time passing and his inching progress toward death. By encouraging Jack to destroy Peter's watch, "to make time stand still," Hook attempts to sever the relationship between a father "who's never there," a crying child who feels his dad "didn't even try" to save him, and their home filled with "broken promises."

Hook's demise comes at the jaws of his tenacious nemesis: the fearsome creature who devoured his hand and now stands as a stuffed croc clock in the town square. In the climactic duel scene, the pirate tries to slit Pan open with his hook but, with Tink's help, Peter jams the weapon into the crocodile's hide. The jarring puncture forces the clock face to slide from the beast's mouth and crash onto the ground. A frightened and retreating Hook trips over it (literally stumbling over time), the straps holding the animal snap, and the reptile falls forward onto Hook, who disappears without a trace inside its mouth. Time has finally caught up with the captain. But symbolically Hook's end comes earlier in his battle with Pan. Encircled by the Lost Boys—each holding malevolently ticking clocks—a terrified Hook hears Peter taunt him: "Tic tock, tick tock, tick tock. Hook's afraid of an olden clock. Hook's afraid of time ticking away." Flicking off Hook's elaborate black wig with his sword, Peter reveals the old, balding, and rather pathetic man hidden underneath. The humiliated Hook begs the triumphant Pan, "give me my dignity." Peter hands back the hairpiece and heeds his children's plea to spare his enemy and return home.

The resumption of time in Neverland, however, is the end of Hook's futile struggle to halt the relentless march of minutes—and he knows it.

7.1 The foppish pirate captain (Dustin Hoffman) as a rival father figure to the adult Peter Pan (Robin Williams) in director Steve Spielberg's *Hook* (1991). Courtesy of Jerry Ohlinger's Movie Material Store.

When boys become men, they leave Captain Hook behind. Though Peter Banning begins as a figure genuinely uncertain of his own manhood and lacking the "rough-and-tumble masculinity"[18] of the pirates and the "potent masculinity"[19] embodied in Hook, his (re)learning to fly integrates his past and his present and allows the rescue of his children because he achieves a "more secure and emotionally open masculinity."[20] In this sense, then, *Hook* explores how men struggle to fulfill the cultural expectations of generically masculine roles.

CAPTAIN HOOK AND THE CODES OF MASCULINITY

The masculine code of honor omnipresent in *Peter Pan* comes from far beyond the borders of Neverland and entails the manifold and dynamic factors that compose and represent masculinity. In a contemporary context, the issue of how to define and what constitutes masculinity has become a fertile, if at times quite contentious, field for cultural analysis, psychoanalytic theory, and feminist critique:

> Masculinity . . . is a vexed term, variously inflected, multiply defined, not limited to straightforward descriptions of maleness. . . ."Masculinity" is not as a monolith entity, but an interplay of emotional and intellectual factors—an interplay that directly implicates women as well as men, and is mediated by other social factors, including race, sexuality, nationality and class.[21]

In particular, Judith Butler has interrogated what she labels as "rigid" forms of gender and sexual identification, helping to remap the contours of the cultural landscape. She often focuses on the "performance of gender," arguing that expressions of "actions, gestures, and speech . . . produced retroactively the illusion that there was an inner gender core."[22] Building on this premise, she contends that "gender is produced as a ritualized repetition of conventions, and that this ritual is socially compelled."[23] This performance of gender is central to the presentation of Hook, both in fiction and film, as well as to the other characters in the narrative, particularly Peter Pan and Wendy.

"As in all great pirates," the literary narrator tell us, in Hook's "dark nature there was a touch of the feminine"—an observation equally personified in that most modern of pirates, Captain Jack Sparrow (Johnny Depp).[24] The very costume worn by pirates seems, to the modern eye, like a haphazard amalgamation of hypermasculine and feminine tropes: earrings and cutlasses, brightly colored sashes and blunderbusses, ponytails and pistols. Hook, himself, is depicted as something of a hybrid of male and female attributes, with his long curls, foppish and ornate clothing, eyes the color of blue "forget-me-nots," and two-cigar holder (perhaps an objective correlative to Hook's dual nature).[25] At times, this "man of indomitable courage"[26] dissolves into a hysterical heap on the deck of the *Jolly Roger*, such as when he beholds the sight of his own strangely colored blood or hears the incessant ticking of the crocodile drawing near; he is also prone to "profound melancholy," particularly when he dwells upon his failure to achieve good form.[27]

Indeed, in her psychoanalytical analysis of *Peter Pan*, Ann Yeoman observes that given "the subtle confounding of masculine and feminine attributes that describes many of Barrie's characters. . . . the symbol of Hook's appearance and personality points to a complex, undifferentiated and dark interrelation of masculine and feminine qualities."[28] For her the swaggering Hook, along with the far more diffident Mr. Darling, both embody "a perverse and degenerate masculinity."[29] Such readings invite comparisons between Peter Pan and Captain Hook concerning the issues of male behavior, for one character is quite incomplete without taking into consideration the other.

Any comparison between the masculinity of Peter and Hook remains difficult due to the iterations of the basic narrative in the various films, as well as in the prose sequels and spin-offs that clog the shelves in the "Children's Section" of most bookstores. So, for example, Dustin Hoffman's droll Hook attacks Peter's lack of fatherly attention to his children, finding him vulnerable because he fails to fulfill that culturally dictated masculine role. Quite differently, Jason Isaac's virile swashbuckler charms Tink, poses a sexual threat to Wendy, and at times becomes Pan's rival for the girl's affection. The seeds for this latter interpretation are deeply sown in Barrie's work, particularly the segment in which the pirates capture Wendy and the Lost Boys. While the Boys are treated in a "ruthless manner," Hook accords Wendy an "ironical politeness" by doffing his hat, offering his arm, and escorting her to the ship. For her part, Wendy is initially "fascinated," and the narrator remarks that "for a moment Hook entranced her."[30] This example of mature masculinity differs markedly from Peter's unrealized sense of manhood. He is, after all, still a boy and thus only a potential man, despite his many accomplishments. As such, Pan's dominant masculine trait is his self-congratulatory cockiness, his arrogant assumption that he possesses the freedom to act precisely as he pleases. His impertinent crowing externalizes not only soaring pleasure at his own cleverness, but also functions as a taunting gesture that infuriates Hook: "There was something about Peter which goaded the Pirate captain to frenzy. It was not his courage, it was not his engaged appearance . . . It was Peter's cockiness."[31] Thus, Pan's boyish confidence in his own masculine superiority tortures Hook, makes his iron claw twitch, and disturbs his rest.

INTRODUCING CAPTAIN HOOK

If the operatic Hook (Ernest Torrence) in director Henry Brenon's 1924 silent version of Barrie's play amuses modern viewers, and the foppish Hook

7.2 The virile Captain Hook (Jason Isaacs) as a formidable challenger for Wendy's affection in director P. J. Hogan's *Peter Pan* (2006). Courtesy of Jerry Ohlinger's Movie Material Store.

(Dustin Hoffman) in Steven Spielberg's baroque adaptation concerns himself mainly with Banning's children, then the virile Captain Hook (Jason Isaacs) depicted in P. J. Hogan's production of *Peter Pan* seems as much a rival for Wendy's affections as a challenge to Peter Pan.

His initial appearance announces a conspicuous departure from his cinematic forbearers. The scene begins with Pan's arrival, along with the Darling children, back in Neverland. In his absence, the island has descended into snowy gloom, its inhabitants collapsing into somnambulistic hibernation. At Pan's return sunlight bathes the island, and as the camera tracks through the forest, the snowflakes stop falling, birds begin singing, and tropical flowers instantly bloom. The ice imprisoning the frozen *Jolly Roger* cracks, freeing the ship and sending Smee (Richard Briers) scurrying to tell his captain that the weather has changed dramatically. Peeking through the half-opened door of his irascible leader's treasure-laded cabin to better gauge his mood, Smee approaches cautiously and informs Hook that winter has abruptly turned to spring—but earlier than expected. To prove his point, he plunks his pocket watch down on the desk; suddenly, from the right corner of the screen, a large hook stabs the timepiece and smashes it to pieces.

A disheveled Hook slumps head-down on a scarlet and gold throne-like chair at his desk, his unkempt hair spilling out and dominating the image. Left arm bare and adorned with a tattoo of Eton's coat of arms (assigned by Henry VI in 1449), he slowly rises and speaks: "I was dreaming, Smee, of Pan. And in my dream, I was magnanimous, full of forgiveness." He pauses to drink from a gilded cup, his long black hair cascading down his naked torso. As he begins the next sentence, his right hand rises from underneath the desk and we view, for the first time in any film, his scarred stump as he continues, "I thanked Pan for cutting off my hand and for giving me this fine hook." As the captain goes on speaking, Smee helps him struggle into a cumbersome leather and metal shoulder contraption, the camera drawing our attention not to their ungainly efforts but to the captain's buttocks encased in a tight pair of black pants. "For disemboweling and slitting throats and other such homely uses," Hook intones dryly as he finally straps on the unwieldy device. He then cranks a small lever that elevates his arm, painfully, affixes a rusty hook, and screws it into place. Telling about the crocodile perpetually searching for an entree to follow the appetizer served up by Pan, Hook plunges the metal prosthetic into boiling water and asks why he was so rudely awakened. Upon hearing that the sun is shinning and the flowers blooming, Hook draws his hand from the steamy cauldron, lifts his now-gleaming hook aloft, and declares with a sinister grin, "he's back!"

Compare such an opening to Hook's entrance in Spielberg's and Brenon's movies. In the former, he is introduced by Smee (Bob Hoskins) in a format mimicking the grandiose preambles spewed forth at a pro-wrestling match: "The cunning kingfish, the bad barracuda, a man so deep he's almost unfathomable, a man so quick he is even fast asleep. So let's give him a very big hand 'cause he's only got one. I give you CAPTAIN JAMES HOOOOK!" The crowd takes up the robust chant like a Jerry Springer audience: "Hook. Hook. Hook." Encircled by lace cuffs sliding outside an elaborately decorated red-and-gold braided waistcoat, a large and gleaming silver hook emerges from the cabin door. The camera swings around to view the man from behind, as the mantra continues and the captain takes a deep bow. Responding to Smee's comment about how greatly the men favor him, Hook turns and retorts: "the fuming spawn, how I despise them." He goes on to call them, "my stupid sorry parasitic sacks of entrails." Considering that the scene opens with Smee bellowing "Good morning Neverland!" into a large megaphone (a not-so-subtle intertexual reference to the film's star Robin Williams who made the phrase famous in *Good Morning, Vietnam* [1987]), viewers are clearly not meant to fear this figure. Indeed, Hoffman's hammy portrayal often slips into sly sentimentality but never reaches within a ship cannon's of the sinister.

7.3 The operatic Hook (Ernest Torrence) as a menacing antagonist in director Henry Brenon's *Peter Pan* (1924). Courtesy of Jerry Ohlinger's Movie Material Store.

Hook's entry into Brenon's silent film is much less elaborate than in the two more contemporary movies, but it confirms how much even his own men fear him. His motley crew is first spied hauling a treasure chest up to the crest of a hill (Catalina Island served as Neverland in the production). Sensing their leader's arrival, they shrink back fearfully from the trunk, as Hook strides into the frame, hands behind his back like an angry schoolmaster. His costume consists of a lace shirt with frilly sleeves, a long coat, a tricorn hat, and a pistol tucked prominently into his belt. One scowling look is enough to understand the title card: "Everyone shudders at the approach of Captain Hook!" He brandishes the hook at the cowering men, recounting how Peter cut off his hand and fed it to the crocodile: "the beast has followed me ever since from sea to sea." Hearing movement below them and sensing the presence of his nemesis, Hook grasps a large clock and hurls it into the mouth of the beast, who hungrily swallows it and begins moving its head in syncopation with the ticking timepiece. Finally, the crocodile slinks away accompanied by the jeers of the pirate crew, their leader toasting his victory with an unforgiving prophecy: "to the day I will shake the hand of Peter Pan with this. Oh, I'll tear him!" Off they go, carrying the treasure box with them.

Menage à Trois: Hook, Pan, and Wendy

In Hogan's adaptation, Wendy first spies Hook, "the dark figure who haunted her stories," at The Black Castle, but the narrator tells us that upon beholding those "piercing eyes, she was not afraid but entranced." Hook first sees her in a magical scene that turns sour when Peter cannot respond to Wendy's intimate questions. The scene begins as Peter takes Wendy's hand and they creep through the foliage to watch the king and queen of the fairies dancing gracefully inside a hollow tree trunk. The children steal glances at each other and, finally, look into each other's eyes and smile. Peter stiffly, quite formally, bows. Wendy curtsies in response. We see a close-up of first his hand and then hers, as they entwine. The pair rock back and forth for a few seconds, tentatively and unsure of the rhythm, then Peter tenderly tosses her backward into the air. Wendy floats alone for a moment, but Peter quickly follows, takes her in his arms, and they begin to dance in circles among the high branches, a shimmering trail of fairy light swirling around them. Below them we see another, more ominous glow; unbeknownst to the couple, Hook sneaks into the forest carrying a lantern. Spinning gently in the air, the couple remains oblivious to the danger that lurks and watches below.

Cut to an agonized Hook: "You did it," he mumbles. He stumbles away and sinks to the ground, landing next to an equally dejected Tink sitting on a leaf. "He's got himself a m . . . m . . ." moans Hook, unable to form the word, though Tink supplies another, "Wendy." The camera cuts back to a twirling Wendy and Peter, as Hook continues mournfully on the soundtrack, "And Hook is all alone." Addressing his gloomy companion in jealousy, the Captain repeats her words, "You too. Banished. The dog." With Tink now perched more familiarly on his hook, the crafty pirate senses an opportunity: "I think you and I should talk." The scene reaches its visual climax as Wendy and Peter stare dreamily into each other's eyes, their bodies bathed in soft, lush, and romantic moonlight, though Pan's (and Hook's) conflation of mother and potential, if unrecognized, lover provides sufficient material for armchair Freudians to start scribbling notes.

Slowly, Peter starts to realize something may be amiss. "Wendy, it's only make believe, isn't it that you and I are . . ." his voice trails off, unable, like Hook moments before, to utter words that frighten him. "Oh. Yes" she answers, her smile fading, looking downward away from him, and sinking slowly to earth. "You see," Peter continues as they descend, "it would make me feel so old to be a real father." Back firmly on the ground, Wendy asks, "What are your real feelings?" as Peter recedes nervously away from her interrogation, both physically and emotionally. "Feelings," he answers, as if the word is totally foreign to him. "What you feel?" She probes, "Happiness? Sadness? Jealously? Anger?" Peter hears Hook's footsteps in the forest. "Love?" persists Wendy without hesitation. "Love," responds Peter, contemptuously slamming his dagger back into its scabbard and scowling, "I have never heard of it." But she doggedly prods him, "I think you have, Peter. I daresay you felt it yourself with something or someone." He whispers roughly in her ear, "Never. Even the sound of it offends me." As Wendy reaches out to touch him, perhaps to regain a shard of the affectionate moment just shared in the sky, Peter leaps backward into the foliage and berates her:

PETER: Why do you have to spoil everything? We have fun, don't we? I taught you to fight and to fly. What more could there be?

WENDY: There is so much more.

PETER: What? What else is there?

WENDY: I don't know. I think it becomes clearer when you grow up.

PETER: I will not grow up. You cannot make me. I will banish you like Tinker Bell.

WENDY: I will not be banished!

PETER: Then go home. Go home and grow up and take your feelings with you (he flies off).

Wendy rushes after him, yelling "Peter. Peter, come back." But she cannot fly without him. The pirate contentedly observes this exchange, leaning against a tree and stroking his hook, a cunning half-smile crossing his face. Later, he will tell Wendy that Peter Pan can never love and that she must understand that about him. But for now, Wendy runs to her house, flings herself on the bed of leaves, and furiously sobs.

This sequence establishes several important threads that will be woven throughout the film's fabric. First, it launches an unspoken, but at times seemingly mutual, attraction between Hook and Wendy, another departure from the two previous cinematic *Peter Pan* adaptations, and one that may make viewers slightly uncomfortable given the characters' age differences: despite her pretense of motherhood, Wendy is still a young girl and Hook a grown man. Second, in keeping with the spirit of the novel, it demonstrates the shallowness of Peter Pan, for he is as much callow youth as charismatic hero: in Barrie's original tale, he forgets things almost immediately after they happen (including the existence of Tinker Bell and Hook), he cannot read or spell or write, he is temperamental and quixotic, he acts quite nasty at various points in the story. Even his acts of heroism, as the book's narrator reveals, have more to do with the "cleverness of me"[32] than with sacrificing himself for the good of others as, for example, does Tink when she willingly drinks poison to save Peter. Lest it be forgotten, the first extended view of Peter Pan in most of the tale's iterations is of a boy chasing his own shadow, a concrete demonstration of his solipsistic obsession. He is a careless youth who thinks mostly of himself, one who is perpetually "gay, innocent, and heartless"[33]—the last words in the novel. In fact, Dan Kiley's much-quoted "Peter Pan Syndrome" accurately reflects the character traits of the boy in Barrie's story: irresponsibility, anxiety, loneliness, sex-role conflict, narcissism, chauvinism. Finally, this sequence sets up an incipient rivalry between Peter and Hook for Wendy, as much for masculine ego and bragging rights as for the control of Neverland. She becomes, in effect, the prize of their deadly competition, and at times, a weapon Hook can use to ensnare Peter.

THE CAPTAIN FLIES

P. J. Hogan includes several scenes that differ from previous versions of the Pan story, such as the previously discussed revealing of Hook's stump. But his most radical deviation comes when his pirate captain performs a miraculous feat denied all his literary and cinematic predecessors: he flies! Such a daring departure from earlier narratives makes Hook and Pan relatively equal antagonists. Previously, one was physically larger and the other compensated for this disadvantage with the gift of flight. Now, both can command the air. The inventive sequence begins with the climatic battle between the Lost Boys, aided by the Darling children, and the pirate crew, highlighted by the glittering swordfight between Hook and Peter Pan. At first, the boy seems to gain the advantage, employing acrobatic dips and aerial dives to outmaneuver his grounded adversary. The turning point arrives when a furious Hook grabs Tinker Bell and viciously shakes her, spilling fairy dust over himself. Suddenly borne aloft, he screams out a joyous revelation: "It's Hook! He flies! And he likes it!" Joining Peter amid the ship's high billowing sails, Hook finds a laughing opponent, who greets him with a sardonic hint of admiration, "Not bad for an old man." The insouciant jibe infuriates the captain and the two recklessly twist and turn in each other's arms, interlocked and madly twirling high into the clouds as one being.

From this point onward, the combat becomes as much mental as physical, each combatant insulting the other with increasing ferocity and inflicting more psychological gashes. Finally, Hook slashes through Peter's emotional armor and opens a raw wound with a palpable hit: "You are a tragedy. She was leaving you Pan. Your Wendy was leaving you. Why should she stay? What have you to offer? You are incomplete. She'd rather grow up than stay with you." Their glinting swords cross, as Hook mercilessly hacks home his point with a dire prediction: "Take a peep into the future. What do you see? 'Tis the fair Wendy in her nursery. The window is shut. I'm afraid the window is barred. She can't hear you. She can't see you. She's forgotten all about you."

Hook kicks Peter in the face, sending him sprawling into a sail, and floats triumphantly toward the stricken boy whose eyes now well up with tears: "And what is that I see? There is another in your place. He is called husband." Hook strikes another mighty blow and Peter smashes into the rough, wooden deck. He lies there panting, looking afraid, and appearing—for the first time in the movie—quite mortal. Hook's sword lifts Peter's chin, its point nicking his throat. Again, he kicks Pan backward, snapping his head against the mast. The pirate grips Peter's throat with his good hand and knocks his forehead with the metal one, causing a garish red gash to appear. Pulling the dazed boy to his feet by the scruff of his hair, the preening Hook mutters: "You will die all alone and unloved . . . just like me." Once more, he slams Peter onto the deck, the camera drawing out the action in slow motion to accentuate his suffering.

Sensing the death of Peter Pan is at hand (quite literally by Hook's metal appendage), the Lost Boys and the Darling children avert their eyes, but one of the pirates forces Wendy to witness the excruciating sight. A tear creeps down her check and, seeing this, a small smile creases Peter's lips. With a jubilant, savage cry, the captain draws back his sharp hook and prepares to slice Peter Pan into bits. Only the desperate grasp of Wendy slows him momentarily, but he shakes her violently to the ground, sending her sprawling next to the prostrate boy. She whispers tenderly into his ear, "I'm sorry I must grow up, but this is yours. This belongs to you and always will." With that, Wendy leans over and kisses Peter gently on the lips, a kiss that lingers even after they break apart. Hook stares wide-eyed; the children gasp, open-mouthed. Suddenly, Peter smiles and sunlight breaks into the gloomy blue of the frame. He turns bright pink and explodes upward, an ejaculatory frenzy that takes everyone—most of all his stunned archenemy—by surprise. Ecstatically, Pan closes his eyes and soars above the *Jolly Roger*. Grabbing two swords, he flips one to Hook, spins him over the water, and bellows, "You are old!" Hook's response is a childlike, petulant whine: "No. I won. I won." Treading air, Hook sees his worst nightmare circling just beneath his feet: the gaping jaws of the crocodile. "Old. Alone. Done for," chant the children, as Hook struggles to summon happy thoughts that will keep him aloft. But it is a futile battle against himself. Finally, he surrenders to his fate, sadly echoing their refrain as he plops into the crocodile's mouth: "Old. Alone. Done for."

The distinctive moment of the kiss separates Hogan's vision of *Peter Pan* from earlier versions of the story. Kissing, of course, inevitably plants one on the path to sexuality, a traditional line of demarcation between childhood (or adolescence) and adulthood. It also can lead to motherhood and fatherhood, roles only play-acted in Neverland but quite real in London. A liminal figure hovering between corporeality and immortality, Peter remains suspended in preadolescent animation and, tapped in this state, cannot understand what more both Tinker Bell and Tiger Lily would like of him—not to mention the insistent Wendy. In Barrie's novel, perpetual youth meant a denial of sexuality, or at least a severe repression of its powers; even an innocent kiss is transformed into a thimble. His portrait of Mrs. Darling romanticizes motherhood without a hint of how she got that way, despite the "innermost box and the kiss" she never grants to anyone, even her husband or children.[34]

But Hogan allows Peter a glimpse into the joys of physical contact, and that fleeting touch hurls him rapturously spiraling into the air. It vividly restores his dynamism. As noted, Hogan's film is far more sexualized than either Brenon's or Spielberg's movies. Not only is Hook a truly menacing figure right up until the film's conclusion, but he seems a genuine physical threat to Wendy and, at times, even a potential rapist. He does actually make her walk the plank, thinking that her death will deal a severe blow to Pan. Since no adult women inhabit Neverland, save for the murderous, web-fingered mermaids, Hook's sexual proclivities remain unknown, though Hogan presents him rather sensually, beginning with the scene previously discussed in which he appears scantily—and tightly—clad. Ultimately, Peter retreats back into androgynous asexuality; no doubt, the moment of the kiss slips from his consciousness as quickly as does the memory of Wendy, Hook, the Lost Boys, and their adventures.

THE NECESSARY RIVALRY

As is often the case in adventure narratives, the hero of *Peter Pan* and its villain are more similar to each other than to anyone else in the story, a fact commented upon by several critics. Yeoman, for example, notes:

> They both have difficulty relating to others; they are isolated and self-centered; each is motivated by a lust for power and control; and each fears the passage of time with the inevitable changes and transformations it occasions.... Both Pan and Hook enjoy extraordinary powers, yet each suffers a desperate and self-destructive loneliness.[35]

In fact, Peter imitates Hook twice in the narrative, once to save the captured children and another when the pirate has been vanquished, on the latter occasion using this enemy's distinctive cigar-holder, wearing his clothing, and bending his forefinger to look like a hook. For his part, Hook is quite bored without Pan to prod and challenge him, and no wonder; as Hogan's film depicts, a Panless Neverland consists of gray skies, lethargic pirates, frozen oceans, and desiccated landscapes. It is Pan's energetic presence that makes Neverland a vibrant place filled with escapades and dangers, with possibilities and play. After all, wicked deeds without a worthy opponent to thwart them bestow upon Hook the pallid rewards of material objects: it is neither greed nor lust that drives the captain to the heights of villainy, but rather the passionate fixation to best Pan and thereby prove himself superior to the boy wonder. Despite Hook's apparent demise in the jaws of the ravenous crocodile, the two adversaries are locked in an endless struggle, a fact aptly demonstrated by the appearance of the "first-ever authorized" sequel to Barrie's story, *Peter Pan in Scarlet* by Geraldine McCaughrean.

WHY HOOK HATES PAN

But why does Captain Hook hate Peter Pan? Obviously, Pan's tossing of the man's hand to the crocodile has instilled an enduring loathing, but we can also assume the two were at odds before this gory episode, since Peter severed Hook's limb in a previous swordfight. Also, as noted above, Hook despises Peter's boyish cockiness, his self-congratulatory crowing. Nicholas Tucker characterizes the conflict between Pan and Hook as a classic example of Oedipal rivalry, one in which "youth is shown defeating age and then carrying off the prize—the idealized parent of the opposite sex."[36] In this

configuration, Peter becomes the heroic father defending Wendy (the stylized maternal figure) and the Lost Boys (their vulnerable offspring) against
Hook (the violent threat from the adult world). Because the same actor
usually performs a Dr. Jekyll/Mr. Hyde split by playing both the ineffectual
Mr. Darling and the forceful Hook (as in the Hogan adaptation), Tucker
contends that this doubling encourages the "most bitter, hostile fantasies of
aggression toward adults who seriously threaten still-surviving, omnipo-
tent, infantile desires for exclusive ownership of the favorite parent."[37] Like
Tucker, Rustin sees *Peter Pan* as a "symbolic attack on the family."[38] In this
type of analysis, Hook embodies far more than an evil fantasy figure; his
kidnapping of Wendy makes him, in Tucker's words, "the black side of any
child's image of the father,"[39] since this deprives Peter and the Lost Boys of
their mother and all she represents. Similarly, Karen Coats, who situates the
book within a Victorian/Edwardian context, sees the story as encapsulating
"the antagonistic relationship between childhood and adulthood . . . and
the truly violent nature of that relationship."[40]

   Such readings correspond interestingly with Steve Neale's psychoanalytic understanding of cinematic identification as aligned with "socially
defined and constructed categories of male and female."[41] He hypothesizes
that cinematic identification incorporates two different "tendencies": individual elements of dream and fantasy, and narcissistic identification. The
latter proves especially valuable in gaining an understanding of the multiple
ways in which a viewer, even an adult, can sustain an identification with
Pan, since it involves "phantasies of power, omnipotence, mastery, and control."[42] In the two more modern movies, in which a man and a boy assume
the role of Pan, this contention seems particularly feasible, though it becomes
muddy in the silent film (and stage adaptations), in which a woman plays
Pan. In Spielberg and Hogan, however, with males—either child or adult—
playing Peter, one can surely acknowledge "the contradiction between narcissism and the law, between an image of *narcissistic* authority on one hand
and an image of *social* authority on the other."[43] In this sense, the battle shifts
from Pan and Hook to Pan and the Darlings; it becomes a fight between the
anarchic adventures possible in Neverland and the restrictions inherent in
London's civilized society.

   Yet, something less conscious gnaws at Hook beneath the surface of his
contempt, a visceral abhorrence akin to the instinctive loathing Claggart
feels for the young and handsome Billy Budd in Melville's seafaring novel.
Hook's hatred harkens to his concept of good form, a socially constructed
sense of what constitutes proper behavior learned during his youth. Those
school-day strictures bind him both to a civilized society beyond Neverland
and to a code of conduct for manhood he deems impossible to realize within

himself. Hook remains passionately obsessed with good form. His notion of what constitutes this quality, and the particular actions that embody such an inculcated concept, come mainly from his school days at Eton, a fact specifically referenced in his recollection of how one needs good form to be eligible for "Pop"—an elite debating society at Eton started in 1816.[44] (One wonders if Barrie was making a slyly conscious pun between the name of the school and Hook's dilemma: his hand having been "eaten"?) Hook cannot shed his early training, and the school's "traditions still clung to him like garments"[45] and shape his thinking about life and his daily conduct.[46] Though lapsed far from this Etonian ideal, Hook still tortures himself with self-imposed critiques founded on the fundamental principle that good form "is all that really matters."[47]

Despite his physical and moral degeneration from those adolescent years, this cadaverous man retains throbbing fragments of a social conscience born during his formative younger days: "far from within him he heard a creaking as of rusty portals, and through them came a stern tap-tap-tap, like hammering in the night when one cannot sleep."[48] Hook's telltale conscience betrays not only his breeding, but at times tempers his savagery. It is often the only thing standing between this terrible man who treats his crew like dogs, and callously kills Skylights for ruffling his lace collar, and the potential victims that surround him. Take, for example, the fury that initially erupts when Hook realizes that the kidnapped children aboard the *Jolly Roger* actually love, not fear, Smee. About to kill his most loyal subordinate, and the closest person he has to a friend, not only because he is loveable, but because "no little children love me,"[49] the captain's sense of proper behavior overcomes his rage, since "to claw a man because he is good form" is clearly to demonstrate "Bad form!"[50] Regardless of Hook's recognition that a pirate's life forever exiles him from civilized society, he clings tenaciously to the ingrained concept of good form as if it were the lone raft of ethical behavior in a sea of wickedness. And it often is just that.

The question Hook continually asks himself is always the same: "Have you been good form today?"[51] Neither fame nor the fear he engenders in others is enough to assuage the persistent pounding in his brain, the unremitting conformation of his failure to reach this standard of conduct. Ultimately, Hook locks himself into a philosophical cage by grasping the inherently paradoxical nature of his incessant contemplation of form: "was it not bad to think about good form?"[52] He realizes that the quintessence of good form is a natural, unthinking display of its characteristics, a feat he sadly concludes is impeccably demonstrated by the intuitive Peter Pan, who unselfconsciously embodies the epitome of good form. Hook's constant need to question and evaluate his behavior, which rarely corresponds with his ideal of good form, drives him to the edge of madness: "His vitals were tortured by this problem. It was a claw within him sharper than the iron one; and as it tore him, the perspiration dripped down his sallow countenance and streaked his doublet. Oft-times he drew his sleeve across his face, but there was no damning that trickle."[53] The ceaseless trickle externalizes Hook's inner anguish and emotional turmoil. Such suffering, perhaps, accounts for the "profound melancholy" in the captain's eyes.

Hook's observance of "form"—whether it be good or bad—links up nicely with his adoption of Cavalier attire; his long black curls and elaborately embellished clothing mimic Charles II (1630–1685), ostensibly because "he bore a strange resemblance to the ill-fated Stuarts."[54] By directly harkening back to the 1600s, Barrie endows Hook with a set of historical associations that establish his character's state of mind as well as his dress. During the reign of Charles II, England emerged as a European power trying to recover from its recent and incredibly destructive civil war and period under Oliver Cromwell while maintaining a cultural identity distinct from the dominant French ideals. At the time Barrie was writing *Peter Pan*, England had the wealth and power to engage in some historical revisionism. The author connects Hook to a period of time in which the British king was redefining "civilized" behavior, not on the battlefield but rather through his interactions with his "merry" followers, most notably the sexual adventurer the Earl of Rochester (John Wilmot) and his many mistresses. This late Victorian and Edwardian approach to history allows Barrie to focus on the relationship between courtier culture and the civilized society that gives rise to Hook's obsession with good form. In turn, it unites him with a two-hundred-year tradition in which public interaction among men and between men and women reflected public standing, allowed for the accumulation of power, and determined social interaction. The seventeenth-century England of the Stuarts, as filtered through the Edwardian glasses of J. M. Barrie, was a place in which manners mattered more than money, and good form was admired as much as deeds of daring. By introducing the concept of good form and linking it to Charles II, Barrie makes a claim that civility had always been the norm in upper-class English society, dating back at least to the Stuarts, though such a contention seems strangely ironic when embodied in a pirate.

For Hook, then, the galling fact that a mere boy can realize good form so effortlessly, so unthinkingly, permeates his entire being. He simmers with bile, envy, and resentment, ready to boil over at the slightest provocation. It is, as William Blake might describe it, "the invisible worm . . . whose dark secret love / does thy life destroy" (11. 2, 7–8).[55] Throughout the various book and film narratives, Hook both wants to emulate and to obliterate Pan. Certainly, a subliminal element of homoerotic attraction exists in their relationship, as well as the discordant parent/son dichotomy that compels them into competitive battles against each other. Then, too, the sheer delight Peter takes in being "youth" and "joy" affronts the captain's sense of mortality and his intelligence, as does the boy's cocky crowing. But at his very core, Hook remains forever aware of the devastating conclusion that the ludic Pan naturally expresses good form in his everyday actions while he, a man with far superior mental capacities, is condemned to endlessly contemplate his own ineffectual attempts to achieve it. Even though Peter has no sense "of who or what he was," Hook understands his lack of introspection to be "the very pinnacle of good form."[56] Thus, good form becomes the structuring absence in Hook's life. The painful anguish and deep sorrow it causes guides his actions and fuels his hatred toward Pan. It becomes the bedrock of the bitter revulsion he feels for his rival, whom he conceptualizes as forcing him to display bad form, against his better instincts and training. No wonder Hook goes rather contentedly to his fate in the novel, jeering Peter with a cry of "bad form" as the boy kicks instead of stabs him. At long last, Hook has received "the boon for which he craved."[57] In the captain's mind, Peter has finally revealed his true nature and, in so doing, proven himself as fallible as Hook, and more important, as capable of bad form.

This discussion of good form highlights a crucial difference between Pan and Hook. The boy lives only in the present and, as a result, has no memory of past events. As such, he retains no sense of personal or communal history and is, in fact, quite ahistorical, since he lives outside society's boundaries and laws. To retain this perpetual stasis, Peter can never grow up, never grow older, never be anything other than what he is at this point in his stunted development. His focus must always be on himself, for to assume any responsibilities for others demands an understanding of the inherent consequences of living in a social environment with a past and a future—as well as a present. It is to grasp that current actions have antecedents and consequences, and that what you do affects those around you. Though he moves and talks and acts, Peter Pan remains perpetually frozen in an endless time warp of games and adventures. Like the "foster child of silence and slow time" (1.2) of Keats's famous urn, he stays forever young but forever lacking connection, completion, or union with anything or anyone outside of himself.[58]

Hook, quite to the contrary, is obsessed with time and tortured by memories. The beast relentlessly pursuing him consumes human flesh and constantly reminds Hook that death awaits just a few ticks away from him—and from us as well. His demise offers unmistakable, if harsh, confirmation that we cannot escape the inexorable jaws of time. Concomitantly, his sharpest memories have triggered his current, traumatized condition: he remembers himself not only as a man with two good hands, but also as one who abided by good form during his school days. The distance between what he was before and how he looks and acts now constantly reminds Hook of the yawning gap between his perception of who he might have been and what he has become.

THE IMMORTAL PIRATE CAPTAIN

Without Captain Hook to oppose him, Peter Pan's seductive adventures are unimaginable. Hook's fearsome presence accounts for much of the narrative's continuing power, and his dark deeds for its sway over generations of adults and children. Most critics characterize Hook as the serpent in the garden, but a more nuanced view acknowledges the captain's sorrow as well as his malevolence: he is a desperately lonely, physically disabled, and emotionally damaged man who has focused his murderous rage on the person who maimed him. While the boy's exhilarating feats may seep into our warm and languid daydreams, the man's vengeful deeds are the stuff of frigid and frightening nightmares. This vibrant figure may have sprung full-blown from the head of J. M. Barrie as an inspired afterthought, but he remains inextricably coupled with his eternal adversary. After all, what would Luke Skywalker be without Darth Vader, Robin Hood without the Sheriff of Nottingham or, in a contemporary literary version of boy-hero versus man-villain, Harry Potter without Lord Voldemort? These deadly combatants are forever yoked together in our minds, for innocence must always be tested against experience; indeed, one would be but a pale intuition without the other to challenge it, as courage without action remains merely good intention. As long as we crave both heroes and villains, as long as we thrill to the glory of flight and shudder at the expression of wickedness, Peter Pan and Captain Hook will breathe within us. They pervade our cultural consciousness as enduring reminders of our reluctance to adhere to the mandate that we must grow up and to the inevitability that we all must do so.

NOTES

Some of the material in the *Hook* section has previously appeared in the author's *Citizen Spielberg* (Champaign-Urbana: University of Illinois Press, 2006). Used with permission of the University of Illinois Press. Thanks to Rae-Ellen Kavey and Delia Temes for their help with this essay.

1. Geraldine McCaughrean, *Peter Pan in Scarlet* (New York: Margaret K. McElderry Books, 2006), 99.
2. Karen McGavock. "The Riddle of His Being: An Exploration of Peter Pan's Perpetually Altered State," in *J. M. Barrie's Peter Pan In and Out of Time: A Children's*

Classic at 100, ed. Donna White and Anita C. Tarr (Lanham, MD: Scarecrow Press, 2006), 207.

3. Ann Yeoman, *Now or Neverland: Peter Pan and the Myth of Eternal Youth: A Psychological Perspective on a Cultural Icon* (Toronto: Inner City Books, 1998), 15–16.

4. Wade Jennings, "Fantasy" in *Handbook of American Film Genres*, ed. Wes D. Gehring (New York: Greenwood Press, 1988), 249.

5. Tzvetan Todorov, *The Fantastic: A Structural Approach to a Literary Genre* (Ithaca, NY: Cornell University Press, 1975), 56.

6. Jennings, "Fantasy," 252–253.

7. Ibid., 251.

8. J. M. Barrie, *Peter Pan* (London: Puffin Books, 2002), 10.

9. Ibid.

10. Ibid., 12.

11. Ibid., 10–12.

12. A precursor of Hook, Captain Swarthy, appears in *The Boy Castaways of Black Lake Island*, a record of Barrie's idyllic 1901 summer with the Llewelyn Davies children at his summer home. Only two copies of the book, which contains thirty-five photographs (all taken by Barrie himself), were ever printed; one Barrie gave to the boys' father, who promptly lost it on a railway carriage; and the other the author kept for himself. In the pictures on biographer Andrew Birkin's website, the stuffed figure of Captain Swarthy the boys strung up appears to be a Black man. As Birkin notes, "although Peter Pan did not figure into the story, many of the other elements were present: a South Sea lagoon, Indians, and a band of cut-throat pirates led by the fiendish Captain Swarthy" (see: jmbarrie.co.uk). Andrew Birkin includes a picture of Barrie playing Hook with Michael dressed as Peter Pan on his website and in his book (140).

13. Barrie, *Peter Pan*, 76.

14. Jill May. "James Barrie's Pirates: *Peter Pan*'s Place in Pirate History and Lore," in *J. M. Barrie's Peter Pan In and Out of Time*, ed. White and Tarr, 73.

15. Michael Rustin, "A Defense of Children's Fiction: Another Reading of *Peter Pan*," *Free Associations* 2 (1985): 142.

16. Barrie, *Peter Pan*, 192.

17. William Wordsworth. "Ode: Intimations of Immortality From Recollections of Early Childhood," in *English Romantic Writers*, ed. David Perkins (New York: Harcourt, Brace and World, 1967), 280. References to this work will be made parenthetically in the text by chapter and line number.

18. Henry Sheehan, "The PANning of Steven Spielberg," *Film Quarterly* 28, no. 3 (May–June 1992): 54.

19. Henry Sheehan, "Spielberg II," *Film Quarterly* 28, no. 4 (July–August 1992): 71.

20. Sheehan, "PANning," 54.

21. Maurice Berger, Brian Wallis, and Simon Watson, "Introduction," in *Constructing Masculinity* (London: Routledge, 1995), 2.

22. Judith Butler, "Melancholy Gender/Refused Identification," in *Constructing Masculinity*, 31.

23. Ibid.

24. Barrie, *Peter Pan*, 125.

25. Ibid., 76.

26. Ibid., 76.

27. Ibid., 76.

28. Yeoman, *Now or Neverland*, 133.

29. Ibid., 140.

30. Barrie, *Peter Pan*, 167.

31. Ibid., 167.
32. Ibid., 39.
33. Ibid., 242.
34. Ibid., 8.
35. Yeoman, *Now or Neverland*, 16/139.
36. Nicholas Tucker, "Peter Pan and Captain Hook: A Study in Oedipal Rivalry," *Annual of Psychoanalysis* 10 (1992): 356.
37. Ibid., 360.
38. Rustin, "A Defense of Children's Fiction," 140.
39. Tucker, "Peter Pan and Captain Hook," 360.
40. Karen Coats, "Child-Hating: Peter Pan in the Context of Victorian Hatred," in *J. M. Barrie's Peter Pan In and Out of Time*, ed. White and Tarr, 4.
41. Steve Neale, "Masculinity as Spectacle: Reflections on Men and Mainstream Cinema," in *Screening the Male: Exploring Masculinities in Hollywood*, ed. Steven Cohan and Ina Rae Hark (London: Routledge, 1993), 11.
42. Ibid., 11.
43. Ibid., 14. Emphasis in the original.
44. See Yeoman, *Now or Neverland*, 109 n174.
45. Barrie, *Peter Pan*, 185.
46. In his July 7, 1927, address to Eton students, Barrie playfully revealed, in a solemnly delivered biographical explication, that Hook had been a former student there, and he talked about some of his activities as a youth at the school (J. A. Hammerton, *Barrie: The Story of a Genius* [New York: Dodd, Mead, 1929], 468). Yeoman, noting the clear references to Pop and Eton, observes that "embedded in the structure of the tale itself lie the values and dynamics of the institution: Neverland suggests an exclusive boy's club, apart for parents, in a world of its own, with its singular population and hierarchy, moral code and set of values" (*Now or Neverland*, 168).
47. Barrie, *Peter Pan*, 186.
48. Ibid., 186.
49. Ibid., 186.
50. Ibid., 188.
51. Ibid., 186.
52. Ibid., 186.
53. Ibid., 186.
54. Ibid., 77.
55. William Blake, "The Sick Rose," in *English Romantic Writers*, ed. Perkins, 61.
56. Barrie, *Peter Pan*, 206.
57. Ibid., 209.
58. John Keats, "Ode on a Grecian Urn," in *English Romantic Writers*, ed. Perkins, 1186.

CHAPTER 8

"Gay, Innocent, and Heartless"

PETER PAN AND THE QUEERING
OF POPULAR CULTURE

David P. D. Munns

"ALL CHILDREN, EXCEPT ONE, GROW UP." This great opening line presents *Peter Pan*'s central themes of adulthood, mortality, and developing sexuality. Growing up connotes progress, but by not growing up J. M. Barrie's central character, Peter Pan, complicates the conventional idea of a successful adulthood as a desirable outcome. Peter Pan fundamentally critiques the appeal of chronological and psychological maturation toward adulthood, since they are the very things Peter clearly lacks. Chronicling the performers and performances of Peter Pan over the last century, Bruce Hanson noted an observation by Sondra Lee, who played Tiger Lily to Mary Martin's Peter Pan: "[Sondra] felt that during interviews, the media [was] too obsessed with the ages of . . . celebrities."[1] For Hanson, the ability of the actors to make their audiences believe in their performances rendered mute any discussion of their age. This assumes what needs to be explained: in a story predicated on an ageless boy, the actors themselves have engaged in a dialogue with the public about the dilemmas of Peter, Wendy, and Hook at their displayed ages.

This dialogue has seen popular culture's representations of Peter Pan age the boy who would not grow up: Peter Pan began as a boy aged four or five and is now widely seen as a teenager. Consequently, this aging has allowed for the appropriation of Peter Pan as a sexual object by popular culture, both straight, in examples like P. J. Hogan's 2003 film, and gay, as seen in the television series *Queer as Folk* (1999 in the UK and 2000–2004 in the United States). Other chapters in this volume pay ample attention to the heteronormative appropriation of Pan, but his presence in gay popular media and the effect that this character has had on gay male culture is equally important.

The transformation of *Peter Pan* into a tale about budding sexuality is equally crucial in understanding this figure as an enduring cultural trope. From Disney's version onward, the battle between Hook and Pan (man versus boy) has been elevated over the relationship between Peter and Wendy (boy and girl). To remain young forever and to have fun is now a byword in many parts of modern consumerist and materialist culture; from clothing labels to music labels, youth sells. One significant expression of the new interpretation of *Peter Pan* makes much of Peter's relationship with Hook, turning their lethal duel into a homoerotic tango defined by mutual attraction and repulsion with, importantly, a dramatic age difference. Gay culture recognized the Peter/Hook relationship in the first mainstream successful gay cable television series, *Queer as Folk* (2000–2005), through the intrigue between the man Brian and the boy Justin. The show illustrated that the traditional pairing of Mr. Darling with Captain Hook, in which the same actor plays both characters, has now been given over to the pairing of Peter with James Hook. Radically reinterpreted by gay culture, the ephebic Pan's desire for eternal youth is woven together with Hook's own obsession with old age and death.

PETER PAN AGES UP

James Matthew Barrie originally conceived of the eternal child as a babe, a figure more or less like a boisterous six-year-old, though the only definite age provided comes in Peter's story to Wendy, that he escaped from his nursery when he was only a week old. In our current imagination, however, Peter Pan is popularly conceived as being about eleven or twelve. Situating him at this significant chronological marker has several important consequences for the narrative. Our conception of childhood itself has changed substantially from the Edwardian context in which Barrie first dreamed up the character to entertain four boys he met regularly in Kensington Gardens. Barrie based "Peter" on the imagined adventures of the youngest Llewelyn Davies brother, Peter, then still in a perambulator. The literary figure emerged from Barrie's experiences with the elder boys, especially six-year-old Michael. For the Edwardians, the relationship between Barrie and the boys was charming, kind, and affectionate. Barrie was adopted into the Llewelyn Davies household as an "Uncle" and eventually, after their parents had tragically died, adopted all five boys as their guardian.

This relationship, when seen through a modern lens in which Peter is older and nearing the age of sexual maturation, suddenly looks suspect. Like Barrie's biographer, Andrew Birkin, modern consumers of Peter Pan express

8.1 A very young Peter playing on his pipes in Kensington Gardens. "Peter is the Fairies Orchestra" by Arthur Rackham from *Peter Pan in Kensington Gardens*, 1906. Used with Permission from Chris Beetles' Collection and the Bridgeman Art Library International, Ltd. London and New York.

disbelief at any suggestion that the friendship between a grown man and three boys might have been entirely innocent, and conclude that there must have been pedophilic intention if not action. Jacqueline Rose saw the absence of heterosexual sexuality in *Peter Pan* as a veiled code for Barrie's own obsession with young boys (which she parallels with Lewis Carroll's infatuations with young girls). Rose links the genre of fantasy tightly with issues concerning sexuality and argues for the impossibility of children's literature, since the book cannot discuss what it is, in fact, about: Barrie's desire for the three Llewelyn Davies boys. The novel itself and "the rest of *Peter Pan's* history," Rose claims, "can then be read as one long attempt to wipe out the residual signs of the disturbance out of which it was produced."[2]

As we will see, such a modern interpretation draws conclusions about Barrie's sexuality from two incompatible and anachronistic lines of investigation: a late-nineteenth-century story tradition of bachelor lives, alongside the late-twentieth and early-twenty-first century-adulation of youth. The latter compels the former to be considered sexually in modern retellings. To conclude that Barrie's intentions were anything other than platonic and fatherly is to impose modern conceptions of predatory adults upon an Edwardian man, and worse, to accept current paranoid ravings that connect pedophilia and homosexuality.[3]

Though Birkin uncovered no evidence to support any speculation of pedophilia, he still explicitly asked Nicholas Llewelyn Davies, the youngest brother, about the possibility. Nicholas Llewelyn Davies's absolute declaration that his and his brothers' relationship with Barrie was entirely innocent must stand unless concrete evidence turns up to destabilize it.[4] Birkin's cultural expectations made it impossible for him to believe in a sexless relationship between an apparently asexual man and three young children, whereas in the Edwardian mind it was entirely conceivable, and in fact true. Partially, Birkin's belief is due to the modern obsession with sexual children and the adults who prey upon them, and partially to the aging of Peter Pan from a true child into a near adolescent who wears his sexuality very close to the skin.[5] The pedophilia question also cropped up in the recent film, *Finding Neverland* (2004), an embroidered biography of Barrie, his relationship with the Llewelyn Davies family, and the story of the making of *Peter Pan*. In it, Barrie's character, masterfully played by Johnny Depp, was absolutely horrified when confronted by nasty rumors about his relationship with the boys.[6] Birkin's book and Marc Foster's film say much about contemporary notions of Barrie and the Lost Boys, predicated on a modern sexual Peter Pan, which came about because Peter Pan has aged to become prepubescent. Moreover, the Edwardian story of Peter and Wendy now dwells alongside a modern one about Peter and Hook. Even the most innocent film versions of Peter Pan produced in the last half-century flirt dangerously with sexual corruption and exploitation, particularly between Hook and Pan and between Hook and Tinker Bell.

In the century since the first stage production of *Peter Pan*, the age at which we believe children become sexual has been steadily driven

8.2 Peter Pan (Jeremy Sumpter) on the verge of adolescence in P. J. Hogan's *Peter Pan* (2001). Courtesy of Jerry Ohlinger's Movie Material Store.

downward. In P. J. Hogan's 2003 film *Peter Pan*, for example, Peter and Wendy are nearly thirteen, and Wendy is embarking on her last adventure before obeying her aunt's urging to prepare for love and marriage, "the greatest adventure of all."[7] More explicitly, in Steven Spielberg's *Hook* (1991), "Granny Wendy" announces that Peter was "twelve nearly thirteen" years old when he fell in love with her granddaughter, Moira, and chose to stay in London. If the film versions remain faithful to Barrie's concept, Peter and Wendy are similar sizes "in both mind and body."[8] Thus, to modern viewers both characters are on the verge of adolescence, rather than in the midst of childhood, and are facing sexual desire and emotional attachment along with imminent death at the hands of pirates.

The icon of the preteen, above all others, now dominates popular conceptions of Peter Pan as a character and a myth. Instead of a boy who shall not grow up and only wants to have fun—a status that absolves Pan from engaging with issues of sexuality that he will never encounter—contemporary characterizations reflect him dealing with the moment, or beginnings, of sexuality. It has changed fundamentally our reading of the story itself. No longer about childhood and the passionate desire to keep old age at bay, *Peter Pan* has become about the beginnings of sexuality and the dance toward and away from emotional commitment.

The aging of Peter is witnessed in the two famous public statues of the title character. Barrie and Sir George Frampton agreed on a design for a public sculpture of Peter Pan in Kensington Gardens sometime in 1911. Barrie convinced Frampton that the statue should appear without pre-publicity or even an unveiling. Instead, a short note simply appeared in *The Times*:

There is a surprise in store for the children who go to Kensington Gardens to feed the ducks in the Serpentine this morning. [They] will find a gift by Mr. J. M. Barrie, a figure of Peter Pan blowing his pipe on the stump of a tree with fairies and mice and squirrels all around. It is the work of Sir George Frampton and the bronze figure of the boy who would never grow up is delightfully conceived.[9]

Delightful, and now famous, Frampton's work shows Peter standing on a woodland scene, looking to the distance, his young face unable to catch anyone's eye, as his delicate fingers play his pipe and a horde of female fairies and other woodland creatures stare up at him adoringly.

Nearly a century later there appeared a second statue of Peter Pan in London. Erected in 2000 by Lord and Lady Callaghan, friends of the Great Ormond Street Hospital for Children, it sits by the hospital's main entrance. The Callaghan statue has Peter sitting alone on a tree branch, looking directly at his audience and seemingly blowing a kiss. A few years later, a small figure of Tinker Bell was added to Peter's upright hand; Peter and Tink are now perpetually connected by, of all things, a thimble. Unlike Frampton's, the Ormond Street representation sees Peter gaunt but lithe, clothed only in a greenish waistcloth, an almost stern expression on his face. In Frampton's statue, Peter is maybe six or seven years old, while at the door of the Great Ormond Street Hospital he is eleven or twelve. In the Kensington Gardens statue, fellow inhabitants of Neverland surround Peter, while at Great Ormond Street, he is alone with the exception of his tiny fairy friend. A century on, Peter Pan has shed his supporting cast: they have grown old and died. Only Peter remains, forever young and eternally desired.

Constructed in the last days of Edwardian England, Frampton's Kensington Park statue of Peter Pan marks the end of a time of innocence. Comparing Peter's Kensington memorial to the one at Great Ormond Street shows the transformation that Peter Pan has undergone over the last century, in particular how he has moved from a figure of innocence to an icon at the beginning of puberty. But even this icon of independent masculine childhood is defined by the often forgotten feminine presence of Wendy peering up over the edge of the stump. She has been forgotten not only by Peter (again), but also in *The Times*' announcement of the statue's appearance. Wendy is perfectly evident in the sculpture, of course. She is the only other human figure, albeit smaller and removed from the center, but far from hidden. Wendy gazes longingly at Peter, evoking that sense of awe and desire with which she meets Peter in her bedroom. From the very beginning, the public persona of Peter Pan has distanced the character from the

8.3 Sir George Frampton's statue of Peter Pan in Kensington Gardens. Photo by David P. D. Munns.

original storyline of Peter and Wendy, concentrating instead upon the persona of Peter himself.

Even Barrie's biographers forget about Wendy. Jackie Wullschläger has but one line on the subject, to the effect that Wendy was a made-up name. If we are going to read into the fiction based upon Barrie's own life, then his relationship to Sylvia Llewelyn Davies(read: Peter's relationship with Wendy) as an enforced platonic friendship always mediated and threatened by Arthur Davies, Sylvia's husband (read: Hook) is a far more convincing interpretation. All the Davies children are the Lost Boys, as they are collectively seen in the holiday photo-story *The Boy Castaways*. Wullschläger is insensitive and uncharitable to readily charge that Hook and Mr. Darling are "sexually mature male villains."[10] Hook and Mr. Darling have become

hypersexualized, but in order to downplay the far more disturbing proto-
sexuality of the children.

"ORDINARY BOY?" "NO." "WONDERFUL BOY!"

The works of Victorian children's writers, from Thomas Hughes's *Tom
Brown's School Days* (1858) to C. S. Lewis's *Chronicles of Narnia* (1950–1956),
sought to understand childhood and in effect elevated its stature to something almost bordering on reverence.[11] "Childhood" became a category that
in and of itself was not necessarily concerned with the child, but with an
adult's conceptualization of the meaning and purpose of childhood. Childhood adventures were good fun, but they also taught the child how to navi-
gate through the world: boarding school stories, for example, were morality
tales concerning the proper relationship between a child and his or her
peers. The authors of such stories, being adults, imposed upon their plots
and characters the lessons that they thought should be learned in such situations. Children's literature thus has affected generations of readers through
thinly, or entirely unconcealed, critiques of the society in which they live.
The stories often idolize children's separation and independence from adult
supervision and thus encourage individual expression. If one thinks of *Peter
Pan*, *The Chronicles of Narnia*, or most recently the Harry Potter series, the
removal of the child characters from an adult world is an important device.
In both Narnia and Hogwarts, the Pevencies and the Wealseys learn important lessons that they carry into their adult lives. On Peter's island, however,
linear time is absent, replaced by a closed circle of characters and adventures. The cast of the island of Neverland is introduced as a parade on a
loop, where "the lost boys were out looking for Peter, the pirates were out
looking for the lost boys, the redskins were out looking for the pirates," and
the crocodile was looking to finish the chief pirate Captain Hook.[12]

Peter discourages all reference to the real world, and delights in the
prospect of eternal adventures. *Peter Pan* stands in contrast to other books
of the adventure genre by downplaying the necessity of returning to normal life armed with important lessons (like those the Pevencies gain when
they return through the Wardrobe). Instead, the book and play, through
their title character, valorizes a static existence where societal norms can be
ignored because there is no possibility of their ever being needed or used.
Moreover, the sentimentalized image of the nineteenth-century child is
challenged by a forgetful, inconsiderate, and crowing Peter Pan—"there was
never a cockier boy"[13]—who displays none of the values of polite restraint
and civilized engagement repeatedly emphasized by other works. Barrie's
experience with children resulted in his downplaying the ideal of innocent
childhood in favor of a three-dimensional characterization of children that

recognizes their humanity; Peter is the most extreme example of an id-driven character in the work, while Wendy and Hook work hard to maintain their commitment to appearances and good form. While Hook plays with Wendy's affections (most notably in the 2003 P. J. Hogan film), Peter is stymied by the desires of Wendy, Tiger Lily, and his faithful fairy, Tinker Bell. Despite their efforts, Neverland responds most directly to Peter, shining when he crows and growing dark when he cries. Hard work, virtue, restraint, and humility are unknown to Peter Pan, and so is the dance of male-female courtship. Recent work by Jeffery Dennis argues that popular culture, until the 1950s, almost entirely portrayed all-American teenagers delaying even the thought of pursuing heterosexual encounters until they are eighteen.[14]

The Edwardian era idolized masculine, playful, and brazen youth. In part that tension was relaxed by the conventions of the British stage, which habitually saw a woman play Peter. Pauline Chase, one of the most significant actresses to assume the Pan role, starred for four seasons at the Duke of York Theatre, from 1906 to 1909.[15] American audiences, with their penchant for continuing the Victorian age indefinitely, widely remember Mary Martin as Peter on Broadway in 1954, and thereafter on NBC television productions in the 1960s, and more recently, Cathy Rigby's performance of the role.[16] When thirty-five-year-old Miles Anderson played Peter for the 1982 season of the Royal Shakespeare Company's production, few reviewers were entirely happy with the performance: "[Miles Anderson as Peter] does not seem to be of a different flesh from the others," commented *The Daily Telegraph*.[17] Girls enacting both Peter and Wendy emphasized the asexual nature of the relationship, "with a masculine star [the] all important illusion faltered and died."[18] Yet Barrie's novel presents only a one-sided portrayal of a longing for courting rituals. Though Wendy is delighted to suspend her journey to maturity for a time in Neverland, Wendy "knew that she must grow up." Wendy is the only child character in Barrie's world who not only acknowledges that she must grow up but also warmly embraces the prospect. Wendy knows that she has much to gain from becoming an adult, separating her from the other children and Peter Pan, who does not acknowledge the process or experience the desire to mature.

The powerful desire for perpetual youth dominates representations of gay male popular culture. Such desire builds upon the distance *Peter Pan* creates between the expectations for the genders through Wendy's embrace of maturity and Peter's absolute rejection of it. Ironically, the British-created Peter Pan reflected an increasingly American approach to life. The prospect of escaping reality to revel in a dream of always having fun and never growing up appears in Americans' embrace of new theme parks across the country. Contrasting the serious 1915 Panama-Pacific international exhibition in San Francisco to the 1915 playful opening of "Toyland," the historian Woody Register noted the appearance of a "Peter Pan culture" among middle-class Americans. Not yet shaken by the horrors of World War I, middle-class grownups flocked to new amusement parks across the United States. In contrast to the industrious and austere exhibitions of the Victorian era and their "noble education," these Toylands were sites of a "great play place."[19]

Toylands became controlled and commercialized realizations of childhood's carefree fantasy and play. According to the leading industry magazine, *Playthings*, such amusement parks were representatives of "Peter Pan the playfellow."[20] One of the leading amusement park entrepreneurs, Fred Thompson, evidently used Barrie's character and world to drum up support for his project, which was only ever half finished. He had planned a "City of Peter Pan" and insisted on divorcing the real world from Toyland as much as possible: "none can enter here who is not willing to play, for the [Grown Up] tin soldiers will guard the entrance against all those nasty modern people who keep on killing the fairies by not believing in them," said one early description.[21] Register goes farther, claiming that one amusement Thompson envisioned but never built, the "Wishing Well," which saw people standing in a bucket and being lowered into the well to make their wish, "invited [middle-class men] to disregard religion, work, civic identity, and the welfare of others, and to subject themselves, their longings, and dissatisfactions, to the alchemical wonders of the marketplace where they could be 'Anything They Wish.'"[22] The removal of oneself from the real world to a place of play and upturned norms and mores is a clear feature of Neverland, which provides lost boys with a landscape in which to avoid the quotidian responsibilities of growing into men.

Peter Pan has been made more real and more visible through pictures and illustrations. Over the last half-century, Peter Pan himself has transformed popular conceptions of awakening sexuality, which has, in turn, altered the changing meaning of the immortal figure. Chris Routh has outlined the most significant illustrators of Peter Pan. The story of Peter Pan was consistently rewritten throughout Barrie's lifetime, both on and off the stage, and subsequently adapted, used as the basis for sequels, and made into movie scripts from that day until this one. Barrie's characters have also changed during the last century, inviting new meanings and permitting new interpretations and appropriations of the story from the culture that surrounds and supports it. Routh lists nearly twenty illustrators of Peter Pan, though one notable absence is Sir George Frampton's statue in Kensington Gardens, which must rank as one of the most ubiquitous images of Peter. Two are worth closer attention here, and draw out several themes about the transformation of Peter over the decades: Mabel Lucie Attwell's "dimpled puffball" children[23] and the brightly colored Walt Disney adolescents. Attwell's children are cherubs, not so much children as toddlers defined by their puffy, rosy cheeks, and altogether innocence. From Attwell and Frampton to Disney, Peter and Wendy have aged as much as a decade. Frampton's and Attwell's Peters and Wendys are very young. They are closer in age, certainly, to Barrie's own image of Peter Pan: the boisterous six years Michael Llewelyn Davies standing atop the creatures of Neverland in Peter Pan regalia.[24] Yet if Attwell's are closer to the original age of Peter, the illustrations lose much of his character: Barrie reportedly complained that Frampton's statue "doesn't show the Devil in Peter," though being a secret and private commission Frampton's work must have been closely watched and guided by Barrie. If Frampton's statue is lacking devilry, then Attwell's children are even further from the imagined.[25] Barrie's children are far from the entirely innocent Attwell puffballs. In tidying up the Darling children's minds each night, Mrs. Darling makes "discoveries sweet and not so sweet." A mother's job, in fact, is to ensure that when her children "wake in the morning, the naughtiness and evil passions . . . have been folded up small and placed at the bottom of your mind."[26] The evil passions are not removed or destroyed, merely tidied up and packed neatly away: in a word, closeted.

Peter Pan as a Teenager

Peter Pan as a popularly conceived male character on the verge of sexuality really begins, ironically, with Walt Disney's 1953 *Peter Pan*. Disney was able successfully to project a boy Peter by drawing upon Bobby Driscoll as a model for their animated film.[27] Utilizing a male star in his early teen years instead of a mature female lead, Disney's Peter directly engaged in latent heterosexual rights of passage, in contrast to the prewar popular culture portrayals of teenagers. Disney's Tinker Bell further added to the overt sexuality of Barrie's story; no longer just a stage-light, Tink assumes female form, becoming a very "sexy little nymph hopelessly in love with Peter," nowhere more so than when Julia Roberts played Tink in *Hook* (1991) and wore a wedding dress.[28] In terms of the Disney brand, Tinker Bell, the curvy blond beauty, has remained one of their most ubiquitous images. Disney thus fundamentally altered the popular conception of Barrie's story. In making Peter both more masculine and older than he had been previously depicted, as well as enlarging and feminizing Tinker Bell, Disney opened up the public availability of Peter Pan as an icon for burgeoning sexuality. In parallel, Hook became more of a sexual predator, given he and Peter's inverse relationship, and moved beyond merely the alter ego of Mr. Darling, the accountant father.

The exaggerated differences in size and age of the three Darling children in Disney's *Peter Pan* further pushed upward the ages of Peter and Wendy. For all the careful elimination of any sexual transgression in Disney's film (it must be the most innocent in terms of plot of any version), Peter and Wendy are now at a stage of protoheterosexual exploration. Through Disney, and because of his new age, Peter is less easily allied with the characteristics that Barrie's Pan celebrates: the forgetfulness, the pride, and the heartlessness— the very qualities without which one can hardly have a decent adventure. In Jacqueline Rose's Freudian analysis of the story, Peter Pan avoids sexuality. "The sexual act which underpins *Peter Pan* is neither act nor fantasy in the sense in which these are normally understood and wrongly opposed to each other. It is an act in which the child is used (and abused) to represent the whole problem of what sexuality is, or can be, and to hold that problem at bay."[29] In Barrie's original story, Peter explicitly does not understand the meaning of a kiss. For Wendy, the kiss is a secret shared between mother and daughter, and a special place on the corner of one's mouth. For the adult audience of the early pantomime, the humor comes from Peter's total ignorance, as highlighted by Tinker Bell's emphatic "you ass" whenever he fails to appreciate Wendy's meaning. The relationship between the two children, Peter and Wendy, occurring in an utterly naïve and innocent way, must surely have been one of the popular moments of the play and kept adult audiences coming back time and again. To understand Barrie's work is to highlight the dueling narratives of childhood innocence and flirtation. Wendy is swept away by Peter. His bravado, his audacity, and his crowing are attractive to Wendy, and later Tiger Lilly, while their infatuation is the cause of jealously in Tinker Bell. Part of Peter's innocence is that he is not swept away, like other men, by the affections of a pretty girl offering a kiss. Surely that innocence is at the core of the narrative's enduring popularity

Harry Potter starts where Peter Pan leaves off. Part of the phenomenal success of the series is the vision J. K. Rowling conjured of a developing Pan-like character. Harry is eleven when Year One begins. Oppressed and tucked away in a cupboard under the stairs by his proudly "normal" aunt and uncle, to whom silliness, odd style of manner and dress—any form of Neverland—are a complete anathema. There are elements in Harry's character that echo his Pan legacy: flying is completely normal, Harry breaks rules and plays Quidditch to have fun. *Harry Potter and the Philosopher's Stone*, opening with Harry as a baby, and then jumping, in chapter two, to Harry aged eleven, bypasses a direct Peter Pan narrative parallel, but develops the story of a boy who desires to stay in a version of Neverland, but who also grows up. The dreamlike quality of Hogwarts, embedded within a wider Wizarding Community, is realized by Harry's return to the world of his "Muggle" aunt and uncle at the conclusion of each of the first six books. And, to make sure that readers are aware of how heavily she is borrowing Barrie's work, after Harry's first adventure Rowling paraphrases Barrie's immortal line—"death is but the next great adventure."[30] As the series developed, one storyline coherently held the books together: the battle between a child and a man, between Harry Potter and Lord Voldemort. Voldemort attempted to kill Harry as a baby due to a prophecy about his own downfall via the child. Of course, it was Voldemort's own act that created his nemesis, just as Peter and Hook are formed from their constant struggle with each other. But Rowling's clearest debt to Peter Pan comes near the end of the last book as the final battle between Voldemort's Death Eaters and the now-dead Dumbledore's Order of the Phoenix rages at Hogwarts School, when Harry realizes that "He and Voldemort and Snape, the abandoned boys, had all found homes here."[31]

Yet drawing the parallels too closely would be a mistake, as Rowling's magical boarding school has a real-place feel more akin to Lewis or E. Nesbit and is deeply indebted to the long tradition of school stories in English children's literature. Nor does Rowling's imagination map youth onto the Edwardian categories of beauty, sacrifice, and patriotism, except perhaps in the case of Cedric Diggory. Rather, whereas Harry embraces his new reality, Peter adamantly refuses ever to face the reality of growing up. Harry fumbles his way through his first romance, dance, and kiss; Peter forever accepts kisses merely as thimbles. Finally, the world of Wizards becomes richer and more concrete with each Rowling book; *Finding Neverland* notwithstanding, Neverland remains in the imagination.

To understand *Peter Pan*'s continuing power and easy appropriation by popular culture, we must forget about Wendy, as Peter himself does, and focus on the pursuit of Peter as an ideal and myth. John and Michael, the Lost Boys, Hook, Disney, and, as we shall see, gay male culture have all participated in the construction and embrace of the desire for youth, enticingly entwined with cockiness and daring situated in all-male communities. Many children's adventure stories emphasize bachelor lives, and groups of male youths rollicking about. Robert Louis Stevenson's *Treasure Island* (1883) and Kenneth Grahame's *Wind in the Willows* (1908) are essentially womanless. Barrie's late-in-life speech "Jas Hook goes to Eton" filled out a particular storyline of the identity of Captain Hook and his history as a pupil at a famous boys' school. Armed with Hook's prehistory, Hook's and Barrie's desire for Peter Pan becomes less overtly sexual—though Stephen Fry remembers boys' schools being about little else except fumbling through sexual exploration[32]—than with the portrayal and idolization of a time of innocence and play, secure within the walls of the school and supported by one's fellows. A recent narrative, *Queer as Folk,* reflects the continuing importance of *Peter Pan* in popular culture, and illustrates the significance of Peter's perceived aging and the homosocial content of his world.

PETER PAN AND GAY DESIRE

Peter Pan, in his continually reinvented guises in popular culture, has aged from a boy to a teen over the course of the past century. At the same time, the emphasis on the relationship between Wendy and Peter has been replaced with a near fixation on the duel between Peter and Hook. One of the most expensive movies at the time, Steven Spielberg's *Hook* (1991), completed this transformation of the central story of *Peter Pan* by leaving Wendy in England and focusing solely upon the battle between Hook and Peter. A decade later, the television series *Queer as Folk* could embrace this all-male modern conception of Peter Pan, and the final part of this essay will draw out how the series has extended the desire to be young. The series' dramatic portrayal of "gay lifestyle" celebrated the embrace of Peter's dictum to stay forever young and to have fun. As the series unfolded, however, the central character evoked Peter Pan's own tension of living without consideration for others or potential negative consequences as both ultimately enticing and desirable but also alienating and self-destructive. While the series initially presents as infinitely appealing gay culture worshiping a figure of Peter and a vision of Neverland, the final lesson reinforces the ultimately tragic nature of Peter as eternally isolated, if also eternally desired.

The original British version of *Queer as Folk* (1999) was acclaimed, innovative, and challenging. The show presented a series of storylines about a trio of gay men: two best friends from high school now nearing thirty who encounter a fifteen-year-old entering gay life centered in Manchester's Canal Street. First made for British television, the show was later remade for an American audience and was aired on Showtime from 2000 to 2005. In its frank and sexually provocative portrayal of gay male life, *Queer as Folk* played with the model of *Peter Pan.* The opening sequence showed Stuart (Aidan Gillen) emerging from a gay nightclub to encounter a "lost boy," Nathan (Charlie Hunnam), anxiously surveying an utterly new world of gay men straight out of his heated teenaged imagination. Stuart approaches Nathan and sweeps him away straight to his apartment. When Russell Davies was writing the script for the British *Queer as Folk,* he thus encountered a problem: "[So] the opening ten minutes of ep.1 were scary and tense. Fortunately, we were still filming, so I was able to go away and write a completely new piece-to-camera for Vince. He becomes your narrator, someone safe, relaxed to lead you into that world."[33] Vince (Craig Kelly) is the childhood friend of Stuart (Aidan Gillen), the Peter Pan–like central character of the show. Davies found that, like Peter's forgetfulness, pride, and cockiness, Stuart's own sexual bravado threatens unfamiliar viewers. If graphic images of gay sex are not enough, the show's first episode stresses the age difference between Stuart and the younger Nathan, as well as the casual nature of their encounter, and the explicitly sexual world Stuart introduces to Nathan.

Russell Davies's editorial decision to incorporate a safe voice in the figure of mild and calm Vince emulates modern remakes of Peter Pan that use the voice of Wendy, usually as a grown woman recalling her adventures, as narrator. Particularly evident in P. J. Hogan's *Peter Pan* and Spielberg's *Hook*, Wendy's narrative role as the safe voice initiates modern viewers into a world that has less to do with adventure and fun than with the budding sexuality of Peter and Wendy, and Wendy's hopes for Peter. With Peter as cocky boy and Wendy as a pure girl, the inherent moment of sexual awakening has emerged as a far more dominant theme in the popular conception of Peter Pan, but the scene is always stolen from Wendy when Peter repeatedly overlooks her in favor of his standing engagement with Hook.

In *Queer as Folk,* Russell Davies pushed the moment of sexual awakening within a homosocial world. In the competitive sexual world of gay clubs as seen through the pilot episode of the British version of the series, Peter's cockiness is no longer a sin but celebrated, and does not need to be excused. Stuart is brazen, forgetful, and prideful, but the other "lost boys," especially longtime friend Vince, would rather be ignored by Stuart than fawned over by practically anyone else. Aside from introducing the major characters, the pilot episode juxtaposes the life of gay nightclubs with anonymous sex, bodies on display, and the imagination of desire with the birth of Stuart's son. Stuart is a father only in the biological sense that he donated the sperm: the child's parents are a lesbian couple. Receiving a phone call in the middle of his first sexual encounter with Nathan, Stuart rushes to the hospital accompanied by Nathan and Vince. Seeing his new son, as well as having to be reminded of Nathan's name, the scene gives another reading of both Peter Pan and gay culture: looking at his child, with Nathan on his arm, the child becomes the crocodile.

STUART: He's a calendar. That kid, he's a clock, a great big stopwatch, staring me in the face. 'Cos he gets older, that's all he can do, d'you know what that means? I'm getting older. (To Nathan) Look at me. Is that old? That's not old. (kisses Nathan) Can't get rid of him, twenty years' time, he'll still be there.[34]

Wullschläger's biography of J. M. Barrie claimed, too simply, "*Peter Pan* is a wish-fulfillment story about the triumph of youth over old age which caught the mood of the new young century."[35] It is Peter who triumphs, not over Hook, but over growing old. Hook and Peter desire youth and brazenness; the fear of old age haunts Hook and keeps Pan locked away in Neverland, where he will never have to face it. The clock swallowed by the crocodile actually acts as a warning to Hook, who can hear the approach of the creature and escape. "'Some day,' said Smee, 'the clock will run down, and then he'll get you.' Hook wetted his dry lips. 'Ay,' he said, 'that's the fear that haunts me.'"[36] While at first sight we may think that the clock is marking time with its relentless motion, Hook's (and Stuart's) greatest fear is that time will stop. Only when the clock runs down will Hook no longer be able to evade the crocodile; one day Stuart will be unable to face any youth, let alone successfully seduce him. As the rest of the series demonstrates, Stuart's drive is therefore to stay in motion and have more fun, more drinks, more drugs, and more men. Peter, too, acts in this way; every adventure is one more active moment that allows him to avoid thinking about what he left behind when he escaped through his nursery window. Hook's and Stuart's failure to halt time, in contrast to Peter's success, mocks them both, and it spurs them onto greater excesses.

In the American version of *Queer as Folk* (2000–2004), Brian (Gale Harold) is the Peter Pan character, and though the scene revealing his reaction to the new baby resonates with the theme that new birth also evokes death, the scene was altered so that Brian's reaction to the birth of his child is return to his childhood friend Michael. Michael (Hal Sparks) echoes the sentiments of the real world, that place you fly away from to get to Neverland: "Still it's exciting isn't it, having a kid." Brian (Gale Harold) will have none of it: "What, having some wrinkled little time-clock ticking away reminding you you're getting older?"[37] Brian's is a classic Pan retort to the aggrandizement of any piece of the real world, especially a child whose sole purpose, at least in Brian's mind, is to remind him of his own mortality. Michael holds onto Brian and calls him Dad, referring to him by the informal version of the same title applied to Peter Pan by the Lost Boys in the cave under the ground. This reminder of Brian's/Peter's existing ties, which extend from the Neverland into the real world and back, allows him to continue his fantasy life, in which flight—through drugs, through music, through sex—is possible only for those who are willing to pay the price. Michael plays the part of the Lost Boys, reminding Brian/Peter that there will always be those who value his Neverland identity over any he might hold in the real world, and that his devoted friends and fans will literally follow him anywhere—to Babylon, the gay Mecca of Pittsburgh, and even to the door of the delivery room to help him cope with the collision of his two worlds and reintegrate him into his preferred one. In Michael's imagination Brian is preternatural, capable of greater than human excess in consumption, in bed, and in generosity, much as Peter seemed to the Darling children and the Lost Boys, who relied on him to lead them and be their hero.

Following the "ticking clock" scene in the hospital, the American *Queer as Folk* (2000) cuts to Brian and Michael on the roof of the hospital and Brian threatening suicide, saying, "Come on Mikey, let's fly, like in all those comic books."[38] Brian's longtime friend Michael remains as hopelessly devoted to Brian as the Lost Boys are to Peter. In a scene comprised of close-ups against the pixilated city skyline, Brian's awareness of life as a limited-term engagement defined not by adventures but by responsibilities forces him to consider "flying." Brian claims to be Superman, but Superman would not push Michael to the front of the ledge.

Peter Pan, on the other hand, would—and he would also lie to his followers, as Brian lies to Michael, and use a familiar and comforting figure to lure them to follow and stay with him. In *Peter Pan*, this is demonstrated by Peter's adoption of the real world term "father," a figure whose power he is happy to adopt but whose responsibilities he finds hideous and expendable. He does, however, know the rhetorical power of the word. 'Father' is used to lure the Lost Boys, and especially the Darling children, into Peter's fantasy life and convince them to remain with him there. Like Peter, Brian pushes his devoted charges to their limits, borrowing responsible and powerful figures from their own lives—Superman is an excellent example borrowed from the mind of comic-book buff Michael—to lend him the power and them the courage to do things of which dreams are made.

Dreaming of escaping by flight remains one of the powerful motifs of *Peter Pan* and certainly is one of the most frequently borrowed by modern popular culture. The iconic flight sequence from the original *Superman* (1978) and its remake *Superman Returns* (2006) both copy iconic visions of Disney's *Peter Pan*, sweeping fingertip flights through city streets and above the clouds. Harry Potter found flying "easy" and "*wonderful*."[39] As *Queer as Folk* referenced, the ability to remove yourself and to travel in other realms is what often separates comic-book characters and preternatural sprites from the ordinary mortals in their care. The ability to fly is one that both liberates the hero from the ordinary world but also separates him, as Peter is separate from the Lost Boys and Brian is from his friends and lovers.

Peter and Wendy's relationship is neither simply one of pure devotion or a nonsexual parody of a married couple. The early commonplace interpretation is that Barrie's play and story concerns chiefly the relationship

8.4 Brian (Gale Harold) and Michael (Hal Sparks) in the latter's comic book store sharing their childhood passion. Courtesy of Jerry Ohlinger's Movie Material Store.

between Wendy and Peter. Nina Boucicault believed that *Peter Pan*, "from beginning to end the story is a rather wistful commentary on human nature, taking as its theme the supreme selfishness of man and the supreme unselfishness of woman."[40] In fact, *Queer as Folk* establishes a significantly different interpretation of the relationship between Brian (Gale Harold) and Lindsey (Thea Gill), who are joined by a long friendship beginning in college that included a few sexual encounters before both characters embraced their homosexuality. With the arrival of Wendy in Neverland, Peter's role as Father becomes crystallized, just as Brian's paternal identity is confirmed when Lindsey has his child. Sitting on the maternity bed, Brian and Lindsey express surprise at their new identities. They refer to each other as "Peter" and "Wendy," clearly referencing some old in-joke, and display trepidation at the prospect of parenthood. The moment does not last for Brian, however; he is merely playing at being "Father." He is an interloper into Lindsey and her partner Melanie's family, as Peter is an interloper into Mr. and Mrs. Darling's household.

Peter remains perplexed throughout the novel, first at Wendy's advances, and later Tiger Lily's desires. He realizes that something is strange about them both, that each wants something from him, but he is unable to envision any role for a woman in the community beyond that of "mother." "'You are so queer,' he said, frankly puzzled, and 'Tiger Lily is just the same. There is something she wants to be to me, but she says it is not my mother.'"[41] Even as Peter Pan rejects a grown-up life, he becomes desired by those trapped within heteronormativity. Everyone wants Peter to be something in Neverland: eternal playmate, Father, eternal nemesis, gallant hero. Yet Peter only plays each of his roles temporally, wistfully, until something else captures his attention. Brian and Peter share contempt for the normative expectations of fatherhood and growing up: their strength is in being queer, in being strange—Tiger Lily, Tink, and even Wendy can only eternally desire what they can never have.

Ironically, any resistance to normal heterosexual development between Peter and Wendy has been systematically downplayed in Barrie's version of the story, but it is one of the significant themes developed in the *Peter Pan* directed by P. J. Hogan. Hogan makes Wendy's desire for Peter, and Peter's inability to return that desire, into an advantage for Hook, who seduces Wendy with the pretense of adult male sexuality and the seemingly sad confession about Pan that, "he cannot love." This leaves Wendy out in the cold, quite literally, and she turns to Hook for comfort. In the American version of *Queer as Folk,* lost-boy Justin (Randy Harrison), Brian's very young want-to-be boyfriend, also turns to other men when Michael tells him that Brian will never love him and that he should just go home. Rather than abandoning the field, however, Justin beats Brian at his own game, literally recrafting himself from a scared high school student to the most desirable man in Babylon.[42] Justin challenges Brian's own claims to being Pan. Justin is younger, and desirable on the dance-floor, and thus reattracts Brian's attentions. If only Wendy had had such a receptive audience—if only there *were* lost girls in Neverland. Instead, the Hogan film gives her the power to revive Peter with a kiss that holds no romance for him but rather allows him to triumph over Hook, while Justin's sexual triumph draws Brian inevitably back to him—because what could be hotter, or more powerful, than the two most desirable men in Neverland/Babylon together?

Peter claims, of course, that he does not really desire anything, except to duel with Hook and to hear another story. Every other character in the book, however, is desirous: Wendy for Peter and the assumption of the role of mother; the Lost Boys for their mothers and the lives they left behind; Hook for youth and the destruction of Peter Pan; the Indians for the Pirates; the crocodile for the remainder of its meal. Even the Island itself is desirous for Peter's return; it only "woke" when it had the "feeling that Peter was on his way back." This idea of desirelessness as a guise for inappropriate desire is one adopted by gay author Paul Monette. He writes of his attempts to negotiate the male homosexual world, one in which he remained trapped "in the amber of wrong desire . . . in a twilight world where no one is ever a child again, and where no one ever grows up."[43] Peter Pan has a similarly inappropriate desire—he absolutely refuses to want to grow up, get a job, marry, and become a father. "'I don't ever want to be a man,' he said with passion."[44] The rejection of adult male roles, especially those that define men as heterosexual through their relationships to women and children, is a marked part of *Queer as Folk*'s depiction of gay male—as opposed to gay female—culture. Brian, Michael, and their friends actively combat the march of time, spending hours at the gym and thousands of dollars on clothes to look younger than they really are. They also aggressively mock anyone whose physique or approach to life make them look his age. Ted (Scott Lowell), the most normal-looking of the characters on the American version of *Queer as Folk* and the one who is most accepting of his age, is the butt of many of Brian's cruelest jokes, including the moniker "dead man walking" when he openly admits to being over the age of thirty. Brian, on the other hand, absolutely refuses to attend his own thirtieth birthday party, which his friends stage as a funeral complete with coffin, preferring instead to spend an enormous sum of money on an Hermes scarf and use it in a performance of autoerotic asphyxiation before donning it with a tuxedo and wearing it to Justin's senior prom.

Like the mother of Brian's son, Lindsey (Thea Gill), and her partner Melanie (Michelle Clunie), Wendy wants to grow up. Most notably, she wants to be a mother—one of Peter's lures is that Wendy could tuck the boys in at night. And she wants to be kissed: she relents "'so [Peter] may give me a kiss.'" Tinker Bell pulls Wendy's hair as Peter kisses her, and promises to do it each and every time there is an exchange of thimbles: "Peter could not understand why, but Wendy understood."[45] The lesbians in *Queer as Folk*, like Wendy, seem to want nothing more than to become wives and mothers. In a frustratingly clichéd depiction of female gay life, the two main lesbian characters, Melanie and Lindsey, have two children, get married, and eventually divorce, so that Lindsey can enter a heterosexual relationship. The women in *Queer as Folk*, like their counterparts in *Peter Pan*, are defined by their biological sex in ways that determine their futures as wives and mothers, even if the marriages are composed of two women and the children have two mommies. From Tinker Bell to Tiger Lily to Wendy, the female characters in *Peter Pan* desire Peter for his ability to help them fulfill their potential to become women, as defined by sexuality and the assumption of the role of wife. Perhaps Barrie can be forgiven for making Peter Pan into the rebel and Wendy into a conformist, since the Edwardian period certainly did not champion open rebellion against marriage and motherhood by its women. But *Queer as Folk* has something to answer for—while its male characters are defined by their ambivalence to adult roles and responsibilities, its female characters, like Wendy, seem to want to grow up "one day faster" than the other (straight) girls, assuming mortgages, responsible jobs, wedding rings, and childrearing at a terrifying pace.

In the 1980s a popular psychology book entitled *The Peter Pan Syndrome* diagnosed the refusal or inability to "grow up" as an actual mental disorder.[46] Gay culture as portrayed in *Queer as Folk* openly celebrates a life of endless clubs, men, and fun and openly mocks any embrace of adult behavior: Brian "doesn't do boyfriends," Michael, Brian's lifelong friend, tells a heartbroken Justin. Brian refuses to even engage with the beginnings of relationships, which he views as a slippery slope into routine, boredom, and death. Ironically, in the final episode of the show, in which Justin refuses to marry Brian, he reminds Brian that he does not need—in fact, will be inherently damaged by—these trappings of adulthood. Season five concludes with Justin's insistence upon the narrative that Brian taught him: that the institutions defining heterosexual life, especially marriage and parenthood, are lethal to the eternal freedom and limitless fun that contribute to their identity as gay men.[47]

CONCLUSION

Barrie's desire to remain childlike fertilized his playful imagination and allowed him to just have fun. The modern world has lost that Edwardian sense of safe, harmless adventure. World War I changed all that: George and Jack Llewelyn Davies both enlisted immediately for war in 1914, but only one returned. George Llewelyn Davies was killed in action in 1915, as Barrie and English audiences were coming to painfully realize death was not an awfully big adventure. It was just awful. The losses of Arthur, Sylvia, George, and Michael and the powerful blow the guns of August 1914 dealt to Barrie's Edwardian playground undoubtedly damaged his sense of safety and security in adventure. Secure in their world, the Edwardians were not pursued by the ticking clock that haunted the twentieth century and haunts us still. The popular image of the Second World War as merely an extension of the First, and then the Cold War as an extension of the Second, resonates strongly with the marking of time until inevitable death. The clock of the *Bulletin of the Atomic Scientists*, showing how many seconds we are away from Armageddon, haunts the early twenty-first century.[48] And so all of us, from Mr. Darling with his clock in his office and Hook with his clock in the crocodile, to ourselves with our clock above an atomic arsenal, gaze longingly at the "gay, innocent, and heartless" youth of Peter Pan, for his is a world we desire, and one we have lost.

This essay argued that popular representations of Peter Pan have gradually pushed the perceived age of the character upward so that he is now widely considered to be, in effect, one day younger than puberty. Tomorrow he will understand what separates kisses from thimbles and know what Wendy and Tiger Lily were asking of him. But not today. In contemporary images and in films, Peter Pan is almost a teenager, and occupies a very different place from his original position in Barrie's Edwardian Britain. No longer free of all sexuality, *Peter Pan* now serves as a vehicle to discuss ideas of developing sexuality and even developing alternative sexualities. Particularly among gay men, a group that fetishizes youth and beauty, Peter Pan remains a hero simply for retaining his good looks and his status as the desired, rather than the desiring. Like Brian in *Queer as Folk*, who furiously plays at being Peter, we see that Pan and Hook are tightly intertwined like youth and age. Through gay popular media, we see that Peter is as much Hook as Hook is Peter. Both are obsessed with growing old and dying, and both characters demonstrate the cultural capital, and power, and eternal appeal of youth.

NOTES

1. Bruce K. Hanson, *The Peter Pan Chronicles: The Nearly 100 Year History of "The Boy Who Wouldn't Grow Up"* (New York: Birch Lane, 1993), 11.
2. Jacqueline Rose, *The Case of Peter Pan; or, The Impossibility of Children's Fiction* (London: Macmillan, 1984), 5.
3. An example is the fundamentalist Christian pastor, Bill Hybels, *Christians in a Sex-Crazed Culture* (New York: Victor Books, 1989), 116; For more detail, see J. Cianciotto and S. Cahill, *Youth in the Crosshairs: The Third Wave of Ex-Gay Activism* (New York: National Gay and Lesbian Task Force Policy Institute, 2006), 40.
4. Andrew Birkin, *J. M. Barrie and the Lost Boys* (New Haven, CT: Yale University Press, 2003), 283.
5. James Kincaid, *Erotic Innocence: The Culture of Child Molesting* (Durham, NC: Duke University Press, 1998), ch. 2; James Kincaid, *Child Loving: The Erotic Child and Victorian Culture* (New York: Routledge, 1994), 276–288.
6. Birkin, *J. M. Barrie and the Lost Boys*, 283; *Finding Neverland*, Dir. Marc Foster, Screenplay by David Magee, Miramax, 2004.
7. *Peter Pan*, Dir. P. J. Hogan, Screenplay by P. J. Hogan, Universal Pictures, 2003.
8. J. M. Barrie, *Peter and Wendy* (London: Puffin Books, 2002), 7. In the novel, when asked how old he is, Peter's only reply is "quite young."
9. The Fine Art Society, *Sir George Frampton & Sir Alfred Gilbert: Peter Pan & Eros: Public & Private Sculpture in Britain, 1880–1940* (London: The Fine Art Society, 2002), 3.
10. Jackie Wullschläger, *Inventing Wonderland: The Lives of Lewis Carroll, Edward Lear, J. M. Barrie, Kenneth Grahame, and A. A. Milne* (London: Methuen, 1995), 129.
11. Kimberly Reynolds, *Children's Literature in the 1890s and the 1990s* (London: Northcote House Publishers, 1994), 3.
12. Barrie, *Peter and Wendy*, 47.

13. Barrie, *Peter and Wendy*, 24.
14. Jeffery P. Dennis, *We Boys Together: Teenagers in Love before Girl-Craziness* (Nashville: Vanderbilt University Press, 2007).
15. Catherine Haill, *Dear Peter Pan* (London: V & A Museum, Theatre Museum, 1983), 80.
16. Tim Morris, *You're Only Young Twice: Children's Literature and Film* (Urbana: University of Illinois Press, 2000), 88; Hanson, *The Peter Pan Chronicles*, ch. 13 and 19.
17. Hanson, *The Peter Pan Chronicles*, 241.
18. Quoting Aaron Stein's review of Freddie Bartholomew's 1936 *Peter Pan* from the *New York Post*, in Hanson, *The Peter Pan Chronicles*, 238. The play is also among the most important lesbian popular culture images because women played both roles—see Stacy Wolf, "'Never Gonna Be a Man/Catch Me if You Can/I Won't Grow Up': A Lesbian Account of Mary Martin as Peter Pan," *Theatre Journal* 49: 4 (1997): 493–509.
19. Woody Register, *The Kid of Coney Island: Fred Thompson and the Rise of American Amusements* (Oxford: Oxford University Press, 2001), 253.
20. Ibid., 254.
21. From the *New York World*, September 28, 1913. Register, *The Kid of Coney Island*, 259.
22. Register, *The Kid of Coney Island*, 266.
23. Chris Routh, *Peter Pictured: A Survey of Illustrated Editions of Peter Pan Focusing on Barrie's 1911 Text* (Children's Books History Society Occasional paper, 1995), 6.
24. Birkin, *J. M. Barrie and the Lost Boys*, 141.
25. Ibid., 202 (picture caption).
26. Barrie, *Peter and Wendy*, 5.
27. Hanson, *The Peter Pan Chronicles*, 167.
28. Ibid., 169; *Hook*, Dir. Steven Spielberg, Amblin Entertainment, 1991.
29. Rose, *The Case of Peter Pan*, 4.
30. J. K. Rowling, *Harry Potter and the Philosopher's Stone* (London: Bloomsbury, 1997), 215.
31. J. K. Rowling, *Harry Potter and the Deathly Hallows* (London: Bloomsbury, 2007), 558.
32. Stephen Fry, *Moab Is My Washpot* (London: Arrow Books, 2004), esp "Falling In."
33. Russell T. Davies, *Queer as Folk: The Scripts* (London: Channel 4 Books, 1999), 8.
34. Ibid., 27.
35. Wullschläger, *Inventing Wonderland*, 128.
36. Barrie, *Peter and Wendy*, 55.
37. *Q.A.F. Queer as Folk* (U.S. version), Dir. Russell Mulcahy. Screenplay by Ron Cowan and Daniel Lipman, Showtime. 2000, season 1, episode 1.
38. Ibid.
39. Rowling, *Harry Potter and the Philosopher's Stone*, 148.
40. Quoted in Hanson, *The Peter Pan Chronicles,* 31.
41. Barrie, *Peter and Wendy*, 100.
42. *Q.A.F. Queer as Folk*, Dir. Mulcahy, 2000, season 1, episode 20.
43. Paul Monette, *Becoming a Man: Half a Life Story* (New York: Harcourt Brace Jovanovich, 1992), 31.
44. Barrie, *Peter and Wendy*, 26.
45. Barrie, *Peter and Wendy*, 29–31.

46. Dan Kiley, *The Peter Pan Syndrome: Men Who Have Never Grown Up* (New York: Avon Books, 1984).
47. *Queer as Folk*, Dir. Kelly Makin, Screenplay by Ron Cowan and Daniel Lipman, Showtime, 2005, season 5, episode 13.
48. *Bulletin of the Atomic Scientists.* http://www.thebulletin.org/minutes-to-midnight.

CHAPTER 9

Peter and Me (or How I Learned to Fly)

NETWORK TELEVISION BROADCASTS
OF *PETER PAN*

Teresa Jones

Dear Mary Martin. I am wirteing you because I like your
Peter Pan show so much. I would like to see it again if you
are not too busy. I will be 10 July the nineth and all I want
is to see you in Peter Pan again. Please do not tell anyone
about this.
Love,
Doris MacDonald
P.S. I . . . now have short hare.[1]

DESPITE THE SPELLING ERRORS, the little girl who wrote
this letter was voicing the opinions and the hopes of the millions of viewers
who saw the original televised performance of *Peter Pan* on NBC in March
1955. When Mary Martin accepted the invitation to develop J. M. Barrie's
play into a musical, she said that she wanted Peter to fly farther than he had
ever flown before.[2] When she agreed to two televised performances in the
1950s and then a videotaped performance in 1960 (at age forty-seven), Peter
flew into the realm of mass popular culture. Consider that the audience for
the televised debut of the musical, approximately sixty-five million viewers,
was as large as all of the audiences from all of previous performances combined in the play's long and impressive history.[3]

As a girl growing up in a small town in the southeastern corner of Kansas during the 1960s, there were two television events nearly as important
as Christmas in my life. One was, of course, the annual winter broadcast of
The Wizard of Oz, and the other was the more elusive, more random airing of Mary Martin's *Peter Pan*. For many girls, Dorothy Gale was the only

243

female adventurer readily accessible at the time; when she crosses the little footbridge and sets out on her own heroic quest, she is a midwestern Odysseus, resplendent in gingham and pigtails with her very own Argus in Toto and Athene in Glinda the Good Witch. However, she predictably and disappointedly returns to the black-and-white world of Kansas, a scene which Salman Rushdie aptly describes:

> ...with Auntie Em and Uncle Henry and the rude mechanicals clustered around her bed, Dorothy begins ... fighting not only against the patronizing dismissals of her own folk but also against the scriptwriters, and the sentimental moralizing of the entire Hollywood studio system. *It wasn't a dream, it was a place. Doesn't anyone believe me?*[4]

We did believe her, but Hollywood seemed determined that we believe something else as well: Dorothy's acceptance of the deficiencies and limitations of her home life, in spite of what was, up to this point, a "radical and enabling film ... which teaches us, in the least didactic way to build on what we have, to make the most of ourselves."[5]

However, Peter Pan—a boy who looks like a girl played by a girl who looks like a boy—not only embodied adventure but also, what Dorothy couldn't, liberation for midwestern girls who didn't necessarily agree with the party line "there's no place like home," that drab and familiar space of prescribed gender roles, rigid sexual identities, and oppressive social mores. What the televised performances of *Peter Pan* offered to mid-twentieth-century American audiences was the fantasy of flying by the nets of heteronormativity (to paraphrase James Joyce's Stephen Daedalus, another literary character searching for escape and transcendence). Mary Martin brought the ultimate performance of gender fluidity in all of its joyous flamboyance, playful confusion, and political/cultural critique right into our living rooms. From the studied androgyny of a female actor playing a male character, she could instantly transform into a seductive siren luring Captain Hook into the forest; a middle-class husband smoking a pipe and reading a newspaper next to Wendy; and a sexually precocious boy dancing with Tiger Lily. Now, here truly was a radical and enabling film, which is all about, according to Marjorie Garber, transgression "without guilt, pain, penalty, conflict, or cost."[6]

The 1960 videotaped production with Mary Martin is still considered to be the standard musical version of Barrie's classic play, though the 2000 televised production (aired on cable network A&E) starring Cathy Rigby provides an important comparison to the earlier image of Peter Pan. In a history and analysis of American musicals including Mary Martin's *Peter Pan*, Stacy Wolf points out that in spite of the characterization of the late fifties and early sixties as a placid time in which happy white, middle-class American families mowed lawns and watched television in their suburban homes, it was also a time of great anxiety and profound uneasiness.[7] Indeed, I would argue that the early network broadcasts of the musical production of *Peter Pan* essentially coincide with an emerging cultural, social, and political rebelliousness of the American middle class in which prescribed gender roles were challenged, normative sexual identities were resisted, and high camp was appropriated by dominant culture. And all was packaged for the largest and savviest consumer group in American history: the baby boomers.

Mary Martin Flies into American Living Rooms

Peter Pan is perhaps the most important thing, to me, that I have ever done in the theatre.[8]

When the reader of Mary Martin's 1976 autobiography, *My Heart Belongs*, is reminded of the other roles she created in the American theater including Nellie Forbush in *South Pacific*, Annie Oakley in *Annie Get Your Gun*, Maria in *The Sound of Music*, and Agnes in *I Do! I Do!*, the weight of that above comment is significant. Playing Peter Pan was, according to Martin, a life-long obsession ("I cannot remember a day when I didn't want to be Peter"[9]), and the opportunity presented itself in the fall of 1953 to produce a musical version of the play with her choice of director and composer. Martin chose Jerome Robbins, whom she describes as a "young pixie" and "another Peter Pan" (Hanson 176).

At about the same time that Robbins was directing and choreographing *Peter Pan,* he was being called to testify before the House Un-American Activities Committee (HUAC), where he ultimately identified eight colleagues as members of the Communist Party. He gave more names than any other HUAC witness—a betrayal, according to biographer Amanda Vaill, for which he suffered remorse throughout the rest of his life.[10]

Bud Coleman's speculation that his own fear of being outed as a homosexual prompted Robbins to "name names,"[11] is supported in Victor Navasky's book *Naming Names*, where he writes that an overwhelming dread of exposure often led people such as Robbins to cooperate in anticommunist purges.[12] Throughout the fifties, there emerged an association between homosexuality and treason, and the nets being cast to snare all forms of political and sexual subversiveness by legislators such as Francis Walter and Richard Nixon in the House of Representatives and Joseph McCarthy in the Senate were both wide and dangerous.[13] Another biographer, Greg Lawrence, also supports this theory, reporting that Robbins was very likely confronted with the choice of naming his communist friends or seeing his gay lovers exposed in the media.[14]

A more suggestive linkage between Robbins's sexual orientation, at which Martin coyly hints, and *Peter Pan* is the sense and sensibility of the production itself. Wolf argues quite persuasively that the musical represents an "explicit rejection of heterosexuality" in which the refusal to grow up is essentially the refusal to become heterosexual.[15] That refusal is performed, for example, in the parody of gender norms and in the subversion of what Judith Butler calls a "naturalized and compulsory heterosexuality" that is exposed in a panicked imitation of its own idealization through the scenes played between Peter and Wendy and Peter and Hook.[16]

One little known fact about the production history of *Peter Pan* emerged in 1982 when Carolyn Leigh, one of its original lyricists, disclosed to an audience that "Leonard Bernstein was supposed to have done the music" (Hanson 176). Just two years after the Broadway run of *Peter Pan*, Robbins would indeed collaborate with Bernstein on *West Side Story*, which is intensely homoerotic despite its heterosexual plot line and which features both eroticized male characters and yet another unforgettable androgynous female character, Anybodys. Gay men have been crucially important in the development, production, and success of American musicals. Both their influence and appreciation is well documented in historical and critical works such as D. A. Miller's *Place for Us,* in which he not only labels the musical as a "gay genre" but also contends that nearly all fifties musicals have a "gay subtext,"[17] and in memoirs such as John Clum's *Something for the Boys*, in which he argues that American musicals are and have always been part of gay culture. Clum posits that what sports are to straight men, musical theater is to gay men.[18] In Martin's *Peter Pan*, homoerotic sublimation and gay subtext become nearly as transparent as Peter's flimsy disguise as the "mysterious lady," the addition of an operatic and balletic parody between Peter Pan and Captain Hook, which I will discuss in more detail below.

Once Robbins was secured as director, the process to create and produce a full-scale musical began in earnest. A young composer, Moose Charlap, joined Leigh to complete the musical team, and the cast, including Australian actor Cyril Ritchard as Captain Hook, was announced in May 1954. During rehearsals, it was decided that the show would be featured on NBC's *Production Showcase*, pending final approval by Martin.

The musical opened at the Curran Theatre in San Francisco on July 19, 1954, with two major departures from Barrie's play. The first was the deletion of what became labeled as Peter's "To die would be an awfully big adventure scene," a significant line found in both Barrie's original play (1904) as well as his prose version (1911) of the Peter Pan story. Robbins

9.1 A joyful Mary Martin crows as Peter Pan. She wanted real life to be just like Never-land—timeless, free, mischievous, and magical. Courtesy of Jerry Ohlinger's Movie Material Store.

himself adapted the three-act book for the musical (without credit) from four earlier versions of the dramatic text, and although he regretted the deletion of the scene, he was quite sensitive to the tension between maintaining the integrity of the source and developing a vehicle for the star performer.[19] This tension would underscore many decisions throughout the creative process: from how to cast Martin's own daughter (Robbins was vehemently opposed to casting her at all) to composing the requisite number of songs for Martin and Ritchard as specified in their respective contracts. As Hanson points out, investors knew they were taking a calculated risk, but they were betting that audiences, though unlikely to pay to see just another *Peter Pan*, would flock to see Mary Martin as a singing Peter Pan (186–187).

The second departure was the inclusion of Peter's return to the nursery as described by Martin herself:

> Peter discovers that Wendy now has a daughter named Jane who has been waiting for Peter to teach her how to fly and take her with him to Never Land. Wendy asks if she can come too and Peter answers, "No, you see, Wendy, you're too grown up."[20]

Martin disclosed that this scene included the most touching dialogue for her in the entire play because it expresses the poignant loss of Wendy's childhood and the "brutal honesty" with which Peter acknowledges it (Hansen, 193). For Robbins, this ending was a critical choice both for his conception of the dramatic structure of the musical and for his development of the dramatic tactic of directing the actors to portray children who were simply and naturally pretending to be Lost Boys, pirates, Indians, and even Peter Pan, as children are wont to do: "I thought, well, that's going to be a wonderful thing, to make a circle of the play, in that Peter flies off again with a new Wendy. I tried to think of a bit of the world as children saw it. . . ."[21]

One explanation or rationale for the alterations might be the necessity of conforming to the "happy ending" prerequisite for conventional musical comedy: both the possibility of Peter's death and the problem of Wendy's maturation have dark, even tragic, undertones. At a crucial point during the project's development, one of several writers involved made the following significant distinction: "What they had was [Barrie's] play with some songs, they didn't have a musical yet" (Hansen 200). The erasure of any lingering concerns about mortality (especially given Tinkerbell's resurrection) as well as the enactment of the natural cycle of rebirth and renewal each and every spring with Peter and a "new Wendy" would provide a happily familiar and wonderfully consoling finale for audiences.

Peter Pan was produced roughly in the middle of what came to be known as the Golden Age of Broadway—from 1943 to 1965—in which the optimism and escapist qualities of the productions were supposed to reflect and reinforce the zeitgeist of the era itself. Mass entertainment was careful to promote the values of what was ostensibly a puritanical and innocent time in which death was hidden, sex was unmentionable, abortion was illegal, divorce was difficult, and many children recited the Lord's Prayer at the start of the school day. Gay historian Charles Kaiser characterizes this period of social and artistic conformity as follows: "The suburban family with three children, a barbecue, and a two-car garage was good for business—and almost no one was questioning the notion that whatever was good for General Motors was also good for the United States."[22]

Kaiser's comment is suggestive of yet another consideration for the alterations in the script: the intended audience—children. Once the decision was made to broadcast a live performance of *Peter Pan* on television, expectations about the potential number of viewers must have soared like Peter himself. Daytime, age-appropriate programming was only recently being produced for this new, readily accessible demographic, and the group that Betty Friedan would, in a few years, ironically describe as the children who will never grow up,[23] might have been on the minds of everyone involved in developing a commercially successful vehicle. Hanson does report that one of the songs from the San Francisco production, "When I Went Home," was ultimately deemed "just too sad" and simply inappropriate for children because of its evocation of loss and separation, and it was removed (199).

With the nearly simultaneous development of television and long-playing albums in the mid-twentieth century, musical theatre was becoming available to mass audiences as both spectators *and* consumers.[24] In fact, RCA, one of the sponsors of the first televised performance of *Peter Pan*, followed the two-hour broadcast with a commercial for the original cast album complete with dancing marionettes of the characters. What is essentially an early example of a "product tie-in" preceded Mary Martin's return, in full costume, to bid farewell to the "little children and the grown-up children" who were watching and then to thank NBC, RCA, and the Ford Motor Company "for making it possible . . . to be with you" (Hanson 218). Direct *and* indirect marketing to impressionable and avaricious kiddie viewers was evidently well underway.

The reviews for the San Francisco production were generally positive but not overly enthusiastic, with one critic writing that whether it was ready for New York "is debatable" (Hanson 195). The highly successful team of Betty Comden and Adolph Green (*On the Town*, 1944; *Singin' in the Rain*,

1952; *Bells Are Ringing*, 1953; *Auntie Mame*, 1958; *Applause*, 1970) were recruited to "doctor" the script by creating lyrics for new music composed by Jule Styne (*Anchors Aweigh*, 1945; *Bells Are Ringing*, 1953; *Pocketful of Miracles*, 1961; *Gypsy*, 1962; *Funny Girl*, 1968) and writing additional dialogue to lighten up the play. Following a much more positively received production in Los Angeles, Martin gave the nod to move the musical to New York, where it opened for the first of one hundred fifty performances on October 20, 1954, at the Winter Garden Theatre. The engagement would be limited because of a $500,000 exclusive contract with NBC, an extremely lucrative deal for the investors (Hanson 213–214).

With the five stage sets adapted for the cameras and the original cast intact, NBC broadcast *Peter Pan* on March 7, 1955, live and in color, in spite of the fact there were only about fifteen thousand color television sets at the time. The lavish musical was part of an ongoing series called *Producers' Showcase*; there were live ninety-minute productions airing every fourth Monday in prime time.[25] Because Disney owned the motion picture rights to the play (the animated film was released just two years earlier, in 1953), the production could not be recorded. However, archival kinescope (the film precursor of videotape) bears witness to what was a delightful performance, "rougher but more spontaneous than the later taped version."[26]

Writing for the *New York Times*, Jack Gould focused as much on the technological magic and cultural significance of this national shared experience through the medium of television as he did on the qualities of the production:

> Surely there must have been a trace of fairy dust from coast to coast this morning. Last night's television presentation of Mary Martin as "Peter Pan" was a joy. Who could say whether the TV premiere was more wondrous than the Broadway opening? It is unimportant . . . for in millions of homes entire families were transported to Neverland in the happiest of circumstances.[27]

NBC received so much mail from viewers asking to see *Peter Pan* again that they immediately announced an encore performance for the following year on January 9, 1956. As Hanson writes in his history of *Peter Pan*: "It is still incredible to believe that a musical of such proportion could be telecast 'live' at all, but a second time is astonishing" (218). Four years later, the bright idea of capturing one final performance on videotape, a relatively new medium, was realized. With a new director and several new actors (the original children had, indeed, grown up), Martin and Ritchard performed Peter and Hook one last time. It aired in 1960 and again in 1963, 1966, and 1973.

9.2 Cathy Rigby flies as Peter Pan. She was variously described by critics as uncomplicated, chunky, and tomboyish. Photofest.

And then, the tape was mysteriously lost or tragically burnt or accidentally erased. No one seemed to know what happened to it until 1988, when it showed up at the Museum of Broadcasting in New York. Working slowly and methodically from two surviving copies, the technical staff at NBC remastered the video, and after much wrangling over rights and much worrying about ratings (a new musical version with Mia Farrow as Peter Pan was broadcast on the *Hallmark Hall of Fame* series by NBC in 1976 and did not do well at all), the network aired the 1960 performance in January 1989. Ratings were excellent; a television critic for the *Miami Herald* rightly predicted that "Yuppies will station their puppies in front of the tube to enjoy the magic they remember" (qtd. Hanson 248). The uncut version was released on home video in 1990.

The year 1990 also marked Mary Martin's death and the debut of another Broadway production of the musical starring Cathy Rigby. Besides the athletic abilities and physical compactness of the gymnast, which were tailor-made for the role (she had won eight gold medals in the 1968 and 1972 Olympic Games), Rigby also identified with the nature of Peter: "I grew up very much like him . . . full of adventure and taking risks. . . . I felt like I was at home with the part." However, there might have been a more sinister connection between Rigby and the character—the intense pressure that she herself never mature: "I had a coach who wanted to keep me a child, didn't want me to grow up. . . ." (qtd. in Hanson 260). Rigby had previously played the role in both an NBC touring company and at a West Coast theater, and, taking a similar path to Martin's, decided that her own Broadway run would be limited. The response was, again, overwhelmingly positive. Ten years later, a live performance of *Peter Pan* was filmed at the Mirada Theatre for the Performing Arts, airing on October 8, 2000, on the A&E Network. Rigby was forty-eight years old at the time of the broadcast.

PETER PAN REDUX

'Cause growing up is awfuller
Than all the awful things that ever were.
I'll never grow up, never grow up, never grow up. Not me![28]

If television programming can serve as just one line of input data on a "cultural seismograph" calibrated to detect and measure change in American society, then even a cursory look at what was being aired along with *Peter Pan* in the mid-fifties and early sixties can ostensibly provide a general idea of what millions of citizens were experiencing at the same time through the same medium all over the country: namely, desire . . . for personal validation, escapist entertainment, digestible information, lavish goods. However, under the seemingly placid surface of middle-class, mainstream American society whose values were being propagated and polished through performances such as June Cleaver, products such as space-age appliances, and trends such as "togetherness," fault lines were beginning to emerge and rumblings were becoming audible. The social and cultural shifts that would energize the Beat culture, women's liberation, civil rights, and gay liberation were already well underway. Allen Ginsburg's *Howl* was published in 1956, followed by Jack Kerouac's *On the Road* in 1957, another performative text featuring the exploits of a boy adventurer, Sal Paradise, and the allure of a sexual trickster, Dean Moriarity. Betty Friedan began *The Feminine Mystique* in the mid-fifties, finally disclosing the "problem that has no name" with its publication in 1963. Susan Sontag elaborated Christopher Isherwood's 1954 sketch of an esoteric code and sensibility in her "Notes on Camp" in 1961. In fact, giving names to what Sontag describes as the "many things in the world [that] have not yet been named,"[29] such as the destructiveness of the mystique of feminine fulfillment or the seductiveness of artifice and play-acting, was fast becoming the thing to do.

And *Peter Pan* kept popping up on network television throughout it all. Garber writes that the mere appearance of a transvestite figure (the tomboy, the fairy, the drag queen) in a cultural representation signals a category crisis, and in *Peter Pan*, "category crises are everywhere."[30] In retrospect, it seems that category crises *were* everywhere in mid-century American culture as well, and the medium of television would indeed be the message for those viewers who were literally born and bred into it.

As discussed above, from the very beginning of commercial television, the burgeoning generation of postwar children were targeted as a prime viewing audience, with the premiere of shows such as *Kukla, Fran and Ollie* and the beloved *Howdy Doody* in 1947. *Disneyland* would debut in 1954, and by 1955, the first live broadcast of *Peter Pan;* American kids could spend their mornings with *Captain Kangaroo* on CBS, their afternoons with *The Mickey Mouse Club* on ABC, and, for the first time ever, watch cartoons every Saturday morning on *The Mighty Mouse Playhouse*.[31]

If there were any lingering doubts about the viability of what were then called "youth-oriented shows," they were quickly dispelled when ABC turned its first profits with *Disneyland* and *The Mickey Mouse Club,* and with the unprecedented success of NBC's *Peter Pan*. The 1955 broadcast was the brainchild of Sylvester Weaver, president of NBC, who not only developed the magazine-format program of *Today* but also devised the television "spectacular," of which *Peter Pan* would be the first shining example. To put the number of viewers, sixty-five million, in context, consider that the year before *Peter Pan* aired, 1954, twenty-seven million viewers witnessed the crowning of Miss America, the first time the beauty contest aired on television; the year after *Peter Pan* premiered, 1956 (the same year of the encore performance), forty-five million people tuned into the first televised showing of *The Wizard of Oz*.[32] Hanson begins his own chronicle of Peter Pan with a recollection likely shared by tens of millions of American baby boomers: that of happily eating a Swanson chicken dinner on a TV tray placed squarely in front of the television set while waiting for Mary Martin to fly into the Darling nursery (10).

The six broadcasts of *Peter Pan* (1955–1973) would span a time of incredible transformation in both American media and American culture. The idealized portraits of the nuclear family experiencing the unremarkable joys of middle-class suburban life in *The Adventures of Ozzie and Harriet* (1952–1966) and *Leave It to Beaver* (1957–1963) came and went, replaced with the debut of the feisty George Jefferson, Archie Bunker's African American next-door neighbor in 1973. The sensational television performances of the young Elvis Presley in 1956 on *The Milton Berle Show*, *The Steve Allen Show*, and *The Ed Sullivan Show* would be but a distant memory in 1973 when the bloated and sequined star staggered through *Aloha from Hawaii*, which was viewed by one billion people. The first presidential debates would air in 1960; all programming would be preempted to cover the assassination of John F. Kennedy in 1963; and ten years later, the Watergate hearings would be a fixture of daytime programming along with eleven soap operas. By the mid-sixties, Americans reported that they got more of their news from television than from daily newspapers.[33]

The mysterious disappearance of *Peter Pan* after the 1973 broadcast might well be read as the loss of any vestige of innocence and optimism that remained in the generation who grew up with the musical. And the caution with which NBC approached the miraculous rediscovery and potential rebroadcast of the original videotape attests to the network's initial appraisal of the production as just too outdated, in both its cultural and production values, to attract an audience. When the decision was finally made to air it again in January 1989, the timing likely proved critical in that the country was once again floating on an illusory wave of economic prosperity and conservative family values that the Reagan era—itself a calculated social, political, and moral evocation of the 1950s—had propagated. Despite or because of growing concerns around a new disease, AIDS; a new threat, the terrorist bombing of Pan Am Flight 103; and a new political scandal, the Iran-Contra Affair, the nostalgic longing for the simplicity and guilelessness of childhood drew baby boomers back to their television sets to watch Mary Martin once again.

Betty Friedan and the Cult of the Child

I'm flying!
Look at me, way up high!
Suddenly, here am I!
I'm flying!

Not surprisingly, Betty Friedan invokes the myth of Peter Pan in her discussion of what she calls the "cult of the child" in postwar American society: "Over the past fifteen years a subtle and devastating change seems to have taken place in the character of American children." That change is characterized by an "inability to endure . . . discipline or pursue any self-sustained goal," a "dreamlike unreality," and a "personality arrested at the level of infantile phantasy and passivity."[34] However, what is a bit more unusual is the connection Friedan makes between these children and their mothers, who, she insists, are also "like Peter Pan, for they must remain young."[35] Friedan's exploration and analysis of the vagaries of the feminine mystique turn on two crucial insights; the first is the injunction that women do not "grow up," that they are neither encouraged nor permitted to develop what Erik Erikson describes as a "working identity out of the effective remnants of childhood and the hopes of anticipated adulthood."[36] The second is the prohibition against their pursuing any dream but one, "the housewife-mother." To illustrate these twin evils, Friedan turns to popular culture, specifically women's magazines, whose content radically changes from the mid-forties to the mid-fifties. There in the pages of a 1949 *Ladies' Home Journal*, she extracts a coming-of-age narrative that draws heavily on the literary elements of Peter Pan; for Friedan, the story is an example of what she describes as the "last clear note of the passionate search for individual identity." It is the tale of Sarah, a young woman "who for nineteen years has played the part of a docile daughter" and is secretly learning to fly an airplane. Her solo is rendered as an expression of freedom, self-reliance, and the courage "to discover her own way of life." Friedan contrasts this empowering, albeit melodramatic, piece of 1949 fiction with the reality for women a few years hence: "The New Woman, soaring free, now hesitates in midflight, shivers in all that blue sunlight and rushes back to the cozy walls of home."[37]

Obviously, Friedan approaches the cultural representation of Peter Pan with some ambivalence: both as a figure of arrested development, symbolic of that which is neither fully formed nor fully realized, and as a figure of ultimate liberation, symbolic of unlimited aspiration and unfettered ambition. There is, however, little doubt as to her thoughts and feelings regarding the repressiveness and restriction of traditional gender roles for women, be they played out by a fictive Wendy or her 1949 counterpart, Sarah. Given that the mid-twentieth century was the beginning of a new wave of feminism in America, the televised broadcasts of a musical version of *Peter Pan* whose central ideological project is experimenting with gender roles would have found an attentive and often receptive audience.

In the musical, Wendy happily and comfortably tries on all of the traditional identities and plays out all of the acceptable roles for women at the time: housekeeper, caretaker, mother, wife. However, her serious and confident approach to this play-acting is undermined by Peter's inability or unwillingness to complete and sustain the performance of mother *and* father, wife *and* husband. In one scene, for instance, the two characters sit side by side, facing the audience, in a tableau of conjugal life: Peter smoking a pipe and reading a newspaper, Wendy knitting and chatting about the children. Peter goes from simply breaking character in a goofy and good-natured way to a more panicked response in which he must "ultimately [seek] assurance that this is 'only pretend.'"[38] Such "pretending" effectively calls attention to the artifice of gender roles, subverting them through parody that Butler aptly describes as a kind of "gender mime."[39]

The "lovely little house" built especially for Wendy by Peter and the Lost Boys also undermines heterosexual norms and gender roles. It is an unabashed bribe, complete with "Home Sweet Home upon the wall, / A welcome mat down in the hall," to keep Wendy in Neverland where she can provide emotional nurturing and unqualified love as well as practice the art of home-making. One of her specified domestic responsibilities, along with making pockets, is storytelling, and a scene added by Comden and Green is yet another parody, this time of the conventional fairy-tale reward for the conventional fairy-tale heroine: love and marriage to a prince.

CURLY: Tell us the end of *Cinderella*.
WENDY: Well, the Prince found her, and . . . they all lived happily ever after.
#2 TWIN: Tell us the end of *Sleeping Beauty*.
WENDY: Well, the Prince woke her up, and . . . they all lived happily ever after.
TOOTLES: Tell us the end of *Hamlet*!

The repetition of the happily-ever-after ending signals predictability and banality rather than communicating fulfillment and bliss. Thus, when the boys ask for the ending of *Hamlet* (a different sort of prince in an entirely different genre), there is presented another imaginative possibility: performance rather than passivity, dynamism rather than stasis, complexity rather than simplicity, tragedy rather than comedy, mayhem rather than marriage.

Garber writes that one way of understanding Peter is as a kind of "Wendy Unbound, a regendered . . . alternative persona who can have adventures, fight pirates, smoke pipes and cavort with redskins."[40] In contrast to Wendy, Peter is not confined in domestic spaces, limited to traditional roles bound by social conventions. Such a view of the character's dual nature—that Peter represents what Wendy would and could do if she were only a boy—resonates not only in the literal embodiment of a female actress playing the male character but also in the literary text that Friedan herself chooses as a way to illustrate, by contrast, what she means by the feminine mystique. She quotes from the final passage of the *Ladies' Home Journal* story when Sarah recalls how her flight instructor, Henry, called her "his girl": "Henry's girl! She smiled. No, she was not Henry's girl. She was Sarah. And that was sufficient."[41] Unlike Wendy, Sarah explicitly rejects the roles of "docile daughter" and "Henry's girl" to be who she is and do what she wants—fly. And like Peter, who crows, "I am what I am! And I'm me!" in the opening musical number of the show, Sarah also offers up a cultural representation of individuality and autonomy for girls and women in the fifties and sixties by engaging in those activities most commonly associated with boys and men.

In addition to the musical number in which Peter and the children build the lovely, little house around a sleeping Wendy (presumably awaiting a kiss from Peter who is, at best, an oblivious Prince Charming), Comden and Green also created what remains one of the most controversial sequences in the musical production of *Peter Pan*: the operatic and balletic parody, "Oh My Mysterious Lady." In the number, Peter disguises himself as a woman—wrapping a long, diaphanous scarf around his head and body, floating through the forest and hiding behind the trees, and singing in a seductive soprano. Captain Hook is mesmerized, mincing and prancing after Peter in an effort to learn the identity of this "mysterious lady." What follows is some of the dialogue preceding what Wolf describes as "a pas de deux gone awry or rendered queer."[42]

HOOK: Have you another name?
PETER: Ay, ay.
HOOK: Man?
PETER: No.
HOOK: Boy?
PETER: Yes.
HOOK: Ordinary Boy?

PETER: No.
HOOK: Wonderful Boy?
PETER: Yes.
HOOK: Do you have another voice?
PETER: Yes. (Peter sings a few high notes.)
HOOK: A lady!

The writers themselves were well aware that the duet "was a risky thing. [Martin] plays a boy and we took a chance having her play this role, singing in a coloratura voice. It worked and it was very exciting" (qtd in Hanson 206). The scene does work but in very different ways for very different spectators. For children, it works as a kind of broad and clever game of hide and seek, with Peter always eluding Hook but often appearing to the audience and with Hook often in reach of Peter but always just missing the catch. For adults, it works as high camp.

When Sontag set out to write about a sensibility, namely camp, she knew that it might not only be difficult for her to define (as it is the "difference between the thing as meaning something, anything, and the thing as pure artifice"), but it might also be imprudent of her to share (as it is "something of a private code, a badge of identity even").[43] One, she surmises, must be both "nimble and tentative," a bit like Peter Pan himself. Her numbered notes on camp encompass an identification of the androgyne as "one of its great images"; a discussion of the performance of gender as "the convertibility of 'man' and 'woman,' 'person' and 'thing'"; a description of its flamboyant mannerisms, duplicitous gestures, and seductive poses; and a summary of its moral and political agenda to "neutralize indignation [and] sponsor playfulness."[44] Nearly any one or all of Sontag's "notes" would fit within a description and analysis of "Oh My Mysterious Lady." As Peter shifts roles, voices, and characters, he exposes the artifice of gender, and as Hook swoons, grabs, and groans, he enacts the errant play of desire. It begins to matter less as to who or what is behind the veil for both audience and actor, as the mystery of gender provides as much pleasure for the spectator as the mystery of identity provides for the pirate.

Wolf and Garber each approach this farcical operatic duet / queer balletic pas de deux in the musical as a performance of drag in drag. The overall composition of the scene, itself a theatrical balancing act of music and movement, is an oscillation in voice and gesture between masculine and feminine.[45] Consider that Mary Martin, a woman who crosses as a man who then crosses as a siren, is counterpointed with Cyril Ritchard, a pirate who, by virtue of his effeminate costume and fey gestures, signals that he is a homosexual and crosses as a heterosexual. The overall effect is psychologically disorienting, culturally destabilizing, and politically sub-versive. In the 1972 groundbreaking book *Mother Camp*, Esther Newton writes of how drag enacts the very structure of impersonation by which any gender is assumed.[46] Thus, it not only exhibits gender identity as simply performed rather than ineluctably given, but it also challenges compulsory heterosexuality—the very foundation of postwar, middle-class American society—as the true, the authentic, the norm. "Oh My Mysterious Lady" problematizes what is already complicated to begin with in the play. Peter Pan as a boyish female hero and Captain Hook as a feminized male villain are already crossover figures; the inclusion of the scene merely reinforces what Garber describes as both "the dream and the nightmare of transves-tism" in the production.[47]

The omission of "Oh My Mysterious Lady" is the most significant difference between the Mary Martin production and the later production with Cathy Rigby. In an interview, Rigby explains that the decision to exclude the scene reflected her desire for a kind of consistency, both with the original dramatic version of *Peter Pan*, which she describes as "the straight play," and with the assigned gender of the character: "It totally took away from the fact that this is a boy. All of a sudden he becomes this woman singing this aria . . . I felt that it would really not fit" (Han-son 261). Rigby's discomfort emerges from her awareness that the scene is really queer, with its flamboyant transvestism, flagrant homoeroticism, and all-over high campiness. Moreover, she is also aware that her char-acter's suddenly becoming a woman undermines her impersonation of a boy, and she seems intent on keeping assumed gender intact and disruptive sexual desire at bay. Drawing on what she describes as her own childhood tomboyishness, Rigby's performance is representative of what Judith Hal-berstam describes as the "preadolescent gender in which the adult impera-tives of binary gender have not yet taken hold."[48] Consequently, for Rigby, the tomboy is understood and played as a liminal figure, one inhabiting the space betwixt and between masculinity and femininity, rather than a transgressive one.

Mary Martin was evidently much more comfortable with the artifice and fluidity of gender in both her own life (Wolf argues that she was bisex-ual) and in the role of Peter Pan. In her memoir, Martin writes that creating a static and familiar identity wasn't "really that important" to her: "Nobody seemed to care . . . whether Peter Pan was a boy or a girl."[49] Certainly, her own long and successful career in the theater—where, for centuries, transvestism was more the norm than the exception—may have contributed to her ease with and ability to switch genders at the drop of a hat or the sprinkle of fairy dust.

PETER AND ME: ME AND PETER

Peter's shadow, which always falls across the backdrop of a theater as he flies away, falls across my memories and the memories
of friends I have never even met.[50]

In the late seventies, I had the opportunity to play Peter Pan in the summer
season of a small repertory company. Because of my stature and features, I
had already been playing boys, children, and other small androgynes. But it
was because of Mary Martin that I had always wanted to play—to be—Peter
Pan. It is, not surprisingly, an ambitious but transformative role for an actor,
one that is liberating both physically and psychologically. Peter Pan really
does defy gravity by flying over, under, and through space, time, gender,
social conventions, and ordinary life, a transcendence that is wonderfully
evoked in the lyrics of "I'm Flying":

Over bed, over chair!
Duck your head, clear the air!
Oh, what lovely fun!
Watch me everyone!
Take a look at me and see how easily it's done!
I'm flying!

The director of this particular production, also my long-suffering acting
teacher, was a middle-aged lesbian; Captain Hook, with whom I shared
a dressing-room, was a thirty-year-old gay man; Wendy was a petite college student in the throes of early-pregnancy morning sickness; and I was a
young wife and mother who had to bind her breasts, but who got to wield a
dagger. What *is* gender, anyway?

Throughout the late eighties and early nineties, literary and cultural
critics attempted to answer that question, theorizing substantively and cre-
atively on the construction and the constructedness of gender as culturally
marked categories. For example, in her 1990 book *Gender Trouble*, Judith
Butler not only elucidated the feminist distinction between sex (the appearance of biological intractability) and gender (the cultural inscription of
meaning), but also parsed the linguistic distinction between construction as
somehow inscribed on the passive medium of the body (determinism) and
performed through the very apparatus of the body (agency).[51] For me, the
most effective and efficient mode of wrapping my mind around such complicated discussions of gender has simply been to recall wrapping my torso
with an elastic bandage to play Peter Pan. When Peter flies through the
nursery window, any fixed notion of what gender is and what gender means
flies out. In other words, to perform gender is to understand that gender is

9.3 Sir George Frampton's statue of Peter Pan and me in Kensington Gardens, London.

performed, and the once-in-a-lifetime opportunity to play the role became a unique opportunity to apprehend in body and in mind how gender is the discursive and cultural means by which sexual identity is produced and reproduced.

As Martin writes, the shadow of *Peter Pan* not only falls across one's memories but also, in my case, across one's scholarship. My doctoral work in English ultimately focused on gender and sexuality in mid-century American drama, and I completed a dissertation on a fellow Kansan, William Inge, whose writings explore Midwestern sexual repressiveness (*Picnic, Bus Stop, Splendor in the Grass*) and whose characters include sad, little misfits such as tomboys and sissies. A closeted homosexual, Inge lived with shame and secrecy, suffering from addiction and depression until his suicide in 1973. After graduation, I concentrated on the theatrical response to HIV/AIDS, especially on materials that were experimental in form and confrontational in tone.

The experience of playing Peter Pan sharpened my understanding and fine-tuned my radar regarding the politics of performance and the fluidity of gender. Take it from me, bottle green tights and a fairy sidekick can queerly position just about anyone.

NOTES

1. Bruce K. Hanson. *The Peter Pan Chronicles* (New York: Birch Lane Press, 1993), 218. All future references will appear parenthetically in the text.
2. Mary Martin, *My Heart Belongs* (New York: William Morrow, 1976), 203.
3. Ibid., 14.
4. Salman Rushdie, *The Wizard of Oz* (London: British Film Institute, 1992), 57.
5. Ibid., 56.
6. Marjorie Garber, *Vested Interests: Cross-Dressing and Cultural Anxiety* (New York: Routledge, 1992), 184.
7. Stacy Wolf, *A Problem Like Maria: Gender and Sexuality in the American Musical* (Ann Arbor: University of Michigan Press, 2002), 14.
8. Martin, *My Heart Belongs*, 202.
9. Ibid.
10. Amanda Vaill, *Somewhere: The Life of Jerome Robbins* (New York: Broadway, 2006), 11–21.
11. Bud Coleman, "Jerome Robbins (1918–1998)," *glbtq: an encyclopedia of gay, lesbian, bisexual, transgender, and queer culture.* http://www.glbtq.com. (accessed May 18, 2007).
12. Victor S. Navasky, *Naming Names* (New York: Viking, 1980).
13. Robert K. Martin, "Newton Arvin: Literary Critic and Lewd Person," *American Literary History* 16, no. 2 (2004): 293.
14. Greg Lawrence, *Dance With Demons: The Life of Jerome Robbins* (New York: Berkeley Books, 2001), 157–172.
15. Wolf, *Problem Like Maria* , 75.
16. Judith Butler, "Imitation and Gender Insubordination," in *Inside/Out: Lesbian Theories, Gay Theories* , ed. D. Fuss (New York: Routledge, 1991), 13–31.

17. D. A. Miller, *Place for Us: Essays on the Broadway Musical* (Cambridge, MA: Harvard University Press, 1998), 16.
18. John M. Clum, *Something for the Boys: Musical Theatre and Gay Culture* (New York: St. Martin's Press, 2001), 33.
19. Lawrence, *Dance With Demons* , 224.
20. Martin. *My Heart Belongs* , 193.
21. Lawrence. *Dance with Demons* , 225.
22. Ibid., 154.
23. Betty Friedan, *The Feminine Mystique* (New York: Norton, 1997 edition), 395.
24. Wolf, *Problem Like Maria* , 8.
25. "Producers' Showcase Television Series," http://www.tv.com/producers-showcase/show/4205/summary/html (accessed January 14, 2008).
26. "Musicals on Television: 1944–1955," http://www. Musicals101.com/tv2.htm (accessed 14 January 2008).
27. Jack Gould, "Television Neverland," *New York Times* , March 8, 1955.
28. *Peter Pan* , Music by Moose Charlap, lyrics by Carolyn Leigh, additional music by Jules Styne, additional lyrics by Betty Comden and Adolphe Green, directed and choreographed for Broadway and television by Jerome Robbins, directed for taped performance by Vincent J. Donehue, featuring Mary Martin and Cyril Ritchard. All references to the play come from the videotape of the 1960 broadcast.
29. Susan Sontag, *Against Interpretation and Other Essays* (New York: Farrar, Straus, and Giroux, 1961), 275.
30. Garber, *Vested Interests* , 182.
31. "1954 in Television," "1955 in Television," "1956 in Television," "1963 in Television," "1966 in Television," and "1973 in Television," Wikipedia. http://www.wikipedia.org (accessed June 9, 2007).
32. Mitchell Stephens, "History of Television," *Grolier Encyclopedia* , http://www.nyu.edu/classes/stephens/htm (accessed June 9, 2007).
33. "1954 in Television" et al., Wikipedia. http://www.wikipedia.org.
34. Friedan, *Feminine Mystique* , 393, 400.
35. Ibid., 93.
36. Ibid., 134.
37. Ibid., 88–89.
38. Ibid.
39. Butler, "Imitation and Gender Insubordination," 23.
40. Garber, *Vested Interests* , 168.
41. Friedan, *Feminine Mystique* , 89.
42. Wolf, *A Problem Like Maria* , 72.
43. Sontag, *Against Interpretation* , 275.
44. Ibid., 279–290.
45. Wolf, *A Problem Like Maria* , 71.
46. Esther Newton, *Mother Camp: Female Impersonators in America* (Chicago: University of Chicago Press, 1972).
47. Garber, *Vested Interests* , 176.
48. Judith Halberstam, *Female Masculinity* (Durham, NC: Duke University Press, 1998), 299.
49. Martin, *My Heart Belongs* , 209.
50. Ibid., 11.
51. Judith Butler, *Gender Trouble: Feminism and the Subversion of Identity* (New York: Routledge, 1990), 1–16.

List of Contributors

Lester D. Friedman is chairman of the Media and Society Program at Hobart and William Smith Colleges. His most recent publications include: *Citizen Spielberg, Cultural Sutures: Media and Medicine, American Films of the Seventies: Themes and Variations,* and *Fires Were Started: British Cinema and Thatcherism* (2nd edition). Coeditor of the multivolume series, *Screen Decades: American Culture/American Cinema,* he is currently working on an introductory text about American film genres.

Martha Stoddard Holmes, associate professor of Literature and Writing Studies at California State University, San Marcos, is the author of *Fictions of Affliction: Physical Disability in Victorian Culture.* She is also coeditor of *The Teacher's Body: Embodiment, Authority, and Identity in the Classroom* and special issues of *Literature and Medicine* and the *Journal of Medical Humanities.* Her current projects include a book manuscript, *Queering the Marriage Plot: Disability and Desire in Victorian Fiction,* and a coedited special issue of *Nineteenth-Century Gender Studies* on critical engagements with nineteenth-century texts using disability studies/gender studies/queer theory.

Theresa Jones is an associate professor in the Department of Internal Medicine, Division of Medical Ethics and Humanities, at the University of Utah Health Sciences Center in Salt Lake City. Previously, she was codirector of the Center for Medical Humanities and Ethics at the University of Texas Health Science Center at San Antonio. Her scholarship includes publications in the area of AIDS and cultural materials, including the book *Sharing the Delirium: Second Generation AIDS Plays and Performance.* She is the editor of the *Journal of Medical Humanities.*

Allison B. Kavey, assistant professor in the History Department at CUNY John Jay College, is the author of *Books of Secrets: Popular Natural Philosophy in England, 1550–1600,* "Mercury Falling: Gender Fluidity and Eroticism in Early Modern Alchemy" (*The Sciences of Homosexuality in Early Modern*

Europe), and "Mercury Falling: Gender Flexibility in Popular Alchemical Texts" (*Chymists and Chymistry*). She is currently working on a book analyzing the natural world and the place of desire and imagination in the *Three Books of Occult Philosophy* by Heinrich Cornelius Agrippa.

DAVID P. D. MUNNS is a visiting lecturer at Imperial College, London, where he teaches in the Master's program in the History of Science and Technology. His dissertation focused on the history of radioastronomy and its relationship to transitions within academic science in Britain, Australia, and the United States. He is currently working on a book about phytotrons, and another about the twisted relationship between gays and fundamentalist Christians.

SUSAN OHMER, the William T. and Helen Kuhn Carey Assistant Professor of Modern Communication, teaches film and television history at the University of Notre Dame. Her book *George Gallup in Hollywood* looks at the origins of market research in the studio system during the 1940s. Ohmer's research has appeared in *Film History*, *Journal of Film and Video*, and *The Velvet Light Trap*. She is currently working on a study of the changing corporate environment at Disney during the 1940s.

MURRAY POMERANCE, a professor in the Department of Sociology at Ryerson University, is the author of *The Horse Who Drank the Sky: Film Experience Beyond Narrative and Theory*, *Johnny Depp Starts Here*, *An Eye for Hitchcock*, *Magia d'Amore*, and *Savage Time*. He is the editor or coeditor of *City That Never Sleeps: New York and the Filmic Imagination*, *From Hobbits to Hollywood: Essays on Peter Jackson's* Lord of the Rings, *Cinema and Modernity*, *American Cinema of the 1950s: Themes and Variations*, and *Where the Boys Are: Cinemas of Masculinity and Youth*. He is the coeditor of the "Screen Decades" and "Stars Decades" series and editor of the "Horizons of Cinema" series.

LINDA ROBERTSON, professor, is a senior member of the Media and Society Program at Hobart and William Smith Colleges. Her publications include articles on the rhetoric of economics and feminist economics (coauthored with Bill Waller), the representation of warfare in film, a college rhetoric and reader, *Discovery: Writing in the Academic Disciplines*, and *The Dream of Civilized Warfare: World War I Flying Aces and the American Imagination*.

PATRICK B. TUITE, head of the MA Program in Theater History and Criticism at Catholic University, has published articles in *Youth Theatre Journal*, *Theatre InSight*, and *The Drama Review*. His essay concerning parades and pageants in Northern Ireland is included in *Audience Participation: Essays on Inclusion in Performance*. Currently a Fellow at the Folger Shakespeare Library, he is working on *Theatre of Crisis: The Performance of Power in the Kingdom of Ireland, 1641–1691*, a book exploring how the theater produced narratives and images to better define Ireland's social order.

Index

Note: Page numbers in *italics* refer to illustrations.